Chosen
by the
Spirits

Chosen by the Spirits

Following Your Shamanic Calling

SARANGEREL

DESTINY BOOKS
ROCHESTER, VERMONT

Destiny Books
One Park Street
Rochester, Vermont 05767
www.InnerTraditions.com

Destiny Books is a division of Inner Traditions International

Library of Congress Cataloging-in-Publication Data

Sarangerel, 1963-
    Chosen by the spirits : following your shamanic calling /
Sarangerel.
        p. cm.
    Includes bibliographical references and index.
    ISBN 978-0-89281-861-7 (alk. paper) — ISBN 978-1-59477-544-4 (e-book)
    1. Shamanism—Mongolia—Miscellanea. 2. Shamanism—Russia
(Federation)—Siberia—Miscellanea. I. Title.
BF1622.M66 S37 2001
291.1'44—dc21
                                                      2001028821

Printed and bound in the United States

15 14 13 12

Text design and layout by Priscilla Baker
This book was typeset in Aries, with Monsignor and Gill Sans as display
faces

Contents

Acknowledgments

I would like to thank all of the people that helped make this book possible. First I would like to acknowledge Dr. Marjorie Mandelstam-Balzer, whose translation of V. N. Basilov's "*Izbranniki dukhov*" provided me with the most apt title for this book "Chosen by the Spirits."

I would also like to thank my friend Soyoltu, who encouraged me for many years to write about Mongolian shamanism.

Many thanks as well to the staffs of the newspapers Inform Polis and Buryaad Unen in Ulan-Ude for allowing me to use their computers in the research and preparation of this book. I would like to also acknowledge Drs. Ganjurov and Khundaeva of the Buryat Research Center for their support and advice in my research.

Thanks also to the shamans Byambadorj Dondog, Sumiya Tserendorj, Dawaatseren, Sanjai Khorbakov, Boris Bazarov, Valentina Baldakhinova, and Nadezhda Stepanova for their teachings and support of my work.

I also want to thank my friend Bayar Dugarov for his support, teaching, and advice in all of the work that I do.

Most of all I thank the spirits of the Sayan Mountains and of the Terte lineage who called me to become a shaman and empower me to do all of the work that I do!

Preface

This book is written as a guide for the beginning shaman as well as for the advanced practitioner. My previous book, *Riding Windhorses*, was an introduction to the shamanic world of Siberia with some techniques for the shamanic practitioner; it has become apparent, however, that there is need for a book for those just beginning on the shamanic path.

In today's world many people are being called by the spirits to become shamans, and many of these people are from non-shamanic cultures. This, I believe, is due to the need for earth-wide healing and the restoration of balance in our world. Human beings have made the mistake of ignoring the voice of nature and forgetting the value of the natural and spirit worlds. While man may forget spirits, spirits do not forget us. They are our ancestors, the carriers of the collective wisdom of life from the beginning of time.

The ancient cultures of both Native Americans and Native Siberians have preserved this sense of communion with the natural world and the ancestors. In our traditions the whole world is alive; the consciousness of the ancestors and living things is around us wherever we go. Shall we not listen to them? It is not surprising, then, that as mankind reawakens to the need to reconnect with these aspects of reality, many people have become interested in the old traditions.

In Mongolian and Siberian shamanism, as well as in other traditions, the essence of shamanic work is developing a relationship with the spirit world. The most important relationship of all is that between the shaman and his helper spirits, a "spirit family" that empowers and protects him during his work. The core teaching of this book is the development of this key relationship between the shaman student and his spirit family. In the tradition in which I was trained, it is said that a shaman is made by the "inner initiation" by the spirits and the ongoing relationship that the shaman has with them as teachers, friends, and protectors.

It is therefore the purpose of this book to present some techniques that can be used by those who feel drawn to follow the shamanic path. According to Buryat tradition, the shaman serves his community by having a special relationship with the spirit world for the purpose of healing, protection, and restoring balance and harmony between man and the natural world. Furthermore, the shaman is a teacher and adviser who facilitates the passing of traditions from generation to generation.

The ideas and techniques described in this book are Siberian; my training is in the Buryat Mongolian tradition. Despite the ethnic flavor of the material, these techniques have power and can be used by shamans from any culture or nationality. Furthermore, those of you who have been exposed to other traditions, whether Native American, European, or otherwise, will find that most of these techniques have parallels in other types of shamanism. This is not surprising, for shamanism touches on universal truths that transcend ethnic boundaries. You may already have encountered these same ideas elsewhere but under different names.

Another thing to understand is that when I am describing shamanic techniques, I often use the term *he* in referring to the shaman. This does not mean that I assume the shaman will be a man, for I am myself a shamaness and practice everything I describe. Unfortunately, unlike Buryat, which has no terms for *he* and *she*, English uses these words. Because it is rather burdensome to say "he or she" every time I make reference to the shaman, I say *Hulicegti!* ("Be understanding").

I will try not to burden the reader with a lot of Mongolian and Siberian terms, although some concepts I present will have Mongolian names either because there is no equivalent in English or because the English equivalent is cumbersome. For example, in Siberian tradition the soul is believed to consist of several parts. As

Westerners tend to think of the soul as a unit, I am forced to use the Mongolian names for the soul parts. I also use the concise and evocative term *gol* instead of the awkward "center of the universe." All of the terms taken from Buryat Mongolian and other Siberian languages are explained where they are introduced in the text. In addition, you will find them in the glossary.

It is my sincere hope that these ideas and techniques will be evocative and stimulating and that they will help you as you embark on the shamanic path.

A Few Words about the Buryat Mongols

The shamanic techniques in which I have been trained come from the Mongolian and Buryat Mongolian tradition. There is actually very little difference between Mongols and Buryats, for the Buryats are the Mongols who live within present-day Russia. Until a few hundred years ago, the Buryat Mongols were part of the Mongolian Empire founded by Chinggis Khan in the thirteenth century.

Buryats, as well as other Mongols, are Siberian in origin and have close cultural links with all of the Siberian peoples. Mongolian belongs to the same language family as the languages of the Buryats' Siberian neighbors, the Tuvans, Yakuts, Altaians, and Evenks. The lifestyle as well as the shamanic traditions of all these peoples have many similarities because they all have a common origin in the Sayan-Baikal region.[1]

The Lake Baikal region was the cradle of the Mongolian people. The ancient inhabitants of the Lake Baikal basin were called the Borte Chino, a name derived from the ancient word *bured,* meaning "wolf." Buryats, as well other Mongols, trace their ancestry to the wolf. In fact, the name *Buryat* comes from *bured,* so their name means "the wolf people." In the centuries before the appearance of Chinggis Khan, the ancestors of the Mongols gradually spread

I

southward into the steppes lying between the great Siberian taiga (the largest forest in the world) and the farmlands of China. The Buryats are the descendants of those Mongols who remained in the original Siberian homeland, although there has been some mixing with neighboring peoples such as the Evenks and Tuvans. Within Russia, Buryats live in the basin of Lake Baikal, the Selenge and Angara River valleys, the Aga Steppe, and the eastern Sayan Mountains. Formerly they had lived in a wider area, but they were ethnically cleansed from many regions under both tsarist and Soviet rule.

Buryats are also a significant minority within Mongolia, living in all of the northern and eastern *aimags* (provinces) of that country. In China they live in the Hulun Buir region of Inner Mongolia, descendants of refugees from Stalinist persecution. The Dagurs, who also live in Hulun Buir, are closely related to the Buryats, having migrated from Buryatia to China to flee Cossack raids in the seventeenth century. The Buryat dialect of Mongolian retains many characteristics of the old Mongolian language of Chinggis Khan's time and is remarkable for its poetic style and rich vocabulary.

Buryat shamanism is part of the great Siberian shamanic tradition, and it is important among Mongolian shamanic traditions because it was in Buryatia that Mongolian shamanism flourished for the most part undisturbed until modern times. In the rest of Mongolia, shamanism was persecuted by overzealous princes who had converted to Tibetan Buddhism and also by the Manchu rulers who had conquered the Mongolian Empire in the seventeenth century, for Buddhism was seen as being a good way to pacify the warlike tendencies of the Mongols. Shamanism, on the other hand, with its emphasis on personal power and responsibility for the community, spawned radical and revolutionary tendencies in those areas where shamanism survived, in Buryatia and in the Dagur region of Inner Mongolia. It is interesting to note that Buryats played a leading role in the establishment of independent Mongolia, and then in the overthrow of communism in Mongolia in 1990.

Among the Buryats, oral traditions in the form of *uliger* (epic poetry) were an important way of transmitting shamanic traditions from one generation to the next. Both the shaman and the bard played important roles in preserving ancient knowledge. The bard is almost like a shaman: his recitations are believed to invoke shamanic power for healing, much like the *hataali* of the Navajos. The invocations of shamans, which start every ritual, are poetic and often reflect the language of the *uligers*.

Buryat shamanism, as well as shamanism among all Mongols and Siberian peoples, was harshly repressed under Stalinist rule but managed to survive in secret until 1990, when the demise of the Soviet Union and of the communist government in Mongolia allowed the restoration of religious freedom. Since then, the number of practicing shamans has grown rapidly in Mongolia and Siberia, and almost every community once again has one or more practitioners.

I am descended from this ancient and proud people. My ancestors belonged to the Terte clan of the Hongoodor tribe, the swan-people of the eastern Sayan Mountains. There is a beautiful story about the origin of our shamanic lineage. About five hundred years ago, my ancestors lived in northern Mongolia in the region known as Huvsgul, and the shamans of my lineage practiced there in the foothills of the Sayan Mountains. At that time there was a civil war among the Mongols in what remained of Chinggis Khan's empire, a war that not only pitted tribe against tribe but also resulted in persecution of shamans by those Mongols who had converted to Tibetan Buddhism. The founder of our clan, a man called Toorei, migrated north into the beautiful Tunkhen valley, which lay between the Sayan Mountains and the Erhuu River. One day when he was hunting he saw several swans come flying down to a lake. When they landed, they took off their bird clothing and he realized that they were the daughters of Han Hormasta Tenger come down to earth to bathe. He stole the clothing of one of the women. When she came out of the water, she cried because she could not go back to the upper world. Toorei emerged from his hiding place and they met, fell in love, and married. They had three sons, who became the ancestors of three clans in our homeland (the Hoimor region of the Tunkhen valley). The eldest son was a shaman. His clan was called Zaarin and his descendants became princes and political leaders among the Buryats. The middle son, who was called Terte, married the shamaness Bagshagui, from whom my shamanic spirit has been passed down. They were the ancestors of the shamans among

Toorei's descendants. The youngest son, Bata, fathered a lineage that produced many Buddhist lamas, one of whose reincarnations is a prominent lama in Nepal at this time.

The destiny of Toorei's three lineages was predicted by his swan-wife. When her three sons became young men, she convinced her husband to give back her swan-clothing so she could visit her family in the upper world. When she put on her clothing, she transformed into a swan and flew upward to the smoke hole of the yurt. Her husband, knowing that she would never return, tried to grab her by her feet. Because he had been tending the fire and his hands were sooty, the feet of the swan became black, as they are today. The swan-woman flew around the yurt three times, telling her family that the oldest son's descendants would be a clan of princes, the middle son's descendants would be a clan of shamans, and her youngest son's descendants would become lamas. Her prophecy was fulfilled.

Bagshagui *udagan*, the mother of the Terte clan, came from an ancient Mongolian shaman lineage related to Chinggis Khan. Her name means "shaman without a teacher"—that is, she received her training and initiation directly from the spirits. The first shaman of this lineage, the first to receive the *udha* (spirit of shamanic initiation), was a contemporary of Chinggis Khan and one of several shamans and shamanesses practicing in the imperial court at that time.[2]

In the old days there were many Terte shamans; now I am one of the few remaining shamans carrying on the traditions of that lineage. In Buryat culture the purpose of the shaman is not only to heal and restore balance in the community, but also to preserve and teach the old traditions. In acknowledgment of this responsibility, I lovingly and humbly offer in this book the shamanic knowledge that the spirits have granted me.

If you would like to learn more about the Buryats and their history, please read the Buryat Home Page on the World Wide Web at www.geocities.com/athens/oracle/8226/index.html.

ONE

So You Want to Become a Shaman?

God has appointed that I must wander both beneath and upon the
earth, and has bestowed on me such power that I can comfort and
cheer the afflicted, and on the other hand I can cast down those who
are too happy. The mind of those who are too much given to striving
can I likewise change, so that they will love cheerful amusement.
I am called Kogel-Khan and I am a shaman, who knows the future,
the past, and everything which is taking place
in the present, above and below the earth.

—ZAARIN KOGEL KHAN, FROM CHADWICK AND ZHIRMUNSKY,
ORAL EPICS OF CENTRAL ASIA[1]

I am sure that the above question is something that many of you
have heard or will hear if you have decided to study shamanism. It is
indeed a legitimate question. Becoming a shaman is a serious undertaking, a commitment no less important than enrolling in college, getting married, or assuming political office. These analogies
are not picked casually: Becoming a shaman has a lot in common
with all three of these commitments. As in attending college, you
will find that becoming a shaman is an experience in learning.

There are no graduations, however; you will continue to learn new things as long as your career as a shaman lasts. You will learn things that no one else may have ever known before and that other people may not fully understand. Becoming a shaman is like a marriage commitment in that you will become permanently connected with the spirits with whom you work. The shaman calling cannot be thrown aside casually because you lose interest in it. Becoming a shaman resembles holding political office in that it entails responsibility. A true shaman not only serves himself but is also responsible for the welfare of the people he serves and for sustaining balance in the world around him.

I do not mean to frighten away people by pointing out what a serious thing it is to become a shaman; I believe many of you will be excited by the challenges that it presents. Becoming a shaman is an adventure. You will have experiences unlike anything you have ever had before, and you will have forces at your disposal that are wonderful and awesome. The important thing is never to lose sight of the purpose of your shamanic work and always respect the spirits that provide the abilities with which you will be endowed.

SHAMANS ARE CHOSEN BY THE SPIRITS

Buryats generally believe that all true shamans are called by the spirits. In fact, in most cultures in Siberia shamans usually come from a long lineage of succession, and some laypeople have confused the passing down of the shamanic spirit through families with the idea that there is actually some genetic transmission. This is a misunderstanding. In shamanic lineages the spirit is not always passed down from father to son, from mother to daughter, or in any such fashion. A shaman's helper spirits tended to follow lineages simply because upon a shaman's death it was easier to call someone closely related to the shaman or who lived within the same village and had some acquaintance with the old shaman and his techniques. In that way traditions could be passed down more easily from generation to generation. Due to Soviet oppression, most of these continuous lines of succession have been interrupted, and shamanic spirits call those who seem to them best suited to becoming shamans, regardless of their heritage.

Although the idea that one must come from a certain family background in order to become a shaman is a myth, nevertheless each shaman, no matter his nationality, has been chosen by the spirits from birth. As the goddess Umai told the shamaness Nishan, she had put the drum in Nishan's hand and the cap on her head before she was even born. Apparently the spirits recognize certain natural abilities and personality traits that make a person especially suitable for shamanic work. You will discover this for yourself when you meet other shamans in your work or through workshops. These traits cannot be described exactly, but I have noticed that all the shamans I have met, whether in Siberia, America, or elsewhere, seem to have a lot of personality traits in common. These traits may be the result of becoming a shaman or they may be inherent to the personality type most likely to become a shaman, but if people are called from birth to be a shaman, are they not really the same thing?

In Western countries most people first learn about shamanism through books or from radio or television. This, of course, is because shamanism has been long suppressed by organized religion and has been revived only in the past few decades through the efforts of people like anthropologist and shaman Michael Harner and the writer Carlos Castaneda. In spite of the suppression, the spirits of the old shamans never went away. Sometimes they expressed themselves through the spirit familiars of witches, through the spirit contacts of mediums, and through other people with a non-Christian spiritual calling. From a Siberian point of view I cannot help but feel sad about the many, many shamanic spirits from the old times who are out in nature, unable to share and express their ancient wisdom with the descendants of the people whom they once served. How happy they must be that shamanism is now reviving. It is no wonder that Celtic shamanism is becoming so popular in Europe and America, as are Nordic, Greek, and Slavic forms of shamanism. This is a natural process as these wonderful, long-ignored ancestral spirits are once again allowed to share their gifts with us.

When I speak of being chosen by the spirits, you may think, "Well, I just read a couple of books and I find shamanism interesting, but I don't feel like I have been called," and come to the conclusion that you are not meant to be a shaman. Don't make that mistake. The very fact that you are reading this book at this time is meaningful. It is the spirits themselves who guided you to look for books about shamanism. It was through their prompting that when you first heard about shamanism you did not just give it passing thought and then go on with your life's journey. Your yearning to know more about shamanism and to learn to become a shaman is a sign that the spirits are calling you.

SIGNS TO RECOGNIZE THE CALLING

In Siberia it is believed that certain characteristics are a sign that the spirits have selected an individual to become a shaman. Sometimes these are unusual marks or bodily characteristics. This is not simply a Siberian concept, however. Unusual moles or marks on the body were called "witch's marks" in European traditions; unfortunately many innocent women have been accused of being witches simply for having a birthmark. Being born with a caul (a membrane covering a baby's head) is recognized worldwide as a sign that a person has a special relationship with the spirit world. A shaman friend of mine in Siberia was born with a double thumb; extra fingers or toes are generally considered a sign of the shamanic calling. Another physical sign of the spirit calling is epilepsy, although there may not be a direct connection between being epileptic and becoming a shaman.

The more common marks of a shamanic calling are ones of personality. In Siberia a sign of the shamanic calling is a frequent desire to go into the forest alone for long periods. This is a characteristic that I have had from earliest childhood. I caused my parents a great deal of worry because of my hours-long wanderings through the woods, singing and communing with the plants and animals that live there. Shamans are often loners. Some may be considered eccentric or "different" even as children. Shamans may be misdiagnosed as being psychologically abnormal, often because they experience unusual psychic phenomena that they may themselves have trouble understanding. Shamans are often perceived as being a little out of touch, a little absentminded.

Have you ever seen glimpses of the future or had repeated cases of déjà vu or other signs of paranormal ability? Many shamans-to-be have these experiences in childhood and are surprised to find that other people do not have these same natural abilities. Have you ever seen ghosts or UFOs or felt that spirits have contacted you? These are all signs that you have been endowed with the ability to see things from non-ordinary reality and are a hallmark of the shamanic calling. If it seems that these things are very general and happen to a lot of people, it is because the spirits call many to work with them, even though only a few may actually accept the responsibility.

Some people get an inkling of a shamanic calling through dreams. Shamans commonly journey during their dreams, often flying through the air. Shamans may have dreams in which they repeatedly meet certain animal or teacher figures that are manifestations of the very spirits who are calling them. They may also have dreams that predict the future or vividly show scenes from the past. If you think that everybody has such dreams, are you really sure? Might not some of these otherworldly experiences be unique to your own dream life?

As I mentioned above, however, one of the most reliable marks of a shamanic calling is the urge to learn how to become a shaman. One of the things you will learn if you are trained as a shaman is to recognize how the spirits often prompt you through urges to do one thing or another. This is a form of communication and teaching by the shamanic spirits.

WALKING ON THE EDGE OF TWO WORLDS

One of the most important parts of being a shaman is that you will learn to experience both the physical and the spiritual world in a very real sense. It is a common assumption in Western as well as other societies that physical reality is superior or perhaps the only reality; in contrast, some spiritual practitioners become so engrossed with the beauty of the spiritual world that they tend to look down on physical reality and even consider it illusory. Both points of view are wrong-headed. Both realities exist, both are equally valuable, and both have their own unique qualities. As you follow the shamanic calling, do not allow these realities to grow out of balance with each other. Balance is an important concept in Buryat Mongolian shamanism, and I will discuss it at length a little later. Treating both worlds with equal respect will give you greater power in both realms. As you become more skilled in your shamanic work, you will be able to pass between the two at will and can enjoy both.

ACKNOWLEDGING THE CALLING

Now that you recognize you have been called by the spirits to become a shaman, the next step is to acknowledge the calling. In the tradition in which I was trained, some shamans choose to ignore the spirits' calling. This may bring undesirable consequences or none at all. In Mongolian tradition the called shaman who does not follow up with shamanic training is called a *butur*. *Butur* is the Mongolian name for the cocoon that a caterpillar makes for itself so that it can grow into a butterfly. Like the chrysalis, an untrained shaman contains the potential for transformation from an ordinary individual into a wonderful butterfly-like being. Sometimes a person will not recognize that he is in the *butur* state and will be discovered to be a potential shaman only when he becomes ill and a shaman is called to treat him. In Siberia the illness is often the spirits' way of bringing in a shaman who can recognize the person's calling and direct him to a teacher for training.[2]

Let me conclude this chapter with a small ritual to acknowledge the spirits' calling and to thank them. In this way you will begin to develop your dialogue with the entities who have called you and can start your partnership with them. This is the first step on the path to becoming a shaman.

Ritual to Thank the Spirits

Now that you recognize the calling of the spirits, the best way to prepare yourself for cultivating your relationship with them is to acknowledge the calling and thank the spirits in a ritual way. Here is a simple ritual that can be performed anywhere where you will be undisturbed for a while. You will be connecting with the sacred in a special way. If there are power objects or other things that are of spiritual significance to you, have them with you for this ritual. From this time onward, make a habit of having certain power objects that you bring out only when you are interacting with your shamanic helper spirits or doing shamanic work.

Materials needed for ritual:

- ☉ Smudge (sage or juniper is best)

- ☉ Incense (sandalwood is especially good)

Place your sacred objects in front of you, preferably on a red or sky blue cloth (use this cloth as a wrapper for your sacred objects when you are not using them). Take the smudge and light it; wave the sacred smoke onto the crown of your head, your face, and your chest; then pass it around your body three times. You may choose to extinguish it or leave it burning during this exercise. The sacred smoke cleanses your spiritual body and raises its energy, thereby setting the stage for shamanic work. You will come to recognize a sensation of being energized when smudging yourself once you start doing it as part of your work.

Light three sticks of incense, hold them before you for a moment, and focus on the burning embers. Wave the sticks three times to Father Heaven, three times to Mother Earth, then three times to each of the four directions, starting in the north and going around sunwise (clockwise). Then wave the sticks all about to the ancestors, nature spirits, spirits of the animals, and all other spirits. Set the sticks in a holder and let them burn throughout the ritual.

You will then do an invocation. Here is one that I normally do when thanking the spirits (although I usually say it in Mongolian rather than in English):

> *Father Heaven, Mother Earth,*
> *Spirits of the ancestors,*
> Tenger *of the four directions,*
> Ongon *spirits* [ongon *spirits are the shamanic helper spirits*],
> *Nature spirits of the mountains, waters, and forests,*
> *Spirits of all the animals,*
> *I honor you and thank you!*
> *Please be watching over me,*
> *Please be protecting me,*
> *Please be helping me,* hurai, hurai, hurai!
> *You who stand before me and behind me,*
> *At my right and at my left,*
> *Above me and below me,* hurai, hurai, hurai!
> *Following me like a flock of birds,*
> *You who have called me to be a shaman*
> *Put the vision in my eyes, the words in my mouth,*
> *Give me the power to become a shaman,* hurai, hurai, hurai!
> Om maahan, om maahan, om maahan!
> Manggalam.

The foreign words that you see in this invocation are power words used by shamans. They have been used since time immemorial because they are known to bring power to whatever intention is being stated. *Hurai* is accompanied by the gesture of moving the right hand in a circle, the full meaning of which will be explained later.

Once you have made the invocation, meditate for a while, focusing on the burning embers of the incense. Fire is sacred in shamanic tradition, for it represents the center of all things and the origin of shamans' power. Imagine yourself sitting in the forest by a fire. Smell the fragrance of the smoke. Imagine that you are a shamanic novice, visiting the forest to commune with your spirits and acquire power. Focus your intention to reach out to the spirits who have called you and to ask them to come and work with you from this day forward in the way they intend. Even if you do not receive any direct communication from them or see a manifestation of them in this initial exercise, you will have nevertheless drawn them in to you, and they will begin to reveal themselves now that you have expressed the desire to follow the path that they intend for you. If your invocation does result in a manifestation or some kind of contact, follow the experience and welcome it with wonder. If you feel like it, write down a description of your experiences after you are done. Now your interactions with your shamanic helper spirits will begin, and it is from here that you begin to become a shaman.

TWO

Contacting Your Shamanic Spirits

Old men of the world
women of the sea
who live in this world
who have become khans *and* [ezen]
with a powerful call I summon you
you came on a golden road
which starts from the top of the cliffs . . .
Oh old men, women
who look at this world
a [mountainous] world
who walk keeping watch and guarding . . .
from the forest you give me sense
from the taiga you give me reason
of what I have forgotten, you remind me.

—Invocation of the nature spirits, Bulagat Buryats,
in Dioszegi and Sharakshinova,
"Songs of Bulagat Buriat Shamans"[1]

Whether or not you have recognized it, you have been in contact with the shamanic spirits who have called you all of your life. What makes this time different is that you have acknowledged their presence and are prepared to cultivate a relationship with them. This chapter will explain some of the types of shamanic helper spirits and how they communicate with the shaman.

Shamanic helper spirits call and partner with a shaman in an intimate and loving way. They are like friends or family, and each possesses a full and unique personality. A shaman develops a genuine relationship with the spirits, and like people they need respect and attention. They repay that respect and attention with their guidance, protection, and power.

THE *UDHA*, POWER ANIMALS, AND SPIRIT LOVERS

In Buryat shamanism as well as in several other Siberian shamanic traditions, each shaman has a unique shamanic spirit who is responsible for the calling of the shaman. The spirit is known variously as an *udha, onggor, sahius,* and many other names, but I will use the Buryat word *udha* for simplicity. The *udha* is usually the *suld* soul of a person who lived sometime in the past, perhaps as long as hundreds or even thousands of years ago. The *suld* soul of the human being is the non-reincarnating part of the triad of souls that each human possesses. After death the *suld* normally settles into nature as an ancestral or nature spirit. Some of them also become *udha* and select certain individuals to become shamans.

An *udha* may or may not have been a shaman during its time of incarnation in a human being. Usually the *udha* has some reason for wanting to be of service to human beings; each has its own history and personality that a shaman learns as his relationship with it develops. With each association the *udha* becomes stronger and wiser. Even now new *udha* are being produced as the human population increases and the need for new shamans grows. Nevertheless, there are many lonely and neglected *udha* spirits who are seeking new partners, even if these partners may be from outside the culture in which the *udha* was incarnated during its lifetime as a human being. In Siberia it is not unusual for an *udha* to cross over into another ethnic group—for example, a Tuvan *udha* may select a Buryat partner or vice versa.

Being selected by an *udha* to become a partner is a tremendous honor as well as a responsibility. In many ways the *udha* becomes like an extra soul to the person it bonds with. This is a benefit to a shaman, as the *udha* carries the collected memories of all of the shamans with which it has bonded, a chain of memories the Mongols call the *sunsnii mur,* "trail of the spirit." Frequently an *udha* becomes a collection of partnered spirits with which it has worked during the lives of previous shamans, so a shaman may actually inherit a family of spirits, although the original *udha* will be dominant.[2]

During the course of his career, a shaman may add more spirits to his family of spirit helpers if they are compatible with the *udha.* For example, I have nine spirit helpers at this time, including two core *udha* spirits, two power animals, and one compound spirit (several acting as one). The most ancient and dominant spirit is Buryat; however, the family has Evenk and Yakut spirits as well.

In Siberian tradition the *udha* is responsible for the acquisition of power animals. Power animals are spirits that take on the form and characteristics of a certain animal. A power animal may be a mammal, bird, reptile, fish, amphibian, even an invertebrate such as an insect or spider (although the most common power animals seem to be mammals or birds). These animal spirits act as the collective consciousness of the species they represent and possess great magical power. The drawing in of the power animals may happen long before a person recognizes himself as a shaman. Have you ever been drawn to certain animals? Do certain animals appear in your dream life or appear to you in other ways? This is most likely a sign that the *udha* is drawing in that animal as a power animal. When you journey as a shaman, you may actually take on the identity of the animal and see through its eyes and run or fly in its body. In Yakut tradition the power animal is also known as the mother animal, which implies the warm and loving relationship that a shaman can develop with his power animal. While this relationship is loving to a degree, the power animal is not a pet. It will always be a free wild animal and should receive the full respect that such an entity deserves. In Siberian tradition, some animals are power animals for all shamans. These include Bear, Wolf, Eagle, Raven, and Owl.[3]

In some rare cases, a shamanic helper spirit, sometimes even the *udha* itself, will become a spirit lover to the shaman. Contact with the spirit may be accompanied by erotic feelings and the shaman may have visions of making love to the spirit. There is nothing abnormal about this. According to some stories, these spiritual wives or husbands are especially powerful helper spirits. Such experiences may be behind European legends about incubus and succubus spirits that come at night to have sex with people while they are sleeping. If you have a helper spirit who does this, try to be open-minded about the experience.[4]

MANIFESTATIONS OF SPIRIT CONTACT

Your spirit helpers have tried to contact you in the past in one way or another. At the time, you may not have recognized their communications for what they were. Below I will describe some of the different ways in which the spirits will send information to their shaman partner. It is likely that you will then recognize certain experiences as messages from your *udha*, power animal, or other spirits.

Revelations Through Dreams

Because dreams are the closest thing to shamanic journeys that all humans experience, it is not surprising that spirit messages often manifest themselves through a person's dream life. (In the next chapter I will describe some techniques to sharpen your ability to use dreams as a means of retrieving information from the spirits.)

Most of us recognize that dreams generally fall into two categories. Many dreams are just psychic noise, images randomly appearing from our past experiences that may or may not tell a coherent story. On the other hand, we have all experienced dreams or segments within dreams that seemed as clear and coherent and real as everyday life. These dreams are the type of dreams that the spirits use to convey information to a shaman.

Have you ever had repeated images of a certain type of animal in your dreams? When you see this animal, does it seem to relate to you in some special kind of way, perhaps talking to you or accompanying you on your dream journey? This may be one of your power animals trying to connect with you at the prompting of your *udha* spirit. Have you ever dreamed of scenes from the past or future, in a distant country or foreign culture? You are getting glimpses of the *sunsnii mur*, the spirit trail.

Many shamans liken the *sunsnii mur* to a river. This shaman river is a tributary of the World River Dolbor, in which all times and consciousnesses merge. The *sunsnii mur* is beyond the confines of time; you can actually see events in the lives of the shamans with whom your *udha* has bonded in the past or from the life of the *udha* itself when it was a human being. What is even more fascinating is that you can glimpse scenes from the lives of shamans with whom the *udha* will associate in the future, after it has left you. These dreams showing past and future are the beginning of the teachings that your *udha* will impart to you.

Your *udha* or one of your other helper spirits may manifest itself in your dreams as a teacher, elder, or even as an ordinary person, but the message that it communicates will be quite vivid and will stand out from the rest of what you see. Take note of these figures that appear in your dream life. If such individuals appear on multiple occasions, you can be sure that this is a sign of their effort to convey information to you.

Chance Meetings and Manifestations

One thing that you will learn in your shamanic training is that there is no such thing as coincidence. Why is this? The simple answer is that because time is irrelevant in shamanism, nothing happens randomly. Things that seem to be related to each other, even if separated by time or space, are connected by a thread of meaning and spiritual purpose. Coincidences are another way in which spirits communicate with us.

Have you ever noticed how many times in your life a chance meeting or simply asking a question at the right time brings you in contact with a person or reveals information that is vital to your spiritual growth? The spirits will introduce into your life certain people who bring important lessons, who, unknowingly, speak the very message that the spirits are trying to convey to you. In the same way, your *udha* will bring you the shaman teacher who suits your needs, even when you may not have been consciously looking for one.

The idea of coincidences reminds me of a former student who first encountered the concept of shamanism after reading an article in a local "new age" newspaper. She had no idea where to start, but she went to a bookstore to seek out more information. When she reached the spirituality section, a copy of Michael Harner's *Way of the Shaman* fell right off the shelf and landed at her feet. She was most astonished at this sudden manifestation and rightly understood it to be a sign from the spirits. Do you remember how you first learned about shamanism? Was it from a book you found seemingly by accident or from an article pointed out by a friend? Did you hear or see a broadcast about shamans and the memory of it lingered? These are all ways in which the spirits will point out the way to your calling and bring the teachings necessary for your growth.

Power animals will manifest themselves in a similar way. Just as they may reveal themselves in a person's dream life with repeated imagery, a power animal may reveal itself in nature. Watch out for unusual sightings of wild animals and repeated sightings of a certain type of animal. I remember that when I first acknowledged my shamanic calling, I sighted eagles, including a rare white eagle, several times in different places. This was particularly significant because, according to Buryat tradition, the eagle was the first shaman and is the special totem of all shamans. Manifestations of animals and the interpretation of their meaning are an important part of shamanic work.

Unconscious Urges

The spirits also often communicate by way of unconscious urges. As you progress in your development as a shaman, you will come to recognize certain urges as being direct messages from your helper spirits. These may manifest as sudden flashes of insight when discussing an issue related to healing or sudden revelations of information that you normally do not know, something that is sometimes referred to as second sight. Cases of déjà vu are examples of this same phenomenon.

TECHNIQUES TO ATTRACT AND TUNE IN

Now that you have decided to heed the call of the spirits, there are a number of techniques to attract and tune in your shamanic helper spirits. The most important skills each shaman needs to cultivate in his training are developing the energy of pure intention and being able to quiet the mind and bring it into sharp focus. If you have not had any training in meditation or self-hypnosis, I recommend you study some materials on these techniques and try them out as part of your shamanic training. The ability to bring yourself into an extremely focused state of mind is essential for successful journeying and for the channeling of spirit energies used in healing and protection rituals.

Clarity of mind brings the best results in shamanic ritual. Even though early Siberian shamans consumed psychedelic mushrooms and some shamans from other traditions continue to use drugs of one kind or another in a ritual context, they are neither necessary nor recommended. Some psychedelic drugs, such as those contained in mushrooms, do aid in concentration and amplify sensation, but they can also be distracting and may become a crutch to reaching the proper state of mind for shamanic work. Furthermore, many of these drugs create a shock to the physical body. This is not helpful, for a shaman should try to maintain his body in as healthy a state as possible. In ritual, Siberian shamans use the smoke of juniper; it has a slight hallucinogenic effect but not enough to produce full intoxication. Many shamans also use alcohol in ritual, but only a small amount should be consumed, for a drunken shaman disgraces himself and the spirits he serves. It is also not wise for a shaman to do shamanic work when he is tired unless he can do some physical exercise to bring the mind to a fully awake state before starting.

Focusing and directing intention is an important part of shamanic work. Intention goes far beyond mere fantasizing or wishing. True intention is charged with spiritual energy that is capable of manifesting the thing intended for. The degree and intensity of the energy will vary with the skill and experience of the shaman, the concentration of the mind in which the intention originates, and the strength of the spirits assisting the shaman. There are a few techniques and tools you can use to focus intention.

An effective technique that is used almost universally among spiritual practitioners is the spoken word. Well-chosen and well-thought-out words contain power and will add force to your intention. In Mongolian and Siberian tradition, the power of a spoken intention can be amplified by following each phrase with *hurai, hurai, hurai!* This magical phrase is probably related to the word *huraaha*, which means "to gather." These words are accompanied by the gesture of circling the right hand clockwise three times. The motion imitates the movement of the sun and gathers energy from the universe to direct it toward the spoken intention. This phrase is commonly used in shaman songs and prayers. Spoken intentions are so powerful that you must be careful of what you wish for; an empowered shamanic intention is likely to manifest with all its benefits or consequences. This is why I advise that all such statements be carefully thought out and artfully phrased.[5]

Another technique to concentrate intention is to create a talisman. Talismans are used in spiritual traditions throughout the world. The most effective technique I have found is to write out the intention on a square piece of paper (its size is not important). Starting from the top, write in a sunwise (clockwise) direction, spiraling in toward the center. Once again, artful, concise, and well-thought-out statements of the intention add energy to it. Red ink is preferable, as red is a color of power in our tradition. Add symbols that have sacred importance to you to enhance the power of the text. Once you have written the intention, fold the top and bottom of the paper inward so that the paper is folded into three parts. Fold in the sides in the same way so that the paper is now folded in nine sections. If the paper is large, fold it again so you have a small square. Tie up the paper with a red or sky blue thin ribbon or thread and keep it with you as long as the intention is in effect.

A proper state of mind is necessary for successful spirit contact. As I mentioned earlier, being intoxicated or drowsy is a hindrance to success in shamanic exercises. Achieving a clear and receptive state of mind may require some practice, but once you get used to doing it you will find yourself capable of going into that state at will no matter what your circumstances are. This is what Siberian shamans do in low-level (non-journeying) work and in situations in which a drum cannot be used.

When beginning to work on invoking a focused state of mind, it is a good idea to practice in a situation where you are free from distractions and worries. If you do this indoors, be sure to isolate yourself from ringing phones and other interruptions. All shamans prefer working in darkness when possible because it aids in concentration; this is of great help when you are starting to practice focusing.

Sit or lie down in a position that you find comfortable and try to empty your mind of all thought. Try to visualize a blank screen or deep, calm, dark water. When you begin, your mind may be like a young child, constantly bothering you for attention. Just let the thoughts flow past; do not focus on any of them. Imagine your mind as being like a cup of water: calm, clear, and receptive.

Repetitive motions or noises often can be helpful in attaining this state. Mongolian shamans sometimes rock gently back and forth in a motion called *twaalah*. If you rock, it should be effortless and comfortable and should not interfere with your concentration.

A more common shamanic technique to help boost oneself into the focused and receptive state of mind is drumming. If you plan to become a shaman, a drum is a tool that you should acquire sooner or later. The repetitive motion and the sound of drumming stimulate the mind into a focused state. This is especially useful when you are doing extended shamanic work, such as journeying. A rattle may also be useful for the same purpose. If you drum or rattle, do not try to keep a steady rhythm; let your mind guide you to the speed and rhythm that suit you. Drumming too fast or keeping a steady beat can become distracting; your hands may get tired, or you may get hung up on trying to maintain a certain speed.

Music may also help in your training to focus the mind. The type of music that works for attaining the proper state of consciousness varies from person to person; the important thing is that the music make you feel comfortable and relaxed without lulling you to sleep. Songs with lyrics in a language you understand may be distracting if you get hung up on the words, but music from any genre—classical, rock, techno, or world music—can be used. Music associated with shamanic practices and meditation often works best. Buddhist chanting, Indian ragas, Tuvan throat singing, Mongolian music, and Native American music are especially effective.[6]

Let go of all expectations. It's easy to think, "I am not concentrating, I am not experiencing anything," and lose patience. Your experience will be unique to you, for each shaman works with different spirits. Try some of the various techniques for focusing that I have described until you find one that works for you.

One last tip for achieving success in your work is to have certain ritual objects or garments that you use only when you are doing shamanic work. The paraphernalia of the shaman, the sacred objects and the costume, bring continuity to each experience and are added to and decorated to commemorate successful journeys and healings. As you start out, have something that you wear or keep around you while you do your meditation or drumming. It can be as simple as a special piece of jewelry, a headband or a hat, or a favorite crystal or other sacred object. When you are not doing shamanic work, put this item away in its own special place. For example, I have a headdress that I wear only during shamanic ritual. It has become like a mental trigger: when I put on the shaman cap, my mind realizes that it is time to go into the focused and receptive state that I need for shamanizing. The simple act of putting on the cap brings me to the brink of achieving the state of consciousness necessary for my work.

MAKING THE BREAKTHROUGH

The core idea of Mongolian and Siberian shamanism is to allow the helper spirits and power animals to work through the shaman in order to accomplish certain tasks. This requires a rapport with the spirits that is deeper than simple flashes of insight. The different forms of spirit contact that I have described in this chapter will be part of an ongoing relationship you will have with your spirit family.

Up to now, you may have had occasional and fleeting contacts, evidence of the spirits' calling you to be their partner in doing shamanic work. Now I present a ritual that will take this contact between you and your shamanic spirits to an entirely new level. I have been describing techniques of creating intention and mental focusing for this very reason. Once you have achieved a state of mental focus and receptivity, you will be capable of establishing direct contact with your shamanic helper spirits and thus will begin your inner shamanic initiation.

Ritual to Welcome In the Spirits

This ritual has something in common with the one presented at the end of the last chapter, but it will put you in more direct contact with your helper spirits. You may find that the contact you seek here has already happened spontaneously during the course of your previous exercise; nevertheless, I still recommend that you perform this ritual, as the relationship that you are establishing with your spirit family is an ongoing process, and all shamans need to connect with their spirits for learning no matter how advanced they have become. Being a shaman is a lifelong process of receiving instruction from the spirits, and this learning is the legacy that you will pass on to your successors in the "trail of the spirit."

Creating a ritual space (see appendix 1) is not necessary for this exercise, but you may choose to do so. A ritual space can be helpful to this exercise because the very act of creating the circle encourages a state of mind that promotes contact with the spirits. This, after all, is the true purpose of ritual. Ritual in and of itself is just a series of actions with sacred meanings, but these actions have an influence on the mental state of the person performing them. At other times all shamans, when the conditions require it, should be able to induce the proper state of mind to contact the spirits as needed without the assistance of ritual action. The mind itself becomes the ritual space. While you are a novice shaman, however, you are training your mind to bring on these mental states at will, and ritual is a good way to get accustomed to what it is like to be in contact with your spirits.

Set up a ritual space if you want to do so; otherwise, sit in a place that is comfortable and where you will not be disturbed. If you are able to, try this ritual outdoors, in nature, where it can be a very special experience.

For this exercise I recommend the use of a drum or rattle in order to help focus your mind. Drums in particular have been used in almost all shamanic cultures as a tool for focusing a shaman's attention. While you are drumming you may want to close your eyes and concentrate on the sound of the drum, allowing all other stimuli to be drowned out by the sound. The drumming does not necessarily need to be loud; drumming hard and fast may cause your hands to become tired and distract you while you are doing this exercise.

Before starting, be sure to smudge yourself so that your spiritual body will be clear of all spiritual influences other than the ones you intentionally call in. Start the exercise by invoking your spirits and intending them to gather close around you. Be sure to state your desire to have direct contact with them, to have them speak to you or to reveal themselves in some way.

Sit comfortably and start drumming slowly and softly, continuing to focus your intention on contact with your spirits. Allow your attention to focus on only the intention and the drumming, as if the drumming itself is the essence of the intention. Let the sound of it carry your intention to the spirits. Visualize your spirits gathering around you. If you do have knowledge of certain spirits or power animals, you may try to visualize them, but it is better to release all expectations, for your spirit family may have other entities whom you have not recognized specifically up to now. By releasing all expectations, you allow yourself to be surprised by what you experience.

Continue drumming and allow your intention to be energized with your entire being, yet keep your mind calm and yielding. The manifestation of your spirits will happen suddenly. There may be a voice in your mind, images, or other sensations. You may actually see one or more of them, see where they are from, or receive information about their name or what they want to do through you. You may experience scenes from the lives of previous shamans in your udha's lineage or even hear the shaman songs. When you feel contact, express your willingness to become the spirits' partner, to receive their teachings, and to let them work through you. At this point you may want to continue drumming, or you can simply allow yourself to relax and let the experience take its course.

Continue with the spirit contact as long as you wish. Do not impose a time limit on it, although you may find that the time that has actually elapsed is much shorter than it seemed in your shamanic experience. If the spirits take you on a journey, let them, knowing that you travel in perfect safety. If you feel like it, write down a description of your experiences after you are done. Now your interactions with your shamanic helper spirits will begin: it is from this point that you begin to become a shaman.

THREE

Bringing the Spirits into One's Being

It was deemed in olden times
When [everything] came to life
After the earth had appeared.
It was always like this
When [everything] began to live.
For the essence of success
I begin to ask.
Say something!
At the campfire I want to shamanize
[to appeal to you]
To the centre of the earth
To mother morning.
With the search of animals
Manifest yourself somehow!
I want to shamanize
Doing magic at the fire in the open . . .

—INVOCATION OF THE ONGON SPIRITS FOR THE SHINKELEVUN CEREMONY IN
VASILEVICH, "SHAMANISTIC SONGS OF THE EVENKI (TUNGUS)"[1]

One of the things that distinguish Mongolian and Siberian shamanism from some (but not all) other shamanic traditions is the idea that the shaman actually embodies the spirits in many of the rituals he performs. This state is known as being *ongod orood,* "embodying the shamanic spirits," and is often accompanied by a sensation of great ecstasy for the shaman. This idea is also found in voodoo, wherein the spirits come into the worshiper and speak, dance, or do other activities. Of all contemporary Western practices, channeling comes closest to embodying the spirits. Most trance channelers learn to cultivate a receptive state of mind that allows the channeled spirit to speak through them. While some channelers have complete amnesia of what happened during a session, a shaman usually has at least partial awareness of what is happening after the spirits have entered.

In my experience, when the spirits enter my body I feel like I have relinquished control of the body but remain aware of my surroundings, even though I usually have my eyes closed during the time of possession. The entering of the spirits is accompanied by a pleasurable feeling, almost like being intoxicated. If the ritual involves journeying, my consciousness becomes like a spirit, capable of flying, traveling to distant places, and all the other special abilities of spirits liberated from the confines of physical reality.

These experiences are the wonderful gift of the shamanic spirits. Always remember that whatever you experience, whatever miraculous things are done in your shamanic work, it is through the powers of the spirits that you have partnered with that these things are possible. The saddest thing possible is the shaman whose spirits have left him because his arrogance, neglect of spirit helpers, or abuse of powers have offended them.

"LIVING WITH WINDHORSE"

Each shaman develops a way of life that cultivates personal power and sustains communion with the helper spirits. I call this "living with windhorse." Windhorse, known as *hiimori* in Mongolian, is personal spiritual power. Windhorse enhances a person's ability to tap into the spiritual part of his being. People who are centered on the needs and desires of the physical body neglect windhorse and are spiritually blind and weak. Those who ignore the spiritual side of their nature are unable to increase windhorse and generally deplete it through selfish and harmful deeds. Concepts similar to windhorse are found in Taoism and Buddhism—no surprise, as both religions developed in cultures with a heritage of shamanism similar to Siberian shamanism, and these ideas became incorporated because they are true.

Each of us is born with a certain amount of windhorse; this is natural, for each human being is a physical organism that was fused with three spiritual beings at the time of birth. The essence of windhorse is the ability to perceive things beyond physical reality and the ability to use spiritual power to manifest what a person focuses intention on. People who are successful or charismatic often have high windhorse, even though they may not realize it. Windhorse may be inherited if a person has a spirit that was formerly incarnated in a person of great spiritual power, such as a shaman or a magician. Psychic abilities are a manifestation of windhorse, as they are an expression of the powers that all spirits possess. There are ways to build up as well as deplete windhorse; a shaman tries to build up as much as possible in order to make his work more powerful and effective.

The terms *gavia* and *buyan* are related to windhorse. They build up or tear down windhorse, depending on how they are used. Both are based on the idea that each person has the responsibility to help keep the world in balance, to avoid causing harm to people or living things as much as possible, and to act to bring greater happiness to all living things. *Gavia* is the doing of things to benefit the community as a whole, such as volunteer service, contributions to culture, or taking a position of responsible and benevolent leadership. A shaman may accumulate *gavia* by his service to the community in which he works and by preserving, teaching, and adding to shamanic traditions. *Buyan* is related to personal behavior, the way one relates to other people and with the natural world. *Buyan* is created by acts of generosity, healing, and respect for nature and other humans, living things, and the spirits. *Buyan* and *gavia* can be regarded as being like a bank account: They can be added to or

depleted according to one's actions. They are depleted by selfish-
ness, hatred, personal filthiness, and disrespect for the natural world,
living things, and the spirits. Acts that increase *buyan* and *gavia* are
like deposits in our spiritual bank account, adding to our personal
power and good fortune.

Just as the accumulation of *buyan* raises windhorse, the deple-
tion of *buyan* decreases it. This is especially true of people who
reject spiritual things and those who use the powers bestowed by
their windhorse for hateful and destructive actions. I deliberately
avoid using the terms *good* and *evil* in this discussion: What is perceived as good or evil differs from culture to culture and even from
person to person, and these words can create confusion. Furthermore, the ideal of Mongolian shamanism is not the unattainable
state of perfect goodness but, rather, a balanced state of benevolent
responsibility. The polarities are between generosity/respect/respon-
sibility and selfishness/arrogance/indifference.

In Mongolian shamanism the ideal way of life is described by
the term *tegsh*, which means "being in balance," and implies acting
in moderation and in consideration of the effects of one's actions
on others. Since ancient times, when the *tenger* sent Abai Geser
into the world to restore balance between creative and destructive
forces on earth, physical and spiritual reality have been in a natural
state of balance. This is at times disrupted by people's selfish and
destructive actions, but in most cases it corrects itself in a process
known in other traditions as karmic retribution. In one's own life
one's windhorse and *buyan* are directly related to one's positive
and negative actions, actions that promote or disrupt balance in the
world. Even though no person is capable of positive actions at all
times, as long as positive and negative actions are in balance, one
can live in health, peace, and safety. The essential meaning of *tegsh*
is to live temperately and conscientiously, being able to accept one's
flaws while having an intention to live a balanced, benevolent life.
Shamans have the special responsibility of restoring balance in
people's lives as well as in the world when the disruption of balance is too extreme to correct itself.[2]

Using one's windhorse in shamanic work will not deplete it. A
shaman may, in fact, give of his own windhorse to those who are
physically or spiritually injured. Rather than depleting windhorse,

this actually increases it, for the Universe immediately replaces what is given, and the *buyan* created by the act of giving increases the total amount of windhorse the shaman possesses. This is one reason that many shamans add some sort of ornament to their ceremonial costume after each ritual: it shows the amount of spiritual merit the shaman has accumulated in his work. The gathering and directing of windhorse is such an essential part of a shaman's work that I sometimes humorously refer to shamanic work as "windhorse engineering." Actually, one word used to describe shamanic ability is *erdem*, which in a nonreligious context means "science" or "technology."

Certain practices keep windhorse strong and build it up. One of the most important is a simple exercise called *ariulga*, which shamans perform every morning before leaving home or doing any shamanic work. It consists of smudging oneself and drinking a small amount of *arshaan* (energized water; the creation of *arshaan* is described in the next chapter). The shaman lights a smudge of juniper or sage (or incense sticks, if neither is available), waves the sacred smoke on the head and chest, then passes it around the body sunwise three times. The shaman then pours a little *arshaan* into the right hand, drinks a small sip, then rubs the rest of it onto the crown of the head. These actions cleanse and protect the spiritual body and bring healing to any illness affecting the shaman.

Another practice beneficial to windhorse is the creation of a *hoimor*, a sacred place within the home. Here you keep your sacred objects such as smudging herbs, shamanic tools, and *ongons* (described below). It is traditional to leave a plate of (nonperishable) food and one or more cups of tea or vodka as an offering to the shamanic spirits. This sharing of food and drink symbolizes the acknowledgment of the spirits' role in your daily life and the sharing of consciousness that will grow during your shamanic work. It is customary to replace the food every so often and then to either eat the old food respectfully or leave it respectfully out in nature.

MAKING *ONGONS*

One of the most important tools in Mongolian and Siberian shamanism is the *ongon*, a symbolic dwelling or sitting place for shamanic helper spirits. An *ongon* can be abstract—a rock, shell, small animal skin, feather, or decorated stick—or made like a doll in order to give a human face to a spirit. Many *ongons* are simple pictures drawn on leather or paper. They are only a symbolic representation; a literal portrait of the spirit is unnecessary.

Ongons are a tool for interaction with the shamanic helper spirits. While the helper spirits usually are clustered in the general vicinity of the shaman at all times, the *ongon* is used in ritual to honor the spirits and to call the spirits. *Ongons* are also a visible reminder of the spirit family that the shaman has acquired. When they are not being used in ritual, *ongons* are kept in the shaman's sacred place *(hoimor)*, either out in the open or wrapped in a sky blue cloth. When a shaman leaves home to do his work, he may take some of his *ongons* with him. The placement of the *ongons* in the ritual space are a reminder of the presence of the shamanic spirits for the shaman as well as for the people for whom the work is being done.

Once you have met and interacted with your helper spirits, I recommend you create *ongons* for them. This is another opportunity for interaction with your shamanic spirits, as they will direct your creativity in the act of making them. It is best to assemble the materials and then meditate a little in order to tune in to them before starting to create with them.

Leather, cloth, paper, feathers, bone, wood, crystals—anything you find significant in your spiritual practice is appropriate material for an ongon. In my own shamanic work I often make an *ongon* for the spirit Zol Zayaach, who brings protection and blessing to households. This *ongon* is made of leather and is painted with the stick figures of a man and woman. Depending on how the spirits advise me or what the individual needs of the family are, I will decorate it with feathers or beads or attach a stone in a small hanging bag. The leather piece is also decorated with various traditional sacred symbols or even magical words. According to tradition, additional decorations (I use beads) are added to Zol Zayaach as an expression of good and fortunate things that happen after the *ongon* has been created. In the same way, you may continue to add decorations to your *ongons* to commemorate successful shamanic rituals or other blessings from the spirits. Some of the ancestral spirit *ongons* I have are carved from wood. They have faces and clothing and generally resemble dolls. The *ongons* I have seen take all kinds of forms, from something as simple as an unusual stone wrapped in birch bark to a rattle carved to look like a raven, from a seashell to painted doll-like *ongons*. The creative expression of making *ongons* is part of your ongoing interaction with your spirits, so you can make them in any form that works for you. Try to keep them small and simple, though, so that they can be carried from place to place easily and will not break. If you have an object that has special meaning for you and you want to designate it as an *ongon,* you are free to do so. It is not unusual for an *ongon* to be created by someone else, but the most important thing is the act of *amiluulah,* bringing the spirit into the *ongon,* which is done only by shamans.

Shamans also usually have what in Mongolian is called a *sahius.* It is similar to a medicine bag in Native American tradition. It is usually a bag filled with the shaman's most sacred objects, and it is an *ongon* of the *udha* spirit. In some cases the *sahius* may be a pendant that is worn around the neck. Keep it with you as much as possible. Others should not handle it without permission.

As your shamanic activities continue, you will make more *ongons.* If you call a spirit for a specific purpose, such as assistance in a healing, you may want to make an *ongon* for that spirit to leave with the patient while he is recovering. You will probably add more spirits to your spirit family during your shamanic career, and you should make *ongons* for them as well. It is not unusual for a shaman to have quite a collection of *ongons* after several years of work. You will come to recognize distinct personalities in the various spirits they represent and find that certain *ongons* are effective for certain types of shamanic work. Some *ongons* will be good for healing; others may be useful for protection, blessing, or weather magic, for example. Employing *ongons* that are helpful for specific purposes will bring better results.

Once you have created and animated your *ongons,* there are a few things you should do to care for them. Never lay them down carelessly, as this is a sign of disrespect for the spirits they represent. According to Mongolian and Siberian custom, you should "feed" them by putting a dab of milk, alcohol, or grease on them from time to time. If you are happy with the assistance of a certain spirit, you can add decorations to the spirit's *ongon*. If you decide to no longer work with a certain spirit, you can dispose of the *ongon* either by burning it respectfully or by discarding it in a place out in nature. Simply throwing an *ongon* away is an insult to the spirit and you may suffer illness or bad luck as a result of its anger.

Ritual to Enliven *Ongons*

This is a very simple ritual to imbue an *ongon* with the spirit for which it was created. It should be done only when the process of creating the *ongon* is completed and the materials you used for making it are put away. A ritual space is not necessary if you feel confident in contacting your spirits without one.

Call in your helper spirits with a simple invocation. Once you have done this, address the spirit for which the *ongon* was specifically made. If you do not know its name, assign one that fits its attributes or use, according to how you perceive it. In fact, many *ongons* in Mongolia and Siberia have such names, as the actual names of the spirits are forgotten, taboo, or both (Zol Zayaach, for instance, approximately means "worker of fortune"). State your intention: that you have created the *ongon* for this spirit and would like the spirit to imbue it with its essence. Hold the *ongon* upward in front of you. You may feel a flow of spiritual energy into the *ongon* as the spirit takes hold of it. You will be able to tell the difference between "alive" and "dead" *ongons*, for the spiritual essence in them will be directly perceptible through your hands.

From this time on, the *ongon* is a physical extension of the spirit for which it was made. Treat it with respect, as if it were the actual presence of the spirit, for that is what it is. Do not allow non-shamans to handle it except in the context of shamanic work, unless you are sure the object will be handled with the honor it deserves.

If, in your shamanic work, you ever handle *ongons* used by other shamans, be prepared to be contacted by the spirits in them. They will often reach out to other shamans when their *ongons* are handled—that has happened to me a couple of times in Siberia.

If the spirit in the *ongon* is one that has joined you recently, you may want to learn more about it. By drumming in its presence and making contact with it, you will learn more about the nature of the spirit and what kinds of work it is good for.

CULTIVATING CONTACT THROUGH DREAM LIFE

One of the ways in which a shaman communicates with the spirits is through dreaming. In Buryat tradition we say that the nine sha- man sons of Bukhe Noyon Baabai, one of the great patron deities of shamans, send shamans important revelations in their dreams. In the last chapter I discussed some of the ways in which inten- tional dreaming may be used for shamanic work. Shamans may be asked to dream about a certain issue or to interpret other people's dreams. Spirits send dreams to the people a shaman serves with full knowledge that the dreamer is destined to ask the shaman about it; therefore, it is important to sharpen the skills of inten- tional dreaming as well as to build up knowledge of dreams and their symbolic interpretations.[3]

The most valuable tool a student needs in order to develop the full use of his dream life for shamanic purposes is a dream journal or other record of dream experiences. There is no need to do this all your life, but it is definitely a good idea to keep a record of dreams for a while, until you feel that your dream skills are well enough developed.

Developing dream recall is the first step. Many people remem- ber very little about their dreams or believe that they do not dream at all. All people dream for hours every night, but the ability to recall dreams must be developed if dreaming is going to be used for shamanic work. Sometimes the inability to remember dreams is a sign of physical exhaustion, a warning from your body that should not be ignored. Prolonged periods of exhaustion and lack of sleep can result in an illness called *yadargaa*, which may lead to progres- sive loss of control of bodily movement!

Keeping a record of your dreams will make you more capable of remembering them. Be sure to note what you saw and experienced, no matter how seemingly ordinary or nonsensical. Developing this habit will train your mind to pay attention to what is happening, and you will remember more and more details of what you experienced. It will also help you distinguish between dreams that are simply psychic noise and those that contain significant information. As you continue your training, you will find that you have fewer "garbage" dreams and more of those that are worth paying attention to.

Eventually you will start to see patterns emerge in your dream life. Are there certain individuals or animals that appear again and again? Their significance will become clear as you observe who they are and what they do. You may tend to go to certain places on multiple occasions. If these places are foreign to you, it may be that they are significant to your *udha* or to another of your helper spirits. Nonsensical or unusual statements are often a way for the spirits to get your attention. For instance, I remember a dream many years ago in which I was carrying on a normal conversation when a person ran up to me and said, "Many people will die in Armenia!" "Why Armenia?" I thought, as I had never been there. The next morning I heard on the radio about a devastating earthquake in Armenia. Since I have become a shaman, it is fairly common for me to get information in dreams like that.

Another benefit of keeping a dream record is that you will come to understand the symbolism of your dreams. You will notice that what happens in the days that follow a particular dream mirrors your dream experience. In starting a dream journal you have already begun transforming your dreams from simply random information to intentional dreaming. If you dream with the intention that this become a way of communicating with your shamanic helper spirits, this will come to pass. Comparing the dream record with the events in your life will show that your dreams are becoming more prophetic and insightful. Once you start recognizing this pattern, you will realize that some of the predictions are in symbolic rather than literal form. Thus, you will start understanding the symbolic language of dreams and will be able to interpret the dreams of other people as well.

The final stage of dream training is intentional and lucid dreaming. In intentional dreaming you dream with the specific purpose of obtaining an answer to a question. Not all shamans have an outstanding talent for intentional dreaming, but many do, and most can do it to a certain degree.

The most important thing in developing your dream life is to make it a means of communication between you and your helper spirits. As a bonus, it is an adventure. You will see glimpses of the past and the future, of far countries or worlds that you may never see with your physical eyes. Dreaming is often a form of shamanic journeying by which you can explore other realities in spirit. In our tradition it is said that some dreams are the memory of a person's soul leaving the body and traveling in the spirit and physical worlds.

DRUMMING, DANCING, AND REPETITIVE EXERCISE

In the last chapter I discussed the importance of developing the ability to go into the proper mental state for making contact with the spirits. I am revisiting this topic because at the end of this chapter I describe a technique for taking this contact to a higher degree and embodying the spirits. Although meditation or mild trance brought on by drumming or music is good enough for initial contact and acquaintance with the shamanic spirits, bringing the spirits into the body is a much more strenuous exercise. It requires a greater degree of intention and receptivity and a deeper form of trance. This is advanced shamanic work and should not be undertaken frivolously. Generally, if a person is trying to embody the spirits just for fun, without a good purpose, they will refuse to cooperate. Embodying the spirits is usually done for healing, for soul retrieval, for driving away hostile spirits, or for the purpose of learning shamanic techniques.

Drumming and dancing are the most common and often the most effective methods of preparing the shaman for the entrance of the spirits. It is no coincidence that drumming and dancing are found in shamanic rituals worldwide. I recommend that you have a drum dedicated to shamanic work. A drum that can be held with one hand while being struck with a stick held in the other is the standard drum used in Siberia. Because the shaman often dances, walks, and jumps around while drumming, the drum should be easy to carry while shamanizing. Many drumsticks have jingling rings on the back side and can also be used as rattles. The rattling noise coupled with the primary drum rhythm is especially effective in achieving a deep trance. You may want to experiment by substituting a sturdy rattle for the drumstick. You can also do what many Siberian shamans do and tie some small bells inside the drum to jingle along with the beat.

Solo drumming is best for embodying the spirits. The reason is that the drumming becomes a part of the interaction between the shaman and his shamanic spirits. The spirits will actually dictate the rhythm and speed until you reach something that is suitable for them. You may speed up or slow down; that is perfectly normal. Siberian shamans may change rhythm and speed several times during a ritual, perhaps even stop suddenly and start again. Experiment with unusual rhythms. Try clacking the drumstick handle against the rim. Note how the tone varies when you strike different parts of the drumhead.

Ideally, as you continue drumming your mind will become sharply focused. You and your drum will seem almost to merge. The beat will feel as natural as your breathing. It will be a total expression of your being. Everything else will fade from your consciousness as your mind focuses on the beat. You may find that your mind is in an almost dreamlike state.

Drumming by other people while you are trying to embody the spirits can work against what you are trying to do. When many people drum together, they usually try to follow a common speed and rhythm. Beccause you have to find the speed and rhythm you need to prepare yourself for spirit entry, the other drummers' rhythm and speed will become a distraction. Siberian shamans do occasionally shamanize with other drummers, but usually only with people they work with often and find compatible. In the story of the shamaness Nishan, it is said that when she first attempted her lower-world journey, the village shamans' drumming clashed with her own and she failed. When she called in her usual assistant, though, she was able to make the journey easily. You will find from your own experience whether certain drummers work well with you.

Dancing often accompanies drumming in shamanic ritual. Dancing or walking around in a circle can be helpful in achieving the trance proper for embodying the spirits. Many shamans dance very vigorously and even jump while drumming. In real shamanic dancing, however, artistry is not the goal, so you should not become discouraged if you feel you are not a good dancer or do not know what to do. Twirling around is common in shamanic dances and helps boost you toward ecstasy (this is the purpose of the whirling dances of the dervishes). Allow the spirits to guide your dance. Let go of expectations and follow the urges the spirits send to you. It is exactly in this manner that you build your rapport with your shamanic spirits through your drumming and dancing.

You may also want to experiment with singing. As with dancing, do not let yourself get hung up if you are self-conscious or do not know what to sing. Shamanic songs are unique to each shaman and will be developed over time. The vision quest (see chapter 6) is the way Buryat shamans traditionally acquire their songs. Experiment with singing tones, repetitive phrases, or even nonsense words—these may evolve into shaman songs at a later time or the spirits may turn them into songs after they have entered your body.

The amount of time spent drumming and dancing before the spirits actually come in varies from shaman to shaman and even from session to session. The actual moment when spirits enter is unpredictable, and the important thing is to work toward the receptive state that makes it happen. I have observed that drumming and dancing rapidly often speeds up the process, as physical strain seems to help boost the shaman's consciousness toward ecstasy. I believe this is why Siberian shaman costumes tend to be very heavy; for example, one shaman costume I used to wear weighed almost thirty pounds, yet when I achieved ecstasy it suddenly seemed weightless. The weight of the costume would normally bring exhaustion fairly quickly, but the spirits will enter and empower the shaman to continue dancing and drumming, sometimes for hours. Shamanizing in extremely cold conditions can have the same effect and is common in Siberia. Chinggis Khan's shaman Teb Tenger was said to have shamanized naked in winter; I have shamanized at temperatures of minus forty-two degrees without feeling cold or suffering frostbite, as the spirits came in quickly and protected me as long as the ritual lasted. Drumming and dancing at a rapid tempo can also bring on this effect and is less dangerous.

RECOGNIZING THE RECEPTIVE MIND STATE

The state of consciousness required to embody the spirits is brought in by great intention, yet it is in itself soft and yielding. Michael Harner refers to this state as "shamanic state of consciousness." In Siberian shamanic practice, however, this is only a preparatory stage for the ultimate ecstasy that happens with spirit entry. Although each person's perception of the receptive mind state may be a little different, there are a few things that will be common to all experiences.

When you have reached this state, you will find yourself so focused that perception of everything besides yourself and your drum fades away. Other noises will seem far away, and if your eyes are open, the reality they reveal seems detached, almost unreal. Your body may feel weightless. Even the motion of drumming seems to require no effort.

The experience of spirit entry is correctly referred to as ecstasy. The sensation is almost like orgasm, an uncontrollable letting go and filling of your being with pleasant feelings. Everyday reality may seem to be blown away and you will be surrounded by light. You may feel as if you were flying into the sky. It will come suddenly with a burst of energy that carries you away. From the time of spirit entry until it is over, you will feel as if you have yielded control to other forces, which is exactly what is happening. During a shamanic session, one or a whole succession of spirits may act through you in your work.

This state is called *ongod orood,* meaning the state of having the *ongon* spirits inside the body. While you are *ongod orood,* you retain awareness of your surroundings, but your senses are heightened through your merging with the spirits. You will be able to see spiritual beings and forces, something that you will need for your shamanic work. You may have the sensation that you are working in two realities at once: the physical reality of your body and the ritual space and the ecstatic reality of spirit.

While you are embodying the spirits, you are in perfect safety; the spirits will not allow any harm to come to your body while they are in it. You may find yourself singing songs you have never heard, doing ritual actions you never learned, dancing dances you have never seen. This is because your *udha* is working directly through you and teaching you the techniques that have been passed down through the *sunsnii mur*, the stream of shamanic experiences and techniques from the lives of all the shamans your *udha* has partnered with before. Just relax, release all expectation, observe, and learn.

EXERCISE: EMBODYING *ONGON* SPIRITS

This exercise is very advanced shamanic work. If you do not yet feel comfortable with the idea of yielding control of your body to other spirit entities, wait until you are accustomed to contact with your shamanic helper spirits and feel confident that they will always protect you. Opening yourself up in order to allow your shamanic spirits to work through you is not dangerous if you do so with the specific intention of embodying them and no other spirits besides them. Your helper spirits will bar the way to any foreign spirits that may try to enter your body. **Warning: Before attempting this exercise, be perfectly honest with yourself. Have you contacted shamanic helper spirits? Do you know for sure that you are a shaman? If you open yourself up for spirit possession without being a shaman, lacking the helper spirits for protection, you expose yourself to the danger of possession by spirits that may cause you harm.**

It is not my intention to frighten you, but the reality is that in the shamanic world not everything is love and light. There are wonderful things to be discovered but also dangers that can bring you spiritual or physical illness. You must have the assistance of the spirits you work with.

When a shaman embodies the *ongon* spirits intentionally for shamanic work, it is always done in a ritual space (see appendix 1). Once you become more experienced in doing shamanic work, one of your spirits may enter spontaneously outside of a ritual if it becomes necessary for some purpose. Using ritual space is necessary for all advanced shamanic work; from this time onward all of the techniques I describe should be done in a ritual space. This is especially important in any procedures in which you are embodying the *ongon* spirits, as a ritual setting will help trigger the proper state of mind required for their entry. All of the rituals I present from now on will first require the creation and consecration of the ritual circle.

As I mentioned earlier, ritual clothing such as a robe, a hat, or a kerchief is advisable in doing any ritual involving entry of the *ongon* spirits, for it will be a mental trigger for inducing the state of mind necessary for the spirits to enter your body. Furthermore, until you are experienced with embodying the *ongon* spirits, a drum or rattle should be used to induce and drive the shamanic state of consciousness necessary for this exercise.

Drumming to the *Ongon* Spirits

When you have created your ritual space and donned your ceremonial clothing, you are ready to begin. If you have not done so already, do an invocation to call in your shamanic helper spirits. While you are doing this, face either the *gol* or the altar. State your intention and willingness to allow them to come directly inside you, merging themselves with your being. Ask them to protect you, and tell them that in your work you will merge only with them and experience and do only what is necessary for your learning as a shaman. Once you have done this, take your drum or rattle and sit down on the back side of the circle next to the altar. Be sure that the area around you is uncluttered so that you will be able to move around easily. If you use a ceremonial pipe, you may want to make a smoke offering before merging with the spirits.

Allow yourself to take a few breaths, then go into a relaxed and focused state of mind. It is normal for a shaman to be silent for a few minutes just before shamanizing to merge with the *ongon* spirits. In our tradition it is understood that the shaman is creating the proper state of mind to allow the spirits' entry. When you feel ready, purposefully and reverently pick up your drumstick (or rattle) and start drumming at the rhythm the spirits will direct you to use. At this point you may want to walk around the circle several times, or you may feel that the spirits will come to you as you are sitting in

The author, Sarangerel, merged with the spirits

place. If you get up and walk around the circle, experiment with spinning around sunwise three or nine times—this often triggers spirit entry. The most important thing at this point is to keep your mind open and keep a dialogue going with your shaman spirits so that they will tell you what they need in order to merge with you.

When you have reached the point of being *ongod orood,* you will have a definite sensation of energy exploding into your being. It may be in the form of light or felt as intense physical sensations. When this happens, do not be afraid! When the *ongon* spirits are in your body, they feel physical sensations the same way you do when you are in a normal state of consciousness; in fact, the *ongon* spirits, who normally experience only the spiritual realm, enjoy the novelty of being in physical reality again after being spirits for hundreds or thousands of years. When the *ongon* spirits are in your body, they will not allow you to be harmed in any way. Even if you do something dangerous, such as walking through fire, they will use their spiritual-magical power to protect you, as any pain or suffering you feel is equally traumatic to them. This is why Evenk shamans walk through fires or step on knives. It is not a display of shamanic power but, rather, a way to strengthen the state of being merged with the spirits. (There are many such practices in Siberia, but I will not describe them because they are extremely dangerous to people who are not truly *ongod orood*, and I do not encourage them in my teaching.) My main point in mentioning these things is that you should not worry about yielding control of your body to the *ongon* spirits because they will not allow any harm to come to you.

When you have become *ongod orood*, do not think too much about what the spirits are doing. It is as if you are a passenger in your own car, allowing someone else to drive you to a place you do not know. You are watching but not controlling. If you sense the spirits are making you get up and walk around or dance or lie down, just be accepting and allow it to happen. If they start making you sing or babble words you do not understand, let them. At this point you are merging with them so that they can teach you about what it is like. In the future when you merge with the spirits in this way, they will use your body to do ritual actions or to direct their power in the ways that they know through their collected shamanic knowl-edge will be most appropriate for the situation at hand. Pay atten-tion to what they do, for you may want to use these same methods even while not being *ongod orood* if the spirits tell you it is appro-priate. While being *ongod orood*, you have broken down all barri-ers between yourself and the shamans who preceded you in the trail of the spirit. In the same way, when you go on shamanic jour-neys, being *ongod orood* allows the spirits to lead you to where you need to go in the most powerful and efficient way.

When you are *ongod orood*, you will be channeling several shamanic spirits and power animals in succession, but some will be more dominant than others. Do not be surprised if you suddenly find yourself swooping like a bird or stomping around and growling like a wild animal. Sometimes when you merge with animal spirits you will transform yourself into those animals—I have seen my teacher turn into a wolf and have been surprised to find that I my-self have left wolf tracks in the snow! You may find yourself speak-ing in a foreign language or with a voice that seems to be too male or female to be coming from your mouth. All these are normal when you merge with the *ongon* spirits. Become comfortable with the experience of doing this so you will be able to induce the state of being merged with the shamanic helper spirits when it is needed in order to accomplish your work.

When you have been able to merge with the spirits, you have made the most important breakthrough in becoming a shaman. I congratulate you and welcome you into the realm of true shamanic power! Once you have accomplished this, you have finally broken down the barrier that most humans have between the physical and spiritual worlds, and you will now be able to go back and forth between both. Continue to practice merging with the spirits and they will be able to use you to bring great benefit and blessing to the world. Your inner shamanic initiation has truly begun.

FOUR

Returning
to the Center

Having gone through the experience of embodying the shaman spirits, you have now had a glimpse of the non-ordinary reality of the shaman. As you continue to explore and learn, you will find that the shamanic experience reveals a version of reality that seems to defy all the rules of physical reality. Random events are shown to be connected, progressions of time and causality are turned around, physical distance and size are distorted or seem irrelevant. As I will explain in this chapter, you are actually tearing through the illusion of physical "reality" and seeing the world as it truly is.

Spirits are free of the limitations of physical senses. Through windhorse and in the state of being merged with the shamanic spirits, we are able to overcome the limitations of physical existence and perceive reality like spirit. Shamans are often likened to cuckoos: just as the cuckoo is born in the nest of a different type of bird, so the shaman is born as a human yet is fundamentally different in the kind of person he becomes. This special relationship with spirit is the cause.

THE TRUE SOURCE OF POWER

The true source of power is the center of all existence, referred to in Siberian languages and in Mongolian with the root word *gal* or *gol*. *Gol* has the essential meaning of "core," "essence," "center." This word is the root of such important words as *gal*, "fire," *golomt* or *gulamta*, "place of the fire," *gol*, "river," and *golduu*, "most important." Fire is a symbol of this core of existence, for it is a place where heaven and earth merge, creating heat, and shamans use it in rituals as the symbolic representation of this center. *Gol*, when used in the sense of "river," is related to this same concept—another symbol of the center of the universe is the river Dolbor, which links all consciousness and ties together the upper, lower, and middle worlds. In this sense the root word *mur* is also significant. *Mur* means "trail," but in the form *murun* it refers to a great river flowing to the sea. Dolbor *murun* is the river of the universe, while the *sunsnii mur*, the stream of consciousness linking shamans in a line of succession, is visualized as a tributary stream of the Dolbor.[1]

The *gol* is the true source of power in that it is through visualizing it that the shaman is capable of doing practically anything he can conceptualize and focus intent on. This is an awesome capability but also requires an acute sense of self-awareness and responsibility, for the ability to shape reality has no limits. The shamanic helper spirits, bearing generations' worth of wisdom and knowledge, do restrain the use of this ability if a shaman's intention may result in imbalance or suffering in the world.

What is the nature of this center of all existence? It is simply the point or axis, depending on your perception, where all time, all space, and all potentialities touch. It can probably be conceptualized as a sort of higher-dimensional place, as it is essentially impossible in the geometry of the physical world as we normally perceive it. In the reality of the *gol* there is no separation among past, present, and future; all times that have been or will be are the present. In the same way, all places in the universe touch at this point. A shaman can leap into any time or place through this point if his work requires it. Furthermore, when you understand that a shaman can go to any time at any place, you will intuitively understand that the *gol* is the place where all potentialities meet. If the shaman can go to any time and place to create a desired outcome, does that not also mean that any number of outcomes that the shaman can visualize become possible? This is the explanation of the miraculous deeds and manifestations that occur during shamanic ritual. The stories of unbelievable shamanic deeds are indeed true, and the amount of windhorse the shamans had to have to make them happen is indeed formidable!

In discussing the source of shamanic power, perhaps it is appropriate to discuss briefly the concept of power. Power in the physical sense is understood as being force, the ability to move something or to create the potential for movement. It can be measured in quantifiable amounts. Spiritual power is similar, but there are some differences. Spiritual power is not quantifiable—it is either available or not. The only constraint on it is when an intention will throw things seriously out of balance, and in such cases it usually will not manifest. While power in the physical world is the creation of movement, spiritual power is the ability to manifest through intention. This intention may be simply to perceive beyond the confines of physical reality, or it may be used to alter physical reality in shamanic work, such as in healing and soul retrieval. Spiritual energy is unlike physical energy in that there is not a set amount required for a given result. A shamanic task such as a healing may require great amounts of physical energy, or may even be impossible, if undertaken by ordinary medical means.

SYMBOLIC TOOLS AND TECHNIQUES

A concept as complex as that of the *gol* is difficult for a new shaman to understand, much less visualize. Thus it is not surprising

that there are a number of symbols and tools for helping the shaman to manifest and use it. Many of these same symbols, used among
Mongols and Siberians who are not shamans, are rooted in the distant past when shamanism and traditional culture evolved together
and influenced each other. Shamanic symbols and ideas permeate
traditional culture, even among people who are not aware of their
shamanic meanings and uses. Many of these symbols are found in
ancient rock carvings, and a number of them are found in other
cultures as well, evidence of a common world shamanic heritage.
They exist because they work, of course, and because they are part
of Universal Truth.

The traditional dwelling of the Mongols, the *ger*, is a good example of the symbolism of the *gol*. The *ger* is circular with a definite orientation to the four directions. No matter where it is set up,
it represents the same place. The circular movement inside represents the circularity of time. Time in Mongolian tradition is seen not
as linear but, rather, as circular, so the past, present, and future
wind tightly around themselves, and therefore, past, present, and
future all touch each other. The center of the *ger* has the significant
name *gal golomt*, "*gol*, place of the fire." The *gal golomt* is the focal
point of an axis that runs up to the sky and down into the earth. At
that very point heaven and earth meet, and the fire (itself called
gal) naturally resides there. For this reason fire is considered sacred. Fire cleanses and liberates. People give to the fire with great
reverence in all kinds of shamanic ceremonies, and the kindling
of fire is a sacred act. This symbolism of the Mongolian tradition
is found throughout Siberia and in many other cultures as well.[2]

The idea of the vertical axis and the focal point of the *gol* is
symbolically represented in other ways. The axis is embodied in the
World Tree, the *turge*, which has its roots in the lower world and
its branches extending into the upper world. The idea of the lower
and upper worlds is actually more a concept of parallel realities
than of worlds stacked like layers in a cake. The lower and upper
worlds are spiritual realms that the shaman accesses in doing his
work. These spiritual worlds are accessed through the center; thus,
the shaman goes to the center and from there travels into these
other worlds. In other shamanic traditions this may be visualized as

a tunnel rather than a tree, but the basic concept is the same. Ritual trees are a representation of the World Tree and will sometimes take the center of a shaman's ritual space instead of the fire. In Buryat ritual the symbolic *turge* tree may be placed in the *gal golomt* itself, which is consistent with its representation of the *gol*.[3]

A site for fire rituals at a sacred tree (barisaa)

Trees represent another important aspect of our spiritual being. Each person in his own spiritual sphere has the same axis running from the sky above his head to the ground beneath his feet. In the chest is the *gol* of one's personal consciousness, the *setgel*. In shamanic work you will learn how to unify the *gol* of your own being with the universal *gol*, and you will eventually understand that wherever you go, you never leave the *gol*. This is the key to great shamanic power.

Mountains have the same symbolism as trees, for they are earth reaching up to touch the sky. In Buryat tradition the world has a spiritual mountain, Humber Uula, that like the *turge* has its roots in the lower world and its peak in the upper world. Of course Buryats do not believe that the *turge* or the Humber Uula exists in physical reality; each is simply a representation of a deeper spiritual truth. Throughout Siberia and Mongolia symbolic representations of mountains or of the *turge*, called *oboo*, are used in shamanic ritual. The symbolic representation of the *gol*

Buryat yohor *dance raises a spiral of energy to send the shaman on his journey. In the background is an eight-sided traditional Buryat yurt.*

in *oboos* links them magically with it. People visit *oboos to* make offerings and tie on horsehair and cloth as physical representations of their intentions. By bringing their intentions to such a sacred place, it is believed that the power may be granted to make their intentions manifest.

A shaman may create a fire, an *oboo,* or a ceremonial *turge* tree as a way of visualizing the *gol* for himself and for the participants in the ritual. The imagery of these attributes adds to the richness and magnificence of a ritual and thereby enhance its power. The massed intention of the people participating in the ritual adds to the shaman's windhorse during his work. In some rituals the participants may dance around the shaman in a sunwise direction, creating a spiral of energy. In much the same way, the merging of time and space at the *gol* can be visualized as a spiraling of all things toward the center.

OVERCOMING ILLUSIONS OF TIME AND SEPARATION

As you progress in your shamanic work, you will come to realize how truly limited physical perception is. Almost all human beings get an inkling that there is a lot more to the world than the usual everyday reality, but as a shaman you will be working beyond this reality on a regular basis. If you think about it, even our perception of ordinary physical reality is extremely limited. We can hear and see only tiny portions of the electromagnetic spectrum and stumble about practically blind to the fantastic world that surrounds us. In the same way, most people are unaware of the true nature of reality. We know differently—we are shamans.

Scientists often speak of the big bang theory, which holds that the entire universe was once concentrated inside an infinitesimally tiny point that, for some unexplained reason, exploded and expanded outward to create the universe as we know it today. Now, if we think about it, in non-ordinary reality, where all time and space merge into a single point and single time, is not the *gol* the original cosmic egg? Not only do we return to the center, but we also return to the Beginning. Nothing could be more sacred.

Shamans live a dual life, one based in physical reality and one based in the spiritual. One is not more real than the other. In the spiritual world, everything merges at the center; if we carry this perception into physical reality, however, the paradox can drive people insane. Unconsciously, non-shamans choose to ignore much of non-ordinary reality to preserve a sense of order and stability in their world. Are we physical beings in a definite here and now, or are we simply all beings in the *gol* rationalizing this whole physical reality in order to make the universe more understandable? If you answer yes to either question, you are right. This is the paradox.

In shamanic work you can dispense with the idea of linear time. There is no time in shamanism. Cause and effect are contemporary and intrinsically linked even if their manifestations in physical re-ality seem to be random. This is the meaning of the phrase *hoyor sagai negende* ("two times becoming as one"), for in saying this magical phrase you use the power of the *gol* to unite the time of intention with the time of manifestation. If you so need to, you can actually shamanize for a time that has already passed if your inten-tion will not create imbalance; the only rule is that this usually works only if you do not know what the outcome is before you do it. You can actually bend time, make it slow down or speed up. In undertaking shamanic journeys it is not unusual for you to feel that great lengths of time have elapsed only to discover when you return that you have been gone just a few minutes in the perception of the people observing you. You are also capable of traveling backward or forward in time through the *gol*. Visualize time as a ball of string wound infinitely tightly around itself. Parts of a long strand touch in many, many places that would be separated by a great distance if the string were unwound. In much the same way, all times touch each other.[4]

All places touch each other at the center. How could they not if the *gol* is the sum total of the universe concentrated in an infinitesimally small point? When you shamanize, you can do work for someone who is a great distance away with the same effect as if the person were in your ritual space. While you may not be able to bring your physical body across such great distances, with some training you can project your consciousness or focus your intention to places separated from you in time or space. In Buryat tradition the ability of a shaman to overcome great distances magically is called *gazar humihe* ("bending space").

As if this were not enough, I present you with another paradox. As I mentioned earlier, each person possesses a reflection of the *gol* within his or her spiritual body. Each human being is surrounded by a blue sphere of energy with the *setgel*, the *gol* of the individual being, at the center. This sphere, in non-ordinary reality, is infinitely big, like a universe within itself. This personal universe is unique for every individual and shapes perceptions of the universe at large. Human interaction, the intersection of these personal universes, is a miraculous thing. As you read this book, my universe intersects with yours. If you think about this, you will come to understand why people's perceptions of reality, of the meaning of things, may seem irreconcilably different. On the other hand, we are all merged in a great stream of consciousness, each one of our universes being like a stream flowing into a great river, the Dolbor *gol*. Like waters flowing from many streams, we mix together and are intimately connected with one another. How is the volume of a great body of water the same as a single center point? This is an intriguing contradiction, two ways of looking at the same thing.

The exercise at the end of this chapter will teach you how to break through physical illusion and limitation and return to the center. In your shamanic work, however, it is not necessary always to visualize this. Using the symbol of fire, tree, mountain, or river, you can access the center and benefit from being able to do so.

CONCENTRATING AND USING SPIRITUAL ENERGY

In many shamanic techniques, you will be concentrating and directing spiritual energy. The Siberian concept of spiritual energy has a lot in common with that of *chi* in Chinese tradition. This is not a coincidence, as the techniques of *chi gong* originated from ancient Chinese shamanism and share their origin from extremely ancient Asian shamanic traditions. Spiritual energy is usually known as *huch*, "force," or *tsog*, which is imagined as being like lightning or fire. The word *tsog* is appropriate because many shamans experience heat or a mild tingling sensation when this spiritual energy is concentrated in the hands. Recognizing the presence of *tsog* is useful not only for concentrating or manipulating it, but also useful in healing, because you can recognize the presence or absence of *tsog* in a person's energy field. This is an important tool for diagnosing spiritual repressions and intrusions, which are the underlying causes of many a human illness.

In order to work with *tsog*, it is necessary to be able to sense the energies within the energy field that is centered in your own body. Have you ever seen a bar magnet set down among iron filings and noticed how the filings arrange themselves into patterns in alignment with the magnetic energy that surrounds the magnet? In much the same way, spiritual energy naturally surrounds each of us. In our traditions spiritual energy is visualized as a sphere of sky blue light that is visible when seeing with the eyes of spirit. An axis runs straight up and down through this sphere, extending up toward the heavens and down toward the earth. Energy comes down from Father Heaven along this axis, streaming into the crown of the head *(zulai)*. Nurturing energy flows up this same axis from Mother Earth, entering through the feet and base of the spine. The hands can draw in energy from either direction. This energy flows up and down the body in rhythm with the heartbeat. These sources of energy are inexhaustible as long as the body is free of blockages and intrusions. Shamans do the *ariulga* daily in order to keep the flow clean and unimpeded.

In the center of the personal energy sphere is the *setgel*, the *gol* of the personal energy sphere, visualized as a starlike point of red light. Its brightness is directly related to the level of the individual's windhorse. Observing this in other people is another important tool for diagnosis. The *setgel* is conceived of as the ultimate seat of consciousness. It is fed by the energy flow in the upright axis that intersects it. The *setgel* of people with a lot of windhorse is thought to be larger than that of other people; it can be enlarged by the practices I described for raising windhorse.

In invoking and directing *tsog*, a person will not and must not give of his or her personal *tsog* energy. People who drain off personal energy when giving *tsog* to other people suffer from some sort of interruption in the energy flow that naturally replenishes *tsog*. In shamanic work, *tsog* should be consciously allowed to flow in directly from above or below and channeled into the hands for transferring to other people or objects.

EXERCISE: MAKING *ARSHAAN*

The creation of *arshaan* (an energized liquid) is a good exercise for concentrating and directing *tsog*. It is also necessary for daily spiritual practice and a regular part of many healing techniques. In Siberia and in Mongolia, people who are going to shamans for healing bring liquids as a matter of course for conversion into *arshaan*.

Arshaan is normally taken in small amounts or rubbed or sprinkled on the body in order to transfer healing energy to where injury has occurred or for cleansing of the spiritual energy field. Putting *arshaan* on the crown of the head keeps the axis of energy flow clear of intrusions or interruptions. Because *arshaan* is necessary for your daily spiritual practice, I present it here as an exercise in concentrating and directing *tsog*.

Before you start, have a bottle or cup of liquid such as water, tea, milk, or vodka (these are the liquids traditionally used for making *arshaan*) at the ready so you can easily pick it up when it is time to energize it. In order to direct *tsog*, you must be standing or sitting upright, with neither your arms nor legs crossed so that energy flow is not impeded in any way. With your eyes open or closed, visualize the spherical field of energy surrounding you. Once you have done this, focus on the sensation of energy flow going up and down your body. When you have tuned it in, you can draw in *tsog* in one of two ways. One is to extend your hands slightly to each side, palms upward, and allow the energy flowing from above to pool in your hands. Think of standing out in the rain with the drops flowing down your body and forming puddles in your palms. Focus on the intention of concentrating *tsog* in your hands. As you do this, you may feel heat or a prickly electric sensation starting to grow in your palms. The second way to gather *tsog* in the hands is to move the hands along the axis of energy flow, scooping up from below and directing it down from above to a point a little in front of the chest.

Now that you have concentrated *tsog* in this way, pick up the container of liquid that you will be converting into *arshaan*. Using focused intention, transfer the *tsog* from your hands into the liquid. The energy will flow naturally into it. The liquid imbued with *tsog* can be applied to parts of the body or to objects for cleansing. You can transfer *tsog* into people's bodies in the same way for healing.

Another way shamans transfer this energy is through breath. When you draw in and direct the energy, you can put it into your breath rather than into your hands. Blowing into the liquid or blowing onto a sick person will transfer *tsog* just as effectively.

You may call your shaman spirits to bring greater levels of energy to a specific target either through your own body or directly from themselves. Allowing the force of the shaman spirits to flow through your body is a low-level method of merging with them; it does not require trance or drumming and you remain in ordinary consciousness. As you become more experienced, you will be able to recognize when your helper spirits are augmenting your personal power in a non-trance state. The very act of concentrating and directing *tsog* may at first require that you go into a slight meditative state, but soon you will find that you can do it easily in almost any situation.

CREATING YOUR OWN *OBOO* OR RITUAL TREE

In Mongolian shamanism the creation of an *oboo* has two purposes. One is to honor the nature spirit of a place, and in honoring it to create a representation of the *gol* so that the spirit can more easily bring blessings to the people who come to pray to it. The other is to create a place where a shaman can more easily access the power of the *gol* by using a representation of it as a tool. An *oboo* usually serves both purposes.

Oboos take several forms. What they all have in common is their symbolic meaning, even though they may be made of different materials. Most *oboos* are made of wood or stones. In general, the people in Mongolia and in some parts of Tuva make *oboos* of stones because they live in the steppe; the forest-dwelling people of Siberia make *oboos* of wood. The most important characteristic of *oboos* is their vertical nature—whether they are piles of stone, piles of wood, or living trees, they represent the union among the three worlds and the union between all places and times. Thus they have great shamanic power.

An oboo *in the form of a* serge *(tethering post) at the source of the Oka River.*

It is not difficult to make an *oboo*. There are certain items that are traditionally put under *oboos*, but they are not necessary. In the past, weapons were often buried under *oboos* in recognition of their power to make peace and to bring protection (the Iroquois peace tree ceremony also involves the burying of weapons). What is most important, however, is the intention in creating an *oboo*. An *oboo* can be created anywhere if the person who builds it has a sincere desire to use it for shamanic work and to honor the nature spirits of the place where it is erected.

Perhaps the easiest *oboo* to make is a *barisaa*, "sacred tree," which is usually made from a young tree, preferably a pine, willow, birch, or larch (but I have used other types of trees in warmer climates). It is not necessary to perform a ritual to start using a tree as a *barisaa*, although the Peace Tree ritual (see chapter 8) can be done to consecrate it. What is important is the intention to use it as a representation of the *turge*, the World Tree, the *gol* in its aspect as a tree. The roots, the trunk, and the branches represent past, present, and future and the lower, middle, and upper worlds. The tree or *oboo* is a vertical object, but in the unity of its components as one object it represents the unity of these things within the *gol*. We, as human beings drawing energy from the earth and sky, are a reflection of the *turge*, with roots in the past and branches reaching up to the future.

If you make a *barisaa*, be sure to do things to honor the tree spirit. Smudge it; give it some milk, tea, or vodka; and decorate its branches with beautiful ribbons—its spirit will be happy and act as a helper for you when you try to visualize the *gol* in your shamanic work. Of course you may also want to do a ritual to commune with the spirit directly, which will make the *barisaa* even more effective.

You can also create an *oboo* from a pile of stones—new *oboos* are not that big, only a few feet high. To create it, walk around it sunwise (clockwise) as you place the stones and stay focused on the intention of making it a reflection of the World Mountain Humber Uula, another manifestation of the *gol*. It is customary to stick a few branches into the top of the pile of stones and decorate it with ribbons in honor of the nature spirit of the place in which it was created. *Oboos* created at mountain passes and on hill- or mountaintops are considered to be especially powerful.

If rocks are not available but you have tree branches and sticks, you may also create an *oboo* by leaning them against each other to form a conical stack. Tie ribbons to the branches to honor the nature spirits. Remember when you create *oboos* that it is not in good taste to climb and scramble on them. It is honorable, however, and a way to add to the *oboo's* spiritual power, to add rocks or branches to it. This pleases the nature spirits; they will increase the power of the *oboo* in return.

When I speak of the spiritual power of the *oboo*, I speak of its spiritual power for non-shamans, its ability to grant wishes when people come to pray, tie on ribbons, and leave tobacco offerings. For the purpose of shamanic work, when you are using an *oboo* as a tool to visualize the *gol*, the size or age of the *oboo* is not so important.

In Buryat shamanic practice, temporary *oboos* are made for rituals, and you can do this in various shamanic ceremonies as your spirits lead you. These are made from cut trees (saplings, from one foot to twenty feet in height, depending on the ceremony), and they are called *turge*, which refers to the fact that they represent the *gol* in the form of the World Tree. The simplest *turge* is a little tree to which a few white ribbons have been attached; the most complicated is the nine-branched tree that the shaman climbs during the ascent to the upper world. (In some places the shaman climbs it in fact, in which case the tree needs to be sturdy enough to support his weight, but usually a smaller tree is used and the shaman climbs it only in spirit.) These trees are stuck in the ground or otherwise propped up within the ritual space during a ritual and then either burned or discarded in a respectful way. One special way to employ a tree ritually is to use a living tree with its roots still attached (a sapling such as you can obtain at a nursery or find in the woods), which you then plant outside later. This becomes a *barisaa*. Birch trees are the favorite type of tree to use as *turge*, but any type of tree is acceptable.

The most important thing about an *oboo* is that as a concrete representation of the *gol*, it gives you a concrete representation of the world center to focus on in your work. Of course a fire can serve the same purpose, but in many cases a fire is impractical.

Also, if you create a permanent *oboo*, you can have a place to use again and again for your shamanic work, and the nature spirits that are drawn to the *oboo* will add to its power as time passes.

EXERCISE: VISUALIZATION OF WORLD CENTER

After the exercise of merging with the spirits, which was described in the previous chapter, this is probably the most powerful exercise in this book. If you complete this, you will have made a significant step in your progress to becoming a fully empowered shaman. Why? Because when you merge with the *gol*, you have unlimited powers, mobility, and the ability to contact any time, place, or spirit entity. In this exercise it is important to merge with the spirits first so they can lead you to the *gol* easily and in a way that will be most understandable for you.

As I discussed above, the symbolic representations of the *gol* have one thing in common: they all have the characteristic (in our traditional thinking) of being places where things that are normally separated are joined—earth and sky, matter and light, physical and spiritual. As Abai Geser said, "Two times being as one!" Abai Geser, in using the *gol* in *gazar humihe* (bending of time and space), would turn around three times in a sunwise direction and then jump from the place of beginning to the time and place of his choice. What is the meaning of this turning around? It is significant, for it represents the other characteristic of the *gol*, that of being a vortex, first spiraling in a sunwise direction and then spiraling out again. This is represented in Mongolian amulets, in which the invocations and intention are written in a sunwise spiral circling in toward the center and then the words specifying their manifestation are written sunwise spiraling outward from the center. It is not surprising that the spiral symbol is found in many shamanic and esoteric traditions throughout the world, for the *gol* is a universal truth known to mystics throughout history.[5]

Those of you who are acquainted with astronomy are probably familiar with the concept of the black hole, which consists of matter spiraling inward in a vortex into an infinitely small point called the singularity. In the singularity, time becomes eternity; matter and energy become as one. Furthermore, some theories hold that the singularity is connected with some other point in the universe where the energy spirals outward again. This phenomenon is similar to the original cosmic egg, the infinitely small point from which the universe was born at the beginning of time. The *gol* is similar to both the singularity of the black hole and the cosmic egg. It is like the singularity because of its vortexlike aspect; it is like the cosmic egg in that—unlike the singularity, which is relatively localized— the *gol* contains everything and connects everything. Imagining the *gol* in its vortexlike form can be useful in visualizing it, in entering it as a gateway to where you need to go, and for tapping the energy you need for specific tasks.

When you do this exercise for the first time, I highly recommend that you use a fire as a representation of the *gol*. If you are not able to make a fire, a candle will do. It should be a large candle, set in a dish or large holder, that will not be likely to go out while you are doing your work. The holder must be stable and not easily tipped over. You want to be able to look down at the candle as you would look at a fire. Why do I suggest fire? The first reason is that the light and energy of fire are reminders of the infinite energy of creation and destruction embodied in the *gol*. Second, the flame or flames are conducive to focusing and inducing the state of mind that the spirits can use to aid you in visualizing the *gol*. Third, fire is connected with Golomt Eej/Umai, the mother of all things, and with Golto Sagaan Tenger, powerful spirits that will aid you in your work. You may want to specifically address them in your invocation before you start. I also recommend that you invoke Buuluur Sagaan Tenger, the heavenly patron of all shamans. He will lend assistance to all shamanic activities undertaken with a sincere intention and a desire to learn and acquire shamanic power.

Once you have established your sacred space, be sure to light a smudge or some special incense to draw in the spirits you will invoke. Light your fire or candle with your mind focused on the intention that the flame will reveal to you the nature of the *gol*. Do everything with a sacred sense, anticipating that something special is going to happen. Think carefully about what you will say in your invocation before you start so that your words will have the maximum

power. Have a cup of vodka and a spoon on hand for making offerings to the patron spirits of the *gol*.

Once you have kindled your fire, sit on the southern side so
that you face the hearth, looking to the north. As you say your
invocation, throw a spoonful of vodka into the fire at the end of
each sentence (if you are using a candle, pour the vodka onto the
ground in front of it). Once you have finished your invocation, say
the following:

> *Golomt Eej,*
> *Source of all,*
> urshoo! urshoo! urshoo!

Then throw a spoonful of vodka into the fire and say:

> *Golto Sagaan Tenger,*
> *keeper of the gol,*
> urshoo! urshoo! urshoo!

Then throw another spoonful into the fire.

Repeat these two invocations a total of three times. Then rev-
erentially raise the cup to the fire so that the ceremonial liquid is
imbued with its power—you are sharing *arshaan* with beings that
control the greatest power of all. Take a sip from the cup, then
throw the rest of the vodka into the fire so that it blazes brightly.
Do you feel a surge of emotions as you do *joroo* (share offerings)
with these spirits?

You may use a drum now if you feel that it will help you in
merging with the spirits for the next part of this exercise. If you do,
drum softly so that your attention stays focused on the flames. Do
you remember how you felt when you merged with the spirits in
the exercise of the previous chapter? In order to complete this exercise, you should already have been successful in merging with the
spirits. You may choose to focus on the fire without drumming if
you feel so comfortable merging with the spirits that the trance
brought on by focusing on the flames is sufficient to becoming
ongod orood. As you center your intention on the flames, clear
your mind of all thought except the intention that merging with the
spirits will give you power and show you the way to enter the *gol*.

As you grow closer to spirit entry, even that thought will dissolve as your mind becomes empty and receptive.

You will recognize when the spirits have come to you when you experience a feeling of lightness. The spirits have heard your invocations and have sensed your intention; they are ready to send you on your way. You may now sense that you are being drawn toward the fire; there is a spiraling of energy as the *gol* begins to open. With the power of your *udha* and *ongon* spirits, leap forward in spirit toward the flame and you will be drawn in! You may feel yourself spinning around as you fall in.

Where are you now? You may find yourself in the in-between place, floating in an expanse of infinite blueness. This place touches all times, places, and potentialities. Fly out in any direction and you can enter any time and place in the past, present, or future; you can even enter other potential realities you have not experienced in your physical existence. Let your *ongon* spirits guide you and explore one or two of those places. You will come out of the *gol* into any of those places as easily as you entered into the *gol,* and you can move back and forth between the *gol* and these places effortlessly, for your *ongon* spirits are guiding you, empowering you, protecting you. It may seem fantastic to you now, but the most advanced shamans can do as Abai Geser did and actually project their physical bodies through time and space. This is called *gazar humihe* ("folding time and space").

You can return to your body whenever you desire, but when you do, pay attention to how you come out of the *gol* and back into your physical being. This is important. You will probably notice when you come back that you flow in through the chest, the location of the *setgel,* the *gol* of your own being. In fact, as you increase in your shamanic knowledge, you will learn that the *setgel* and the *gol* are connected in a special way and that you can actually enter the *gol* through the reflection of the *gol* in the *setgel.* When you look at the human spiritual body, this reflection is a tiny, flame-colored point of light in the center of the chest region that glows brightly in proportion to the amount of windhorse you have. Keeping your windhorse strong not only fosters your spiritual and physical health but also strengthens this connection with the infinite within your own being. When it is strong, you can use it to tap into the energy of the *gol* and as a gateway in your journeying when you do not have some other representation of the *gol* to assist you in your work.

In July 2000, when I traveled with my friends in the Sayan Mountains, we visited a sacred place where mysterious old shamanic art was painted on a cliff. Two petroglyphs drawn there showed two stick figures (believed to depict shamans) whose chests were represented as circles with dots placed in the center. It is easy to understand that the circles represented the *setgel* with the *gol* in the center.

If you have accomplished the visualization of the *gol*, I congratulate you for your success. When you are able to do this, you will have taken another huge step toward the acquisition of shamanic knowledge and power. From this time forward you will understand the symbolism and meaning of things in Siberian as well as in other shamanic traditions in a new way, in a way that people who have not made this journey will not be able to comprehend. You have discovered that our universe is more wonderful and paradoxical that most people could ever imagine. May the spirits continue to guide and teach you so that your shamanic work will bring blessing to all!

FIVE

The Shamanic Journey

As my moon, my sun began to rise
I burned the golden herb of my wondrous mountain—
The six-jointed juniper—
Fumigating myself.
And carefully refreshing myself with its aroma,
I then mounted my steed and donned my cloak.

And now I am galloping with my shoulder blades,
Nodding my head with the bird feathers,
Opening and closing the all-seeing eyes,
And dropping my head in a bow.
And so I come to that which has a name,
And so I come to this that has become known.

—SAAIA SAMBUU, FROM KENIN-LOPSAN
(TRANS. BY M. MANDELSTAM-BALZER) IN *SHAMANIC WORLDS*[1]

The journey, called *yabdal* in Buryat, is an important part of the shamanic experience. In journeying we travel with the shamanic spirits and fly either as free spirit entities or in the form of some animal that is powerful in the context of the work being done. Many people who have read about shamanism have the idea that the

Siberian shaman is always flying off here and there on journeys, but the truth is that only a small fraction of shamanic work requires journeying. In many cases, trance and embodying the spirits in full possession are not necessary either. Later in this book I will advise you on how to determine the level and type of work required for various situations.

The judicious use of journeying does not downplay its power. Think of it this way: Do you always use the same tool for every repair? Do you always use a hammer to drive in a tack, or do you first try to push it in with your fingers? Journeying is an effective technique when applied for certain purposes, and in some cases it is the only way you can achieve the desired result.

PURPOSES FOR JOURNEYING

When a teacher shaman conducts a group journey of students for instructive purposes, he can extend the protection of his *ongon* spirits to all of the participants on the journey. But unlike many other shaman teachers, I generally do not take students on a journey until I feel they are ready for it. Journeying is a genuine out-of-the-body experience and the student should have established at least some sort of rapport with his shamanic helper spirits before going on a full-fledged journey by himself, for the helper spirits assist in protecting a shaman during the journey. The world is not all goodness and light—there are hostile spirit entities that will attack shamans during a journey if they are not well balanced or lack the protection of helper spirits. Spirit attacks can lower a person's spiritual energy, what we call *suns daraad*, "soul repression," and result in spiritual intrusions or, in the worst cases, even soul loss. Because we journey to bring healing, blessing, or restoration of balance, it is a disservice to those for whom we are doing the work if we become injured ourselves during the journey.

Because you are just beginning your shaman work, you may want to do some exploratory journeying in order to acquaint yourself with the spirit worlds and sharpen your journeying abilities. Although many people assume that you have to drum for journeying, this is not always the case. As described above, drumming brings you to a state of consciousness that is useful for shamanic work. The altered state that you use for embodying the spirits can also prepare you for flying or running in spirit for shamanic journeys. As you practice achieving this state of mind, you will eventually be able to do it at will, even when a drum is not available. Siberian shamans learned to work drumless during the years of Stalinist repression, when drumming could reveal that shamanic work was being done. Being a shaman often meant a death sentence in those dark and terrible times. Today, being able to work drumless gives a shaman a certain freedom. If you find this difficult, do not worry: you can learn to do it once you become familiar with the sensation of the altered state.

Most journeying is for one of three purposes. First, a shamanic journey may be done when the shaman has to retrieve something from some location in the universe. The most common journey of this type is a soul retrieval. This may be a brief middle-world journey or a lengthy and dangerous lower-world journey. A shaman may also journey to bring blessing back to his community, such as in the Clean Tent ritual or in the *shinkelevun* ritual of the Evenks, in which the shaman brings back hunting luck.

A second purpose for a journey is to gather information or meet with spirit entities that are not in the physical (middle) world. For example, a shaman may need to go to the lower world to talk to the spirit Erleg Khan or to speak with someone who has died. The shaman may travel to a specific place in order to meet its master spirit, such as the journey to meet the mountain spirits. This may be performed in order to find and bring back a spirit for introduction into an *ongon* that will bring blessing for a specific undertaking. A shaman may travel to a different time or place in order to get information needed for a specific task. In many cases, however, a shaman will get information simply by divination, then use journeying as the next step if more detailed or special information is necessary.

A third reason for journeying is to return something that is out of place. This usually happens in the context of healing or taking care of hauntings. In these situations the shaman is returning a spirit that has lost its way when traveling to the lower world and needs to be sent back by the shaman personally. In many cases the shaman can get the same results by simply ordering the spirit back to the place where it belongs; journeywork is necessary when the spirit either is excessively attached to a person or place or outright refuses to leave.

In the next sections I will describe the basic cosmology of Mongolian/Siberian shamanism to give you some frame of reference with regard to what you will experience while journeying. Nevertheless, you may find that your perception of how these various parts of the universe appear is not exactly as how I describe it. For example, if in your journey the lower world does not look the way it is described in my or Michael Harner's teachings, do not be overly concerned. Our different perceptions of places like the lower world are equally valid and are what works best for us individually. Thus, I would advise you to do some exploratory journeying to familiarize yourself with the structure of your universe so you will learn to recognize certain landmarks along the way. These landmarks are an important tool for the shaman. Known as *olokhs* in some traditions, they appear differently to each shaman. Usually you will pass nine of these landmarks on the way to your destination. Although frivolous journeys just for "kicks" are a waste and abuse of your shamanic abilities, exploratory journeys are important in making a new shaman understand the realities he will be working with.[2]

STARTING FROM THE CENTER

In the previous chapter you learned to use tools for visualizing the *gol* and how to merge your *setgel* with the *gol* for shamanic empowerment. Journeys naturally start from the *gol;* for this reason, a fire, a ceremonial tree, or another symbolic representation of the *gol* are almost always used in journeying. Journeys start from the center, but you will not remain there: it serves as a gateway or passage to the other times, places, and realms of existence you will be visiting in your work.

The universe is generally considered by all Siberian traditions to comprise three worlds—an upper, a middle, and a lower world. All three are inhabited by spirits; the middle world is unique, however, in that it also contains physical reality. The upper world is considered to be located beyond the sky, not in outer space but, rather, in some dimension beyond it. Doors to the upper world are believed to open sometimes; when they do, bright light streams out because the upper world is thought to be much brighter than the other worlds. The upper world is the home of spirits who play a great role in human fate, the *tenger*, *zayaans*, and *khans*. A shaman may travel to the upper world to communicate with these spirits and negotiate blessings for certain people or for his community. Upper-world spirits are generally invisible to physical sight, and a shaman traveling to the upper world may likewise be invisible if the upper-world being lacks shamanic abilities. Each human being contains an upper-world spirit within his being. (See "The Spiritual Structure of Human Beings" in chapter 6 for a discussion.)

The lower world is also a spirit realm and is visualized as being below, although not literally so. Journeying there is generally visualized as a downward movement through some sort of passageway. The Buryat expression *gazarai urhe* means "smoke hole of the earth," a hole in the earth through which shamans may pass to enter the lower world. There are other routes by which a shaman may travel to the lower world. Visualize these passages as tunnels or watercourses such as the source of a spring or the river Dolbor, which is believed to flow into the lower world. The lower world is generally perceived as somewhat dark—it reminds me of the light on a cloudy day, a little grayer than normal. The lower world is inhabited by human souls between incarnations. It is not an unpleasant place but seems rather natural and unspoiled by modern technology. Some Mongolian shamans visualize the lower world as having much more water than the middle world. As is the case in the upper world, lower-world spirits are usually invisible in this world and we are often invisible in theirs.[3]

Our universe, the middle world, is unique in that it has physical reality in addition to a spiritual dimension. Physical living organisms are inhabited by at least two spirit entities; humans have three, one from each of the three worlds. The middle-world component of the human being, the *suld*, lives in the natural world after a person's life; it is immortal but never incarnates again. Nature is permeated with millions of these beings, all of whom are capable of communicating with shamans.

The *gol* is the connecting point of all these places, and most shamans start with upward movement from it. Even the lower-world journey may start with flight upward from the *gol*. As you recall, when a person becomes *ongod orood,* the sensation at the moment of its happening may seem to be like moving upward toward the sky. This is the sensation of shaking loose from the confines of the physical body, for the *ongon* spirits usurp control of the body temporarily when they enter. When you journey, it usually starts with embodying the shamanic spirits, because they accompany and protect you during the journey and help you break through to the spirit worlds.

Your sensation of travel might be one of flight, running, or falling. As you practice you will find that there are certain ways you travel that are unique to you and your needs. You may find that you remain pretty much in your usual form during the journey, especially if you are using a shaman steed (see page 72). Or you may take on the form of one or more animals during a journey. I have known of Buryat shamans traveling as several animals in succession, such as a fox, then a squirrel, then a hawk, and so on, finally returning to human form upon reaching their destination. These transformations come naturally according to the individual requirements of the journey.

Because you merge with your shaman spirits during a journey, you will experience the same distortions of time that occur while embodying the spirits. The journey may appear to take a long time, although the people watching your ceremony feel it lasts only a few minutes. This is perfectly normal. Perceptions of size and distance likewise become distorted when you are outside the physical body. Your body may seem gigantic, like a mountain, or it may seem microscopically small. Some of the unusual things you see may be the result of seeing from the perspective of being much larger or smaller than usual.

Because all journeys start from the center, distance is essentially meaningless. Buryat legends speak of shamans able to travel at the speed of lightning—this is how others perceive the idea of shamans being able to traverse any distance with a single step. The story that unfolds during your journey, the landmarks that you see, are part of the spirits' lesson to you and should be understood as being significant. Just as you learn to understand the symbolic meaning of dream images, you will also learn to understand the meanings of what you see on your journey. Shamans traditionally recite the sights and events of the journey after returning; you may want to go the extra step and keep a record of your experiences so you can study them and learn the spirits' lessons. Although movement in journeys on one level is instantaneous, our interpreting it as a journey is a way of making rational and useful the tremendous amount of information that is revealed.[4]

Some shamans continue drumming through the entire journey; others lie down during the journey while a competent assistant continues the drumming for them. This is a matter of choice and depends on what works best for you at the time. A lot of shamans prefer doing their journeys in a dark room or at night because darkness helps in maintaining an altered state of consciousness. Journeying is a serious matter, but it is nevertheless a joyous and wonderful experience. Enjoy the adventure!

Before setting out on a shamanic journey, it is important to have a specific destination or goal in mind. In any kind of shamanic work you need to focus and direct intention toward certain goals so that you can manifest the energy to produce the desired results. In journeying, if you do not have a specific destination, such as when you are searching for something like a lost soul, direct your intention toward what you are looking for. Journeying always carries some risk for the shaman of soul loss or of getting lost or hung up somewhere. If this happens, even if you return to ordinary consciousness, you will be disempowered and out of sorts until you have recovered your complete self. Getting lost or hung up is usually caused by journeying without a specific goal in mind. When you journey simply for exploration, be sure to keep your spirits close around you and follow their wisdom, for they will keep you safe.

COMPANIONS ON THE JOURNEY

A shaman does not travel alone. Whenever you leave your body, your spirit family will surround you for protection and guidance, and your power animals will run with you in their usual form. Each shaman visualizes his spirits differently, and as you develop your relationship with them you will recognize the various forms they take. They may even manifest as a certain physical sensation, smell, or sound. Whether or not they are directly visible or otherwise perceptible, the shamanic helper spirits are always around you. Visualize them as being like a flock of birds that cluster around you wherever you go, whether you are journeying or doing other shamanic work or if you are in everyday reality. The truth is that they never leave you. Remember the responsibilities of being a shaman: not only do you serve a community of friends, family, and clients, but you also have an ongoing relationship with these spirits, who should be recognized and honored. This is one reason that shamans generally take their *ongons* wherever they go to do ritual—the *ongons* are a visual reminder to the shaman as well as to the participants in a ceremony of the presence of the helper spirits. While you journey it is also likely that your *udha* and other spirits are inside your body, directing the course of the journey.

In addition to the helper spirits, you may use a spiritual mount in your journey. The drum, or the sound of the drum, can be visualized as a horse or other animal that you ride into the spiritual realm during your shamanic quest. Imagine that the beats of the drum are the hoofbeats of your steed as you travel toward your destination, even if you are flying. You may want to experiment with visualizing different types of shamanic mounts; the usual favorites are horses, deer, wolves, dogs, snakes, and giant birds, but you are free to use any animal that you find helpful in your travel. A shamanic steed is not necessary, but it is often a part of the journey experience. You may just as often become an animal yourself and travel in that form. The most important point is to allow the journey to take the course determined by your spirit helpers. They have guided many shamans before; they know the best and easiest route to where you are going and will present the experiences necessary for what you have to learn.

The Dolbor Night Road Journey

The journey I present here is a variation of the lower-world journey performed by Mongolian and Siberian shamans for the purpose of soul retrieval. In such a case, once the shaman reaches the lower world, he will look about for the missing soul with the help of the spirits. This version of the Dolbor journey is for exploration and learning, but you may later choose to adapt it for your own purposes once you have become familiar with it.[5]

In the previous chapter I presented the *gol* experience in terms of it being like a vortex, singularity, or point. In the Dolbor journey we experience the *gol* as a flow, a body of water linking all consciousness and all three worlds. Each of us is a source of the river as well as an integral part of it. The Dolbor as a river is natural, majestic, and awesome, and the journey is full of ecstatic and beautiful experiences.

I have already described the necessity of preparation by creating sacred space and invoking the spirits, so I will dispense with that part of the ritual. The Dolbor journey is traditionally performed at night; hence it is called a night road journey. The invocation of the spirits is usually done around sunset, and drink offerings may be poured out in front of the entrance of the building where the ritual is being done. In addition to the offering of sacred smoke, an incense burner is placed by the entrance to the sacred space.

The Dolbor journey is usually done with drumming, either by the shaman or by an assistant. Before journeying the shaman drums and dances until he has merged with the *ongon* spirits and is in an ecstatic state. On reaching ecstasy, the shaman will sit or lie down, depending on whether he has to drum for himself.

Visualize the Dolbor as having many small creeks flowing into it, each one representing the individual consciousness of every human being. The source of the river is in the upper world, at the upper reaches of the *turge*, the World Tree, and each of the small streams of consciousness flows into it until it becomes a mighty stream flowing into the lower world. The Dolbor journey starts as a middle-world journey to find the spring that is the source of the individual shaman's consciousness.

I find my spring in the depths of the great Siberian taiga, but you may find your spring in a different place. Once you have found your spring, follow the creek that flows from it to the Dolbor. You may change into a fish or other water creature, fly along it like a bird, or run along the banks of the creek in the form of an animal or human. It is common for shamans doing this journey to shape-shift many times, becoming several different animals in succession and at other times gliding along the route as pure spirit. You may even bob along on the water like a cork. This can be a joyous experience. Be sure to note what your surroundings are like—the trees, mountains, and other landmarks. Is the creek deep and serene, or does it burble along with lots of rocks and little waterfalls? What kind of beings do you meet on the way? Never feel so hurried to reach the Dolbor that you ignore those entities who desire to speak to you on your way—they may have valuable instructions about what you will see on your journey.

When you reach the Dolbor itself, the experience of the mighty flow of the collective consciousness of all beings is ecstatic and overwhelming. Once again you may decide to go down the river through the water, in the air, or along its banks. You may go a great distance following the course of the river until you reach the entrance to the lower world. Be sure to observe the land along the banks of the river and note what kind of country you are traveling through. The Dolbor is said to be full of rapids and waterfalls: do you see many of them on your journey?

The Dolbor is perceived by Siberians as flowing northward, and the entrance to the lower world is at its mouth, where it enters the Arctic Ocean. Many shamans have seen this entrance as a huge sinkhole in the earth, where the Dolbor crashes down in an enormous cataract, rushing into a cavern leading to the lower world. You may find a long, narrow bridge that you can walk across into the cavern and then follow the path to the lower world. You may also fly over the falls or allow yourself to be carried by the waters downward into the lower world.

In one way or another you will eventually emerge in a place similar to the middle world, but the light may appear a little dimmer than is typical of this world. This is said to be because in the lower world there is only a half sun and a half moon. Many shamans will meet the keeper of the entrance to the lower world, Mongoldai Nagts, "Mongolian Uncle." He is usually perceived as a wise old man, and a shaman doing a soul retrieval may ask Mongoldai Nagts about the location of the soul that is missing. Although he is generally friendly, he should be treated with the respect that an entity of his power and responsibility deserves. Mongoldai Nagts allows shamans to pass into the lower world, but he bars the passage of most spirits into and out of the lower world. It is believed that without his assistance the spirits of the dead would travel back to the middle world unrestricted, and there would be far more wandering of the souls of those who have not yet died into the lower world.

Because you do not have a specific purpose for staying in the lower world, you probably will not want to linger. Keep your shamanic spirits close around you, for there are spirit entities in the lower world that may attack you in order to eat or steal your soul. As long as your protection is strong, they will not succeed. It is likely that you will not meet such creatures, but I would be remiss not to warn you about them. The lower world has many beautiful and natural places, but some are ominous and frightening. You may see people living there—the souls of people between incarnations. In some cases a shaman may even encounter someone he knew in the past. If you interact with someone you know, be sure that he does not try to follow you back when you return (unless you are doing a soul retrieval for that person).

The most frightening place in the lower world is Ela Guren. This is where the souls of the most cruel and evil people are banished so that they do not return to our world. The souls of people like Hitler, Stalin, Mao Tse-tung, and other evil tyrants of history are likely to be there; only the spirits know for sure. Shamans who have traveled there say the entities are aggressive and try to keep the shaman from leaving. If you ever travel to Ela Guren, keep your protection strong and get away as quickly as possible.

Once you have finished your exploration of the lower world,

return to the Dolbor and head upstream. The best way to travel is to fly, allowing the power of the drumbeat and the spirits around you to carry you through the air. You will follow the Birds' Way, the path of the souls returning to the middle world when they are to be reborn. You may turn into a bird, with the shamanic spirits surrounding you like a flock of birds. Fly up into the sky, over the waterfall at the entrance to the lower world, through the mist, and straight up into the heavens. As you ascend you will find yourself borne up by the winds, as if you were light as a feather, and you will find a path of stars marking your way. The Milky Way, the seam of the sky, the pathway of the soul birds, is but a reflection in the sky of the Dolbor below. If you look down, you will see that the sky road you follow runs above and parallel to the course of the Dolbor.

Before you a most amazing scene will appear. High in the sky—actually beyond the sky, for the Birds' Way will bring you into the upper world—you will come to the source of the Dolbor. In the heavens, beside a gigantic tree, you will see a spring and a pool, the source of the Dolbor. Beside the tree is a house of logs, the dwelling place of Umai, the mother goddess and the keeper of human souls. If you see her, be sure to pay her respect, for she may show you some special things. The souls of living things are under her care. They perch like birds on the branches of the tree until the time of birth. You may see birds plunging into the waters of the pool to travel down to the middle world, where they will enter into babies at the time of birth.[6]

While you are in the upper world, you may want to linger and explore. Let your helper spirits guide you. When you have finished, plunge into the waters of the Dolbor and let it bring you back to your stream. Allow yourself to become familiar with the sensation of being immersed in the waters of Universal Consciousness. Do not hurry on your return; let the experience flow easily and observe what is happening around you as you go downstream to the place of your beginning. When you reach your stream, go up its course until you once again reach the spring from which you started.

The Dolbor journey is often quite long, and you may find yourself fatigued by the time you return. Be sure to thank the spirits for the visions they have brought you.

When doing the Dolbor journey for soul retrieval, the shaman will normally go straight from the lower world to the beginning place, but because this exercise is for exploration and learning, I wanted to show you the entire course of the World River. In going to the lower world, flying up the Birds' Way to the source of the Dolbor, and then traveling back to the middle world, you actually follow the course that all human souls take from death to rebirth. In this sense the journey I have presented is a type of rebirth experience. May it bring you rich experiences, great joy, and much learning!

SIX

Working
with the Spirits

Two times nine Hongoodor
Two times five Shoshoolog!
Having many white deer
By the great white lake!
Having dappled horses
And great shaman robes!
Ninety-nine Shoshoolog [shamans]
[Each] having nine drums and drumsticks!
You who dance on the mountaintops
You who have a spider web as a footbridge!
Having an indefatigable great father
Having a great wild mother!
Your nine sons
Who wash in a lake in the Altai Mountains,
Who have many steeds,
Who are the masters of many waters,
Tens of thousands of Urianhai,
Seventy thousand Zanhatai!

Your nine daughters
With a khan in the south!
Who made their own city in the south!
[You spirits] with a hundred and eight lights,
And fifty-eight shaman rituals!

—INVOCATION OF THE PROTECTOR SPIRITS OF THE HONGOODOR TRIBE,
IN BAZAROV, *TAINSTVA Y PRAKTIKA SHAMANIZMA*, TRANS. BY THE AUTHOR[1]

As a shaman your work is primarily with spirits and in the spirit world. What makes shamans so important in human society is their relationship with the spirit world, which serves as a bridge between the spirits and the community. In Buryat culture, the shaman is not only a healer and magician but also the preserver of the traditions passed down from the ancestors. He has access to the knowledge of the ancestors through the oral traditions he is taught by other human beings, but in addition he communicates directly with ancestral spirits and learns their ancient knowledge from them. You will as well, regardless of the ethnic heritage of the ancestral spirits who become your helpers.

Healing, blessing, protection, and working with the forces in nature all require interaction with spiritual entities, some benevolent in nature, some destructive. In this chapter I will describe the various ways in which you will work with spiritual entities. You will also learn how all things, not just human beings or animals but even geographical locations and "lifeless" objects, have a spiritual component mirroring their physical existence. It is for precisely this reason that the spiritual workings of the shaman can bring concrete results in mundane reality.

THE SPIRITUAL STRUCTURE OF HUMAN BEINGS

Mongolians have an interesting expression, *sab-shim,* meaning "container and contents" or "container and essence." This word is appropriate when thinking of the physical human being. The body is simply a container, a physical component of a composite of many things. To give an ordinary example, if you see someone who has a case of beer and you say "Give me a beer," you are asking for a can with the beer inside. Without the can the beer cannot be transported, yet you have no use for the can once it is empty. Just as the can and the beer are different substances in their nature but are usable only in their unity as container and contents, so the human body is a container that has little resemblance to the spiritual entities that reside in it while it is alive.

Siberians and Mongols believe that each human being is the result of the fusion of at least three distinct spirit entities. Understanding and visualizing these three components in yourself and in others are important diagnostic tools for healing and other types of shamanic work. In Buryat Mongolian as well as in other languages, the three parts have their own distinctive names, with no counterpart in English. For the sake of convenience, I will use the somewhat inadequate word *soul* in describing them collectively but employ the Mongolian terms to describe them individually. The three souls have their origin in each of the three worlds, the upper, middle, and lower. They are described as follows:

1. *ami*   upper world   reincarnates

2. *suns*   lower world   reincarnates

3. *suld*   middle world   non-reincarnating,
                            becomes nature spirit

The upper world is the origin of the *ami* soul; "*ami*" is related to the word for "breath" or "breathing." The *ami* regulates breathing and other bodily functions. It enters with the first breath of the baby and leaves with the last dying breath. It is rather unstable, especially in children, and is the soul most often found missing in cases of soul loss. Outside of the body it is visualized as being birdlike. In some Siberian cultures the *ami* is secured inside the body by tattooing a picture of a bird on the body. According to legend, in the time between incarnations the *ami* lives as a bird on the World Tree in the upper world until the womb goddess Umai sends it down to settle into the body of a baby being born.

Although the *ami* is mostly concerned with bodily function, it is a fully conscious being and brings reincarnation memories with it. The *ami* tends to follow family lineages in its succession of incarnations. What people often attribute to "genetic memories" are actually the memories of the *ami*. In this way all humans carry the memories of their ancestors, even if they are buried deeply in the subconscious. Identical twins are believed to share one *ami;* this is supported by evidence that some identical twins seem to have a telepathic link.

Animals also have the *ami* soul; thus, hunters kill with respect, for the deer killed this year will return to the same forest in the next spring. For example, what happens if a hunter kills a deer badly and violates the taboos? The *ami* soul of the deer will tell all the deer to be born in the next year to avoid a certain village or a certain hunter. In such cases, a shaman will be called to placate the spirits of the game so that hunting luck returns to his community.

The *suns* soul is a lower-world soul. It also reincarnates but does not follow any specific succession. For example, a person who was born a Mongol in this life may have been an American in a past life and may reincarnate as an African. The succession of incarnations is determined by the spirits according to a person's fate, *zayaa*. The idea of *zayaa* is similar to that of karma in Eastern religions such as Hinduism and Buddhism. A person living a destructive life now may reincarnate into a life of suffering in order to learn of the need to live benevolently and in balance. Likewise, a person living a benevolent life in which he accumulates much *buyan* will probably reincarnate into a life of happiness and prosperity. Just as Umai is in charge of determining the time and place of the incarnating of *ami* souls, the lower-world spirit Erleg Khan is in charge of the decision to reincarnate *suns* souls. Erleg Khan is conceived as being like a judge, assigning *suns* souls to certain incarnations according to their past actions. He is also believed to destroy the souls of those who have been so evil in their past lives that there is no good reason to continue their existence. People such as Hitler and Stalin are the kind of beings whose *suns* souls would likely be annihilated so they no longer would be able to bring destruction to humankind.

Suns souls are often visualized as traveling through water when outside the body. The river Dolbor is a river of souls flowing with its current to the river's mouth in the lower world. Animals that live in water are believed to have a special link with spirit. This is connected with the principle behind the making and using of *arshaan*, that liquids can contain and transmit spiritual power. *Suns* souls can fragment into thirteen parts, although they usually function as a whole. Up to twelve of them can be lost without serious consequences, although the human organism will be weakened by their loss. Generally, however, the *suns* does not normally fragment, and in cases of soul loss usually leaves the body in its entirety. It is interesting that "core shamanic" practitioners often seem to perceive loss of soul fragments rather than whole souls in their soul-retrieval work. It may be because of the fragmentation of the *suns*, or perhaps it appears that way to them because non-Siberian traditions do not always recognize the compound nature of human souls.

The *suns* is the part of the human soul triad that leaves during shamanic journeys and dreaming. The *suns* soul seems to be more dominant than the *ami* in the consciousness of human beings. The *suns* is much more frequently the source of reincarnation memories than is the *ami*. Some people who have performed hypnotic regressions in order to help people recover reincarnation memories note that the person being regressed remembers more than one life in a given time period. This may be due to the fact that the subject is recalling experiences from the past lives of more than one soul. In the case of shamans, the memories of the helper spirits, most especially the *udha*, may be the source of memories so compelling that they seem to be past-life experiences.

The *suld* soul is the unique property of human beings. The *suld* is non-reincarnating, but this does not mean that it ceases to exist after death. When a person dies, the *suld* will find a place in nature, usually a tree, a rock, a river, or a hill, that becomes its residence. It will still travel about to visit people and places it knew while alive. The *suld* begins its life with the birth of the child, and it is the unique personality of an individual, for it is shaped by the experiences of only the present life. Its blending with the *ami* and *suld* entities brings the complexity and depth of human consciousness. The older souls bring the knowledge and wisdom of past generations; the *suld* faces the world with wonder at every new

discovery. After death it joins the millions of other *suld* souls residing in the natural world, whom shamans can invoke for assistance
and advice. Some of these *suld* souls will mutate into *udha* spirits
and then associate with shamans; the exact reason and process for
this remain a mystery.

While wandering *suns* souls are often the source of illness, free-
ranging *suld* souls have a much milder effect on the living unless
they are specifically invoked for some purpose. The *suld*, after set-
tling somewhere, may have an influence on the mental state of
people who live there—for good or bad, depending on the personality of the *suld*. The Peace Tree ritual specifically addresses and
heals the mental state of *suld* souls that are disturbed because they
were released into nature as the result of a violent death.

The *suld* soul resides at the crown of the head, where the energy flow coming down from Father Heaven enters the body. Touching this part of the head is generally taboo, and hats, which cover
that part of the head, are treated with great respect. The *ami* and
suns are mobile and may leave the body temporarily without any
serious consequences, but the departure of the *suld* from the body
results in death very quickly. The *suld*, being a middle-world entity
and unique to a single life, like the body, may be the soul most
closely associated with the human brain.

The spiritual body of a human being is roughly spherical in shape
and extends far outside the confines of the body. The outside of the
sphere is highly charged with *tsog* energy and may be palpable as a
mild electric or prickly sensation on the palm. Try sensing this on
another person by bringing your palm in toward his body. Even
non-shamans can often sense the energy concentration on the edge
of the spiritual body. In diagnosis of illness you may want to feel
the shape of the spiritual body—spirit intrusions often manifest as
depressions on the normally rounded and smooth surface of the
soul sphere.

The upward and downward flow of energy from Mother Earth
and Father Heaven creates a definite and often visible axis inside
the spiritual body. This axis is pierced by seven holes correspond-
ing to the seven chakras: at the base of the spine and at the lower
belly, upper belly, chest, throat, forehead, and crown. The *ami* and

suns souls move in and out of these holes, creating a sine wave–like pattern going up and down in rhythm with the heartbeat. When you observe them, they may be visible as distinct, small points of light moving up and down the body. If you learn how to visualize them within yourself and others, you can read a lot about the physical health of the body and detect cases of soul loss.

An explanation of the complex nature of the human organism is important for the different types of work that you will be required to do. Practice visualizing the spiritual body of yourself and others as much as possible so you become accustomed to sensing the spiritual body and the component souls.

VISION QUESTS, BURYAT-STYLE

When I titled this section "Vision Quests," I did so with a little humor, as Buryats do not practice the vision quest exactly as Native Americans do. They do something similar, however, in the training of shamans. An ongoing theme in this book is cultivating your relationship with your shamanic helper spirits—learning how to communicate with them and how to gain their assistance in accomplishing certain tasks. To achieve this connection, it is helpful to isolate yourself so that you can work with them without the distractions of other people.

Among the Buryats, a shaman in training goes into the forest to commune with his spirits and to develop the rituals and power songs that he will use in his work. In a similar way, shamans awaiting public initiation fast and shamanize together in a *ger* (a traditional dwelling) for several days in preparation for the ritual without leaving the ceremonial area and without interacting with non-shamans. These extended periods of shamanic work cut off from contact with non-shamans are conducive to accelerated learning and enhance communication with the spirit world. This kind of exercise is not done until the beginning shaman has shown definite evidence of a calling from the spirits.[2]

Try this "vision quest" for yourself when you are able to. You may choose to go away for a few hours or for several days, depending on your circumstances. Planning ahead, designating a certain time, and preparing properly all help to focus your intent and will bring better results. Going to a remote natural place is best, but it can be a beach, a forest, mountains, a desert—the type of place is not so important. What is important is that you can drum and commune with the spirits without being interrupted, in a place where your drumming will not disturb others. It is best if you are far enough from other people that you will not hear dogs, traffic, or other nonnatural noises.

Be sure to dress comfortably and appropriately and take everything you need, so that once you find the place where you will do your shamanic work you do not have to stop and run back for something you have forgotten. I have mentioned the use of extreme cold as a way to induce an altered state of consciousness, but I do not recommend this until you have become experienced in your shamanic work, as it can be quite dangerous.

If conditions permit, you may want to build a small fire to use as a focusing point in your work, as it helps you visualize the *gol*. Fire has a mildly hypnotic effect on many people when they gaze into it for an extended period. You may use rocks and sticks to construct an *oboo* for the same purpose, or you may want to focus on a tree. Large, unusual, or lightning-struck trees are natural sources of spiritual power and can be helpful in your work. Before you start, be sure to smudge yourself and any shamanic instruments, such as drums and rattles, you may be using.

The exercise of exploration and learning I am recommending here does not have any other requirements. Each time you try it, it will be different, depending on the length of time involved and what kind of response you get from the spirits. The exercises described earlier in this book for contacting and merging with the spirits and for visualizing the *gol* are the best way to start; from there, just let the spirits guide the course of the experience. This exercise as it is traditionally practiced usually involves drumming and singing alone for an extended period. If you prefer meditation, however, that may work just as well for you. Try to do this exercise every once in a while; the rewards of things learned and experience will be well worth the time you invest in it.

INVOKING AND WORKING WITH SPIRITS

The material in this book up to now has been concerned with developing your relationship with your helper spirits. However, your shamanic work entails working with other spirits that will not be helpful and possibly may be hostile. These spirits may be invoked for help for a specific purpose but will not become a member of your spirit family. Still other spirits that you will meet will want to become your helper spirits and will work with you in the future. This section explains how you will work with the various types of spirits.

Invoking the Spirits

In certain situations you will want to invoke spirits for a specific purpose. In invoking spirits, keep in mind that spirits have personalities and egos, just as human beings do. In fact, if you think about it, human beings' personalities arise from the souls inhabiting the body, who are themselves spirit entities. Disembodied spirits have no less personality than incarnated ones. Keeping this in mind, address spirits in the same way you would a human being. Just as people enjoy being spoken to politely and respectfully, spirits also like being addressed with pleasant words and thoughts. Conversely, spirits can be offended by selfish, disrespectful, and demanding requests. For this reason, shamans often use well-thought-out and even artistic language in their invocations of the spirits. Shaman prayers in Siberia are like poetry, and specific expressions and words of praise may be used again and again if a shaman addresses certain spirits repeatedly. Spirits like phrasing in invocations that expresses awe for their power or beauty or expressions that are tender and affectionate.

Invocations of spirits should be tailored according to the character of each spirit as you have experienced it in your shamanic work and according to the ranking of the spirit (see below). For example, to invoke Erleg Khan, the judge of the lower world, I use wording that is solemn and full of awe. If I am addressing the benevolent *tenger* spirit Bukhe Beligte, however, I use tender and affectionate language to appeal to his love for all living things. To address a nature spirit or an ancestor, I use more familiar language, as these spirits were once human beings like myself. Developing invocations is one of several aspects of shamanism that challenge and stimulate creativity. The spectrum of shamanic activities requires the shaman to be a bit of an artist in many ways.

Just as it is good manners to offer food and drink to guests, it is polite to do the same for the spirits as a gesture of respect and generosity. The spirits cannot actually consume the food or drink, of course, but they can enjoy the essence of them. They will imbue them with spiritual power that will pass to anyone who eats or drinks the offering after the ritual is over. When you are invoking spirits, it is often helpful to regard them in the same way you would human beings: always afford them the respect and understanding they deserve.

Tenger, Zayaans, Chotgor, and Other Kinds of Spirits

Mongolian and Siberian shamanism recognizes many different types of spirits, ranked mostly by origin and by their effects on human beings. While there are a great variety of names for them in Siberian languages, I will use the Mongolian names in order to explain them more simply. Before starting, understand that the terms *god, goddess, deity,* and so on are not adequate to describe these beings, as they are not considered gods in the European sense of the word. These spirits are nonphysical beings that have humanlike personalities and emotions but possess great power and can be called for assistance in shamanic work or for blessing and protection in daily life. The primary deities of Siberian shamanism are Father Heaven and Mother Earth; although they are given human titles, they are nonhuman in form and transcend conception as human personalities. They are generally benevolent toward all living things and spirit beings, and the flow of energy between them empowers everything. On the other hand, they are both attentive to human appeals and shape the fate of all beings. For this reason, they are the objects of worship by all Mongolian and Siberian peoples.

The most powerful spirit beings are the *tenger.* These generally are upper-world spirits and are conceived of as being associated with the four directions. They are believed to be descendants of Esege Malaan Tenger and Manzan Gurme Toodei, who reside in the upper world. At the beginning of time they split into four groupings associated with the four directions. The *tenger* most often called on are Han Hormasta, the leader of the western *tenger;* Atai Ulaan, one of the eastern *tenger;* Bukhe Beligte, son of Han Hormasta; Tatai Tenger, *tenger* of storms; Erleg Khan, lord of the lower world; and Uha Loson Khan, *tenger* of the waters. If you wish to appeal to the *tenger,* you may address them collectively. One of them may over the course of time reveal himself or herself to you and develop a deeper level of cooperation. Many of the deities invoked in other cultural traditions may be regarded as being *tenger;* you will know yourself if a certain being with which you feel connected could be considered one of the *tenger.* Because the *tenger* are universal, and those described at the end of this book are known in many cultures (just by different names), when you read about them you may recognize some of the beings you address in your own spiritual practice even though they are here described with Mongolian names.

Tenger do not generally join a shaman's spirit family—they are available to all people who call on them.

Tenger are called sky spirits because their home in the upper world is beyond the sky, yet the implied meaning is that they control natural forces, which they do. *Tenger* are often appealed to in situations in which the environment is out of balance—to avert bad weather, for example, or to bring rain.

The upper world is also the home of two other types of powerful beings called *khans* and *zayaans.* They are considered to be less powerful than *tenger* but are believed to be descendants of the *tenger.* Some of them are the *suld* souls of great heroes who have been elevated to the status of upper-world spirits. Chinggis Khan is generally thought to have achieved the status of *khan* spirit; some of the most powerful shamans have also become *khans.* *Khans* tend to visit the earth frequently and are mediators between mankind and the higher-ranked *tenger.* *Zayaan* is related to the word *zayaa,* meaning "fate" or "karma." *Zayaans* may be appealed to in order to change what seems to be inevitable or to reverse the harm of bad deeds. *Zayaans* are given great and serious respect. Address them by the term *hairhan,* meaning "beloved," but with an implied respect for their great power. *Khans* and *zayaans* can be appealed to collectively or individually. Study the pantheon in appendix 2 and the mythology of Mongolia and Siberia in order to familiarize yourself with the names and personalities of these spirits if you want to invoke certain ones specifically. In your shamanic practice you may develop a relationship with individual *khans* or *zayaans* after they reveal themselves to you, and you may learn their names and character through direct experience. There are thousands of them, and it is impossible to make a full listing. Mongolian and Siberian mythology specifically mentions only a few of them, and shamans discover new ones all the time

Keep in mind that not all *tenger, khans,* and *zayaans* that you may discover or invoke to work with you will be Mongolian or Siberian in origin. Wherever you live and whatever place may be the land of your ethnic heritage (or the origin of your *udha*) will have its own heritage of heroes, shamans, and other figures of great spiritual power. This is why Siberian shamans have stressed to me that a shaman needs to be familiar with his heritage so that he can identify and work with the *khans* and *zayaans* that are part of his native community. Also, when a shaman travels it is helpful to have some knowledge of the spiritual heritage of a place if he intends to do much shamanic work there. Of course, with the assistance of the *udha* and other shamanic helper spirits, it is possible to reach out and ask the spirits of a place which *tenger, khan,* or *zayaan* spirits may be the spiritual patrons there. All *tenger, khans,* and *zayaans* have spiritual influence everywhere, of course, but the knowledge of these spirits from cultures outside of Siberia and Mongolia where shamanic practice was suppressed for a long time has been largely lost. It is the responsibility of shamans in those parts of the world to rediscover them. For instance, if you live in North America, it is wise to become familiar with the spirits that Native Americans worked with in your region and then to inquire shamanically whether they are available to assist you in the role of *tenger, zayaan,* or *khan.*

All three worlds are inhabited by spirit beings that have been incarnated as either humans or animals at some time or other. You will find that most of the beings you work with belong to these spirits, especially those who once were human. Animal spirits can be perceived as individuals or as collective manifestations of their type. While you may have the collective spirit of Eagle or Wolf as a power animal, you may also interact with the individual spirits of eagles or wolves. In the same way, in hunting rituals a shaman may appeal to the collective spirit of Deer or Bear for favor in the hunt.

Of the three types of human spirits, the *ami* souls in the upper world interact the least with human beings. The reason is unclear; it appears that they do not have any great desire to wander back to the middle world until they are sent there to reincarnate. *Ami* souls, in my perception, seem to have rather mild personalities, unlike the other two souls, and lack the same attachment to the living that often draws lower-world spirits into the middle world. It is possible that the assurance that they will soon return to the same family that they left only a short time before makes them generally uninvolved in human affairs between incarnations.

Lower-world spirits are the most frequent cause of illness and psychological disturbance. These spirits, whether friendly or hostile, have a negative effect on human beings when outside a human body. They have strong and distinct human personalities and should be addressed just as if they were a person. Human *suns* souls sometimes get hung up in the middle world after death, usually because they are still attached to a person or place, and therefore remain in the vicinity of relatives, their home, or a favorite place. In some cases, intense emotion toward some person or place will even cause a *suns* soul to come back from the lower world before its time to be reborn. Of *suns* souls who are benevolent in nature, the most dangerous are those of parents or grandparents who are close to a child, for a child's own souls will be aware of the presence of the spirit and may be drawn out of the body to get closer to the *suns* of the deceased loved one.

Some *suns* souls are downright hostile. Usually the hostility is directed at someone who wronged the dead person. In cases of *suns* souls of people who died suddenly, prematurely, or of suicide, the hostility is due to jealousy of people who have fulfilled and happy lives. These unfriendly beings are known as *chotgor*, and they are the main cause of human illnesses (when you read the description of the Mongolian-Siberian pantheon in appendix 2, you will notice that certain spirits are patrons of illnesses. This does not mean they cause the diseases; rather, it means they have control over them and can be invoked to stop illnesses and epidemics). Shamans, having the protection of their helper spirits, can interact with *chotgor* and send them back to the lower world, where they belong.

As mentioned above, *suld* souls settled in nature do not have the same negative effect on living human beings as *suns* souls do, but those who are sad or mentally unsettled can affect the emotional well-being of people around them. For example, have you ever been walking somewhere and suddenly felt a rush of sadness or dread and not know why? You may have had a fleeting contact with one of these entities.

When shamans die, their *suld* souls tend to be attracted to shamans who are still alive. Some of these become *udha* spirits, but others remain settled in nature and are still available as helpers for shamanic work. In Siberia there are many places that are recognized and revered as the dwelling places of the *suld* souls of great shamans.

As in the case of *tenger*, *khans*, and *zayaans*, nature spirits are found everywhere and have universal influence (by that I mean that I can call for the assistance of a nature spirit from Siberia when I am in the United States or vice versa, if I have some knowledge of the spirit and some experience working with it). Thus, it is important to interact with the nature spirit of the place where you live or where you are visiting to do shamanic work. For example, one of my teachers told me when I went to do shamanic work in the Appalachian Mountains that I should not only invoke the spirits of the Sayan Mountains who are the patrons of my shamanic lineage but also know the spirits of the mountains where I was working and invoke the spirits of the forests and rivers of the region in which I was born. In the same way, you should keep this in mind, even if you do not know the names and specific identities of certain nature spirits, for the master spirits of mountains, lakes, and rivers are powerful and can assist you in your work. Think about where you were born, where you live, and where you are doing your shamanic work. What kinds of mountains, rivers, lakes, or other natural features that would have master spirits of great power are located in those places? The majesty, uniqueness, and size of these places are usually directly related to the power and character of the nature spirits that have taken up residence in them. In a lot of cases these spirits are older and wiser than the average nature spirits found in trees and rocks. Most important, let your shamanic helper spirits assist you in contacting and working with such spirits: not only is it your prerogative to do so as a shaman, but the spirits will be pleased and bring you blessing when you acknowledge them as well.

Suld souls of the ancestors comprise the largest share of nature spirits, but there are other entities residing in nature who have never been human beings. In Evenk they are called the *ojan*, the "old ones," and occasionally they can cause mischief. It is said they like to interfere with shamans on their journeys if they are not offered a share of the food set out for the ritual.

Another type of spirit found in all three worlds but which you will most often encounter in this world is the *burhan*. *Burhan* are quite powerful and can be formidable foes if hostile. While they seem to occur naturally, they usually manifest at events in which humans are traumatized or shocked in some way, and they can cause severe illness or soul loss. There are also benevolent *burhan* spirits under the authority of Golto Sagaan Tenger, patron of the *gol*, who are available to help shamans.[3]

Calling Spirits for Specific Purposes

In shamanic work, it is common practice to call spirits for a specific purpose. A shaman may wish to add power to a specific intention in order to augment his own power and that of his helpers or to assign a spirit as a caretaker for an ongoing process of healing or protection. This is done because certain spirits are not appropriate for permanent addition to a shaman's spirit family and because the spirits that bond to a shaman are not supposed to be left to work with another person after a ritual has been completed.

When you are doing shamanic work of any kind, it is a good

idea to call the *tenger, zayaans,* and other high-ranking spirits for general assistance and protection. When you acknowledge them, they will remember you as well. You may also want to call specific beings for certain purposes, such as Tatai for weather work, Bukhe Beligte for earth healing, and Erleg Khan for soul retrieval. They will add power to what you do, even if the alliance is a temporary one simply for the purpose of a ritual.

When you are doing healing, soul retrieval, or protection work, you may wish to call a nature spirit to assist you and to remain with the person or place involved after the ritual is over. In these cases, make an *ongon* for the spirit so that it remains with the patient or is displayed in the place being protected. You can simply call for a nature spirit to come to you for assistance at some point during your ritual work without knowing its name; a spirit that is in the vicinity and is friendly and helpful will come. Your helper spirits will not allow a hostile spirit to come; only one that is appropriate will be drawn to you. If you feel so inclined, you may journey to find such a spirit and make a deeper contact with it, but only you will know whether that is necessary. The general rule is that journeying for a spirit is done when an illness is especially serious, when protection is being invoked against a powerful being such as a *burhan,* or when bringing blessing for a major undertaking or for an entire community. Once the ritual is done and the spirit has settled into the *ongon* you have created for it, it will continue the process of healing, protection, or blessing.

Adding Spirits to Your Spirit Family

The initial group of spirits that call you to be a shaman will be joined by additional spirit beings as you continue your shamanic practicing. This is a natural process, and a shaman with a long career may have quite a large collection of *ongons* of the various spirits that have joined him. It is not unusual for a shaman to have a variety of helper spirits whose origins are from several regions and ethnic groups. Usually the spirits will contact you when you travel to a specific place for shamanic work. They are often drawn by the presence of a shaman and will want to join the shaman's spirit family.

Because persecution of shamanism around the world in the last few centuries has resulted in a lot of unbonded *udha* spirits residing in nature, it is not surprising that they are drawn to shamans. Some of the spirits you may attract are the *suld* souls of shamans or beings that want to do good for living things. If you feel like doing so, welcome them and learn from their knowledge of the old shamanic traditions.

"Mastering" Spirits

Some spirit entities, whether *suld* souls or *burhan*, may be quite strong and are difficult to overcome in the process of a healing or other ritual. Although some are hostile and cannot be changed, at times they can be "mastered" and redirected to become a shamanic helper spirit. In such cases the healing and restoration to balance affects the spirit as well as the person on whose behalf the ritual was done. *Burhan*, for example, are powerful and can be worth mastering and enlisting as helper spirits. Spirits associated with a particular place or useful for certain types of work because of their personality or history may be worth mastering as well. You will be able to decide for yourself whether a spirit is worth mastering. On the other hand, do not fool yourself into thinking that you have mastered a hostile spirit when you have not and associate with it without its being healed of its malevolence. If you do, the malevolent spirit will have conflict with your *udha* spirit and cause you mental disturbance until you either truly master it or drive it away.

Λ Deep Mystery of Buryat Shamanism:

Journey to Find the Cup of the Great Mother

One concept of Mongolian and Siberian shamanism that has been poorly understood is that of the female aspect of the world of the great spirits with whom shamans work. In addition to Mother Earth, one of the two chief spiritual forces of the world, there are also the great mothers, the mothers and grandmothers of the *tenger, khans,* and *zayaans.* It is said that when Ekhe Ekhe Burhan (Great Mother Spirit) created the world, separating heaven from earth and unfolding our present existence out of the unity of the *gol,* she gave birth to the two great mothers of all of the sky spirits. The greatest of these is Manzan Gurme Toodei, mother of all the western *tenger* and ancestor of all the patron spirits of shamanism.

Manzan Gurme Toodei lives in the highest reaches of the upper world, and she is the possessor of the greatest power and spiritual knowledge of all of the sky spirits. She possesses two great shaman mirrors in which she watches all that happens on earth and in the sky. She holds the great book of fate in which is written all that has happened, all that is happening, and all that will happen. She possesses a higher magic than that of any other of the sky spirits, and she is the one to which the sky spirits appeal when their power is not sufficient to solve the problems threatening the balance of order in the universe. Her most mysterious attribute is her great silver cup, which is the key to her power.

Shamans who have taken the journey that I will now describe have each in their own way come to understand the teaching of the silver cup, a profound and powerful teaching for all shamans. I will not reveal what they have seen, but the visions that they have experienced all bring back the same answer with some slight but not significant variations. What I can say is that the shamans who have undertaken this journey have had an emotionally moving encounter with the Great Mother. The central figure of this journey is female, but that does not mean that this is an experience that cannot be equally experienced by men and women. After all, are we not all mothers' children, no matter what our background?

Many people are surprised at the appearance of the Great Mother, for she can take on many different forms; in fact, she may shift forms over the duration of the journey. If that happens to you, remember that this is normal, for she is a reflection of all women. She may appear as your own mother, as an old woman, even as a girl. This is typical of shamanic journeys: In the spiritual realm, certain entities appear in unexpected forms and keep changing shape. The symbolism of the forms they take has meaning that you will understand with experience. You must be prepared for the silver cup to take on unusual aspects as well. It may look like a small silver bowl or it may be as big as a lake. Manzan Gurme Toodei may touch it to your head, pour its contents over you, or ask you to drink. You may find yourself turned small and you may plunge into the depths of the mysterious liquid it contains.

When you undertake this journey, treat it as you would any other journey. Doing it in a ritual space using a drum or other shamanic instrument will get the best results. You may want to start with an invocation of Manzan Gurme Toodei. Here is an example (although I recite this invocation in Buryat Mongolian rather than in English):

> O grandmother Manzan Gurme Toodei
> You who swaddled a thousand protector spirits!
> O grandmother Manzan Gurme Toodei
> Who rocked ten thousand shaman spirits in their cradles!
> Come to this place as I honor you,
> Bring your sacred silver cup,
> Come reveal yourself to me,
> Bless me with the silver cup!

This invocation is added onto the end of whatever invocations you may do in setting up your sacred space. Notice that in this invocation, the salutation and the statement of the intention are said twice; in Mongolian and Siberian shamanic custom it is believed that repeating such statements in slightly different ways pleases the spirits as well as adds to the power of the invocation itself.

When you go on your journey, enter into the *gol* with the intention of going to that place where you will find the Great Mother. You may come to her instantly once you enter the *gol*, or the spirits may take you on a symbolic journey before she reveals herself. In Buryat folklore the way to Manzan Gurme Toodei's house sometimes reveals itself as a rainbow connecting heaven and earth. Trust what the spirits reveal to you, for each journey is a way by which they teach you.

I cannot tell you exactly what happens when you finally come to her; you must learn this for yourself. I can give you a few hints, though, about what to pay attention to. What does she look like? Is she naked or clothed? What kind of clothes is she wearing? What does the cup look like, and when you ask her to bless you with it, what does she do? What does the cup mean? What does she tell you? Follow the vision as far as it takes you and you will know when it is time to return.

I wish you all a good journey, for I have found that Manzan Gurme Toodei is a good teacher and will bring profound and emotionally moving knowledge.

SEVEN

Healing and Psychopomp Work

Where are you,
Where have you gone?
Your girlfirend who was joined with you for life
Is alone and in great sorrow,
She sits alone in the yurt
Looking at the wall with tears in her eyes,
Remembering her happy life with you.
She cries and sings of her grief.
The children of your body
Cry "Daddy, where are you?"
With sighs and tears.
Come to us!
Hear our summons and come quickly here!
A hurai!

—Alar Buryat invocation to call back the soul, in Sanjeev, "Weltanschauung und Schamanismus der Alaren-Burjaten," translation by the author[1]

In all shamanic cultures, the shaman is one of the chief practitioners of healing, and a large portion of your work as a shaman will be healing. In this section, as we examine the various types of healing work, you will see that all illness has a spiritual component. In Siberian as well as other shamanic traditions, the primary cause of illness is believed to be spiritual. The injury to the spiritual part of the human being suppresses the body's ability to heal itself naturally, and the symptoms of illness are a danger signal of the spiritual injury. Just as some kinds of medicine only suppress symptoms of a cold but do not actually combat the viral infection that caused it, so healing the physical illness without addressing the spiritual issues that underlie it means the patient has not truly been healed. For this reason I will classify healings according to the spiritual needs that must be addressed. It must be understood that shamanic healing should not replace healing by traditional medicine but, rather, should be used to reinforce the physical treatments administered by physicians. In Siberia and Mongolia, shamans have always worked in tandem with herbalists, bonesetters, and other traditional doctors except in cases when other healing practitioners were absent.

Keep in mind while doing healing work that if it is impossible to do healing for a patient in person, healing from a remote location is an option. The only requirement is that you use some object, preferably something belonging to the afflicted person, as a proxy representation of the person. If an item belonging to the person is not available, use something like a placement of rocks to represent the person. While shamanizing, visualize the person ahead of you and you will be able to diagnose and treat as if he or she were present. The results will be the same as if the person were at the healing. The reason is that all places are unified through the *gol*, and in doing this work you are transcending the illusory physical separation between you and the person you are healing.

DIAGNOSIS

Before any healing work can begin, it is necessary to diagnose the cause of the illness. Possible causes include intrusions, soul repression, possession, soul loss, and pollution. Interviewing your patient will often reveal probable causes of illness. Has the patient had unusual contact with death or with some spirit entity (extraterrestrial encounters may fall into this category)? Was the patient close to a relative or friend who has died? Does the patient have any known enemies? Has he or she killed an animal needlessly, or injured another human or animal? Has the patient been traumatized psychologically recently or in the more remote past? Traumatic experience and physical trauma often attract *burhan* spirits that must then be removed.

Divination can be very helpful for making a diagnosis. Mongolian and Siberian shamans have a great variety of divination techniques that are useful for diagnosis, some of which are described at the end of this chapter. Tarot cards can be used as well if a spread is done with the purpose of diagnosing a patient. You may know other divination techniques that you have used for fortune-telling, and you may adapt them for this purpose.

The most common technique for diagnosis of spiritual disease is direct examination of the spiritual body. For this reason I recommend practicing techniques for visualizing the spiritual body and for using your hands to sense the *tsog* energy surrounding people's spiritual bodies. As you gain experience in doing this, you will be able to see if a soul is missing and to spot intrusions. You may feel intrusions as indentations, heat, or stinging when you pass your hand over them. In other cases, you may find that there is nothing specific invading the spiritual body, yet it is somehow weakened; this may be the result of soul repression or pollution. When you are doing diagnosis, you may have thoughts pop into your head, hints from the spirits about the nature of the ailment. Do not hesitate to ask the patient about your perceptions, no matter how far-fetched they seem. You may find that sometimes the patient's condition has an unusual cause. This could be why the person you are treating has not responded to previous treatments for his or her illness.

In cases of soul repression or possession, you may distinctly sense a foreign presence in or around your patient. These entities usually betray themselves readily because they tend to express hostility toward shamans, knowing that you will be driving them away. It is not uncommon for multiple entities to be intruding into a patient's body field, either because a person has been traumatized multiple times or because other spirits are latching on to someone whose resistance is already weakened. Your shamanic helper spirits will shield you from damage by any hostile spirits you deal with.

If the illness is particularly serious or if you cannot pinpoint the underlying cause of a patient's condition, you may wish to journey to get advice from the spirits. You can be sure that your helper spirits will guide your experience so that you learn everything you need in order to restore the patient to balance.

INTRUSIONS, SOUL REPRESSION, AND POSSESSION

I have grouped these conditions because they all represent various degrees of what is basically the same problem. One or more spirit entities either are hanging around in the vicinity of the patient and disrupting his spiritual balance or have intruded within his spiritual body to some extent. Some spirits are more tenacious than others and will require drastic action; others can be removed with relatively little trouble. If some of the techniques for removing these spirits seem overly simple, do not forget that when you are doing them you are not acting just as a human being; instead, your spiritual power is being augmented many times over by your *udha*, your helper spirits, power animals, and any other spirits you have invoked before starting.

Soul repression is the interference of foreign spirits with the proper functioning of the spiritual body. It may manifest as a general lack of energy, as fatigue, or as malaise. A patient may feel sick, but neither gets seriously ill nor feels fully healthy. It may manifest as chronic headache or even as rashes. The lack of energy is due to the presence of the foreign spirit, which disrupts the flow between the patient's spiritual body and the earth or sky. The spirit may be disrupting the free movement of the *suns* and *ami* souls within the body. Repression of the *ami* may affect breathing, producing asthmalike symptoms.

The culprits in soul repression are usually *suns* souls that have not gone to the lower world or that for some reason have returned. In many cases they are the *suns* soul of people the patient knew in the past who have died. In other cases soul repression is the result of a curse (more commonly seen in Mongolia and Russia). The repressing spirits may simply be *chotgor*, loose *suns* souls causing mischief because of jealousy. An animal spirit, usually one that has been killed by human cruelty, may occasionally manifest as a *chotgor*.

Fortunately, *chotgor* who are repressing a patient can be driven away easily. Use a shaman fan *(dalbuur)* to sweep them away; many *chotgor* will run away from the shaman when the *dalbuur* is waved in the direction of the patient. Charging at the patient with a knife and shouting at the spirit will scare it away as well. *Suns* souls that are attached to the patient in some way may be more tenacious. You may find that after you have chased them away, they come back when you walk away from the patient. If this happens, make a simple *ongon* or talisman, call a nature spirit to empower it, then leave it with the patient. In this way the nature spirit will continue the process of shielding the patient as long as is necessary. In the most extreme cases, if the spirit still refuses to leave or if it belonged to someone recently dead, you may want to journey to take the spirit to the lower world. (This will be discussed in more detail below.)

Intrusions in some ways resemble repressions, but they involve a partial penetration of the spiritual body of the patient in some localized area. As with repressions, intrusions are usually fairly easy to expel. Because intrusions are localized, the symptoms manifest as ailments of particular body parts. They may take the form of lesions, rashes, pain, organ dysfunction, even tumors in severe cases. If you detect intrusions while diagnosing a patient, you will usually discover that he has been experiencing discomfort at the site of the intrusion, whether or not you had been told of it beforehand. An intrusion in the reproductive organs can cause infertility, impotence, and other sexual dysfunction. An intrusion may be the result of sudden physical or psychic trauma or may simply be a spirit hanging around for some reason, as in the case of repression.

Sudden movement, fire jabbed at the affected area, waving the shaman fan, or shouting at the intruding spirit could be enough to drive it away. Intruding spirits are especially afraid of fire, and jabbing at the affected area with a burning match will dislodge even some of the more stubborn intrusions. If the intruder does not leave with these methods, pluck out the intrusion with your fingers (imagine tearing off a burr when doing it), then blow it away from yourself and from the patient. You can also grab the spirit from the intrusion site, bring it down to the ground, and will it to go back to the lower world through the earth. If you are lucky enough to have a shaman mirror, you can absorb the intruding spirit directly into the mirror and then place it on the floor or ground facedown so the spirit passes into the earth. Sucking out the intrusion is another removal technique; be conscious of your helper spirits' protection so that you do not accidentally incorporate the spirit into yourself while sucking it out. Visualize it as being localized in the front of your mouth and then spit it onto the ground forcefully.

Tenacious intruders require more extreme measures. Take one or two of your *ongons*, place them on or around the patient, and invoke your helper spirits to forcefully remove the intruder. The intruding spirit will be picked up by the *ongon* and held there until you can deal with it further. When an intruder spirit is this difficult to remove, it is necessary to take it back to the lower world. Once you have cleared your patient of intrusions, you will journey to the lower world to settle the spirits there. Use the Dolbor lower-world journey (see page 73) as a model if you do not have experience with lower-world journeying.

Sometimes you will find that the spirit you are dealing with is neither a *suns* nor a *chotgor* but, rather, a *burhan*. *Burhan* spirits are very strong, perhaps even stronger than some of your helper spirits. These spirits usually enter a patient because of severe trauma, such as rape, abuse, an accident, or some other drastic event. Frequently, rather than simply intruding, they will totally possess a patient, which will bring on very severe physical or mental illness. Whether a *burhan* is intruding or is in full possession of the patient, you will need to confront it directly and struggle with it. Because the *burhan* may very well be as strong as some of your helper spirits, you will have to embody them in order to get rid of it. You will also be required to interact with it on a much more personal level than you usually need to with stray *suns* souls or *chotgor*.

People may find the concept of spiritual struggle rather uncomfortable or strange, but it is something that a shaman will at times be faced with. Because the spiritual world mirrors the physical world in many ways, some spirits are benevolent in nature and others are destructive. Progress and destruction are both natural processes and each must exist in order to sustain balance in the universe. Nevertheless, when destructive beings throw a person or the environment out of balance, it is a shaman's job to remedy the situation, even if doing so is unpleasant.

When you confront a *burhan* or other strong spirit that is intruding on or possessing an individual, the process of removing it may uncover deep and traumatic issues for the patient. Be sure to reassure the person you are treating that he is in a safe place and ask him to be open-minded about what may follow.

You must first drum or otherwise bring yourself into a state of mind to allow your shamanic spirits to enter your being. Once you have achieved this merging with your spirits, directly confront the spirit intruding on the patient. You may do this in the context of a shamanic journey or you can simply approach the patient (it is best for the person to be lying down within a ritual space). Either way, the spirit should be immediately visible or otherwise perceptible. Ask it why it is associating with the patient and what needs to be done for it to go away. A number of things may happen. The spirit may tell you about the event that first attracted it to the person it is affecting. Perhaps the spirit has some emotional need that it wants to fulfill by associating with a human being; in this case, ask your spirits to assist you in bringing emotional healing to the spirit. If you calm it in this way, you may find either that it will leave or that it wants to remain with you as a helper spirit. Many spirits, whether former human souls or other nature spirits, ultimately have a desire to make some kind of change in the physical realm, either positive or negative according to its personality. If the spirit you are confronting feels that it is getting gratification from causing destruction in the person it is afflicting, it may be unwilling to leave, and you will have to struggle with it. Try bribing it by promising a food or drink offering that you will make after the ritual is over—usually this is something simple such as a cup of liquor or a can of beer that you pour out on the ground for it. If it still refuses to leave, visualize all of your helper spirits as being fierce or warrior-like and direct your collective force against the spirit. Grab onto it, pull it away, and carry it outside, leaving it on the far side of a barrier—a wall, street, or alley. If it struggles hard, weaken it by ritually stabbing it with a knife or imagining that one of your helper spirits has eaten it (when you go outside, it will be vomited out in a weakened state). Visualize a barrier of tremendous force surrounding the patient so that the spirit you have removed has no way of returning. You may also invoke the *tenger* and other spirits of great power to bring suffering and pain to the intruder spirit if it tries to intrude on or possess a human being again.

At this point the defeated spirit goes away and will find other ways of exerting its power in nature that will not directly affect human beings. Remember, most spirits like to express themselves in some fashion in the physical world, either destructively or constructively. When you have overcome a spirit, you have mastered it; occasionally, if it and your helper spirits are compatible, it may be added to your spirit family. Because helping a shaman is a way for a spirit to exert power in the physical world, it can bring satisfaction to it as well as achieve positive results for the shaman and his community.

When you encounter possession, you will usually find a generalized sickness of the individual, mentally or physically. This may manifest as chronic illness or as repeated episodes of medical problems from which the patient does not fully recover. A person suffering from possession may have mental disturbance or nightmares or simply an inability to be mentally calm and relaxed. The person may seem to have a psychic cloud hanging over him. While intrusions are localized, a possession affects the entire being. In that way it resembles soul repression, but it is more extreme. In treating possession, if you cannot use the techniques described for repression, the more drastic measures described for the most difficult type of intrusion will be necessary. Once again, you will usually uncover deep issues of abuse or trauma that must be resolved.

In cases of possession, when you have removed the possessing spirit it is a good idea to create an *ongon* for the patient and imbue it with a nature spirit. It will not only protect against the return of the extracted spirit, but it will also help the person who is recovering to adjust to a certain feeling of emptiness he may experience after the disease spirit is gone. The trauma that brought on the possession created a feeling of loss, a spiritual void that was then filled by the spirit that entered the person. So even though the spirit brought physical and mental suffering, it filled a certain need that the person had at the time of the trauma, and its removal will again bring this emptiness if you do not address it in your work. It is significant that the issues brought up by the original trauma usually surface during the course of the healing. Allow your helper spirits to advise you as to the best way to heal this emptiness, and allow them to make the person whole again with their power. Take your drum, place it on your chest to absorb windhorse, then place it on the chest of the person you are treating and allow the energy to flow in, to fill up the hole in his or her being.

SOUL RETRIEVAL

Absence of the *ami* or *suns* soul is another cause of physical or mental disease. When you diagnose your patient, the absence of a soul will be quite apparent when you examine the spiritual body. In general, people with soul loss will often be unable to recover from some physical illness or injury or will seem disoriented or mentally scattered. People with soul loss are usually easy to recognize even before spiritual examination because they seem overwhelmed by the simplest tasks or are obviously mentally depressed. The feeling of being overwhelmed occurs because two souls rather than three are responsible for all mental activity and the regulation of bodily function. Soul loss is called *suns geeh*, meaning "wandering off of the soul." This means that the soul is not lost or stolen but drifts away from the body. The most common reasons for soul loss are being frightened and sustaining physical shock by injury or serious disease. At death the souls go away permanently in much the same way, and in cases of severe illness a soul may leave prematurely because it thinks the body is ready to die.

The *ami* soul is much more mobile and is more often responsible for soul loss. Because it is a body regulator, it is not surprising that loss of the *ami* usually manifests as physical disease or fatigue. I believe that the perception of the *ami* outside of the body as a bird is appropriate. Birds by nature become frightened and fly away easily; similarly, the *ami* can pop out of a person's body very easily when the person is frightened. The *ami* is also animal-like in that it normally plays a lesser role in the formation of conscious thought: it is more subconscious, just as most bodily functions are subconscious. For this reason I have found that loss of the *ami* does not cause as much mental confusion as does loss of the *suns*, but a person lacking it will usually feel fatigued and overwhelmed in general. Children more commonly than older people lose the *ami*, but loss of the *ami* still is the most common form of soul loss in people of any age. Children lose the *ami* because they frighten easily and their *suld* is still not well developed, so their spiritual body is "soft." Young children are much more in touch with the *ami* than are older people, whose personality is more fully developed, and children are still acting out the instinctual impulses of the *ami*. The spiritual body starts becoming harder after the fourth year of life, about the same time that most children who were sickly as babies become fully healthy—and this is no coincidence.

When the *ami* leaves the body, it is usually not hard to find. It always remains in the middle world, and often it is not very far from the body it has left. Usually it leaves because of pain, fright, abuse, or great danger. You may see the *ami* as a birdlike being perched somewhere nearby. Call it gently, coaxing it to come to your hand or to reenter the body it has left. If it comes to your hand, place it on the patient's chest so that it is reabsorbed, or blow it into the chest. Once it enters the body it will return to its normal flow pattern without further intervention. You can follow the same procedure for restoring the *ami* soul no matter what form it takes. If the *ami* is not in the immediate vicinity of the body it left, you will have to journey to look for it. Sometimes it will fly off to a person to whom the patient is emotionally attached or to a place it likes. Sometimes the reason it goes to some place or another seems irrational. When you journey to find it, just ask your helper spirits to locate it and bring you to it. Once you have recovered it, return it to the body as described above.

Loss of the *suns* has more dramatic mental effects and may be more difficult to treat. Because the *suns* contributes much to conscious thought, its absence may manifest as mental confusion or as a drastic change in personality. The *suns* usually leaves the body because of great physical or emotional trauma; it is much more stable than the *ami* and is therefore not so easy to drive out of the body. Even though loss of the *suns* may not be the primary cause of physical injury or disease, its loss often is coupled with serious medical conditions and hampers the body's recovery from them. Another cause of *suns* loss is the sudden death of someone whom a person is close to, especially in the case of a small child whose mother has died. The *suns* of the child is so attached to the mother that it may follow it to the lower world; in much the same way, a person may have soul loss over a dead spouse or lover if the bond was especially strong. Suicidal thoughts and the expectation of death can also cause loss of the *suns;* a person can actually worry himself to death in that way.

Loss of the *suns* usually happens at death. A person lacking a *suns* is in fact partly dead and will indeed die if the soul is not recovered. Lost *suns* souls are a shamanic emergency! Lost *ami* souls can be coped with for long periods, even years, but a lost *suns* soul will eventually result in severe mental illness and rapid physical decline. This is why in the elderly the onset of mental confusion often is soon followed by medical breakdown of the body and death: the *suns* soul, believing that the body is about to fail, leaves for the lower world prematurely—before the actual moment of death. Loss of the *suns* is a serious situation also because it is believed that after a certain period, usually a couple of years, the soul becomes "wild," meaning that it loses all attachment to its former body. Thus it becomes much more difficult to find and to keep inside the body if it is returned. Once the *suns* has become wild, death is virtually inevitable.[2]

Suns souls, unlike *ami* souls, usually wander far from the body. During dreams and shamanic journeys, the *suns* soul leaves the body temporarily and returns with no ill effects—while the body is asleep, the *ami* and *suld* are capable of handling the minimal amount of bodily and mental functions going on during unconsciousness, and the shamanic helper spirits protect the shaman's souls and body during the journey. There is always a certain amount of risk of soul loss involved in these journeys out of the body, but cases of soul loss during sleep or journeying are not common. Occasionally a hostile spirit will steal an *ami* or *suns* soul, usually when it is already out of the body. The Buryat curse "*Chotgor* take him!" can come true. A spirit entity such as a *chotgor* may be powerful enough to force a soul not to return to the body. The reasons for this differ with every case. A *suns* soul that is out of the body may wander as far as the lower world, especially if it believes the body is dying or if it is looking for someone who has already died. Thus, looking for a lost *suns* soul is much more challenging than is looking for the *ami*.

Finding and retrieving a *suns* may entail a long and complicated journey. The famous epic of Nishan Shaman describes such a journey and is a teaching story of how lower-world soul retrievals are accomplished. The Dolbor journey is the model for this type of retrieval. Once you start your journey, it will go quickly if the *suns* is in this world; if it is not, you must go down to the lower world and look for it there. During your journey your spirits will probably explain the reasons and circumstances of the loss if you do not know them already. If the case you are working on involves a spirit that has prevented the return of the soul, you will confront it on your journey. You must negotiate with it much as you would negotiate with an intruder spirit. Ask why it has done what it did and how it can be placated; fight and subdue it if you have to.

In the lower world, people and animals often appear similar to how they appear in the physical world, and the *suns* may look similar to the person to whom it belongs. However, this is not always the case, as spirits can shapeshift easily. You may even perceive the *suns* with some sense other than sight. In whatever way you perceive it, you can make the *suns* (or any spirit, for that matter) small and place it in your drum, ear, mouth, or some other place on your person so you can carry it back to the body it belongs to. When you journey back, place the *suns* on the body or blow it back in, and it will return to its normal function.

While the *ami* and *suns* will leave the body for various reasons, the *suld* never leaves. Just as the body is unique to this lifetime, so is the *suld*, and the two are closely associated until the body dies, at which time the *suld* settles in nature. If the *suld* leaves the body, the body dies almost immediately.

The results of soul retrieval and restoration can be dramatic, and a change may be apparent immediately after the reincorporation of the soul. In some cases the full effects will not manifest until a few hours have passed, but the change will definitely be noticeable within twenty-four hours.

All shamans will, at one time or another, be faced with terminal cases, cases in which the body is so seriously deteriorated that any restoration of the souls can be only temporary. If you are confronted with such a situation, be honest with the people who have called you to do shamanic work. There is no disgrace in a shaman admitting that a condition is incurable because a person is dying. You may be able to reverse an apparently terminal illness if it is possible to do so by returning a person to balance and restoring the souls to the body, but every person's *zayaa* requires death sooner or later, and no shaman alive can change that. If a person is dying, the best thing to do is to try to keep the souls calm and in the body and to cleanse and balance the spiritual body as well as you can so that the person dies with dignity and a minimum of suffering.

POLLUTION AND CLEANSING

Sometimes when the Mongolian shaman does a diagnosis he will declare that a person has been *bohirson*, or polluted. The concept of pollution is not a physical one but, rather, that of a spiritual trauma as the result of contact with death, sexual abuse, rape, curses, or substance abuse. Although these traumatic experiences may lead to repression, intrusion, possession, or soul loss, they may also result in pollution, which leaves the spiritual body in a weakened condition. This is called pollution because it often manifests as a dirtiness in the spiritual body. In the case of substance abuse, the physical abuse of the body can also be an abuse of the spiritual body; if the polluted condition is not healed in the spiritual body, it is difficult to detoxify and get rid of addiction.

As with all spiritual disease, pollution manifests as a weakness or darkness of spirit. The body is weak and listless and the person may seem depressed or disempowered but cannot pinpoint a cause. Sometimes pollution causes facial tics or partial paralysis of the face. In other cases the pollution of the spiritual body manifests as blood disease, electrolyte imbalance, or sugar-level problems. It can also appear on the skin as rashes of unknown origin. When you examine the spiritual body you will see that the light that usually fills the sphere of energy surrounding the body is dim, hazy, or full of specks. This is a symptom of a trauma to the spiritual body that interferes with energy flow and suppresses health as well as mental well-being. Pollution, like repression and possession, affects the body overall, and its effects are general. The main difference is that there is no specific spiritual entity causing and maintaining polution, although one may have caused it and then left long ago. The dirtiness in and of itself causes the problems, and cleansing techniques quickly restore the person to health and balance.

It may be surprising to note that even temporary contact with spiritually destabilizing things such as death, crime, extreme negative emotions, and consumption of mind-altering substances can cause mild pollution. Thinking hateful thoughts or being the object of hatred is also polluting. Many shamans as well as non-shamans regularly use cleansing techniques to rid themselves of any pollution that they may have picked up inadvertently in their daily activities.

Cleansing is known as *ariulga*, meaning "making pure." In *ariulga*, certain substances are charged with spiritual power and dispel pollution when applied to the body. These substances are *arshaan* and the various types of sacred smoke, including juniper, sage, fir, thyme, and incense. Salt, sand, and seeds (usually grains) also absorb pollution and bar its reentry into the spiritual body. The most basic form of purification is the smudging of the affected person with sacred smoke. The smudge is passed around the body three times, followed by the drinking of a minute amount of *arshaan* and applying a small amount of it to the crown of the head. This is usually the *ariulga* for everyday use, when pollution is mild.

If the pollution is stronger, pass the sacred smoke around the body nine times and sprinkle the body with *arshaan* three times three. Pass the sacred smoke around three times, sprinkle three times, and repeat until the total is nine. If this does not cleanse the person completely, wait a little, call the spirits for assistance, then repeat. Before you do it the second time, throw a little sand, salt, and grain onto the person being treated, circling around him three times. Once you have done this, the person's spiritual body will be entirely clear. You may want to recommend that the person continue a daily routine of smudging and taking *arshaan* if he will still be in contact with some sort of polluting influence. Make a bottle of *arshaan* for the person to take home and use in the morning before going out.

WORKING WITH SPIRITS OF THE DEAD

In your shamanic work you will interact all the time with spirits of people who have lived as human beings in the recent or distant past. Indeed, most of your helper spirits will have had past lives as human beings, and your *udha* spirit will carry the memories of many lives. In healing work, *chotgor* spirits as well as nature spirits are actually *suns* and *suld* souls. In this section, however, I will be discussing how you interact with the spirits of people who have died for purposes other than healing or calling for assistance.

The usual reasons to contact spirits of the dead are for information and for conducting them to the lower world when they get hung up in the middle world. This may involve either invoking a spirit or journeying, depending on whether you are contacting a *suld* or a *suns* spirit.

The information you seek from someone who has died could be in regard to an issue regarding the person's family or descendants. In other cases, shamans contact the spirits of shamans of the past for teaching or advice—this is usually a student contacting the *suld* of his former teacher. When you are looking for information, you can usually invoke the *suld* of the person you need to contact or journey to the place where it has settled in nature. Of course you will probably need the assistance of your shamanic helper spirits to find the place where the *suld* of the person you are consulting is settled. In most cases, however, setting out food offerings and beckoning the spirit with a well-thought-out invocation are enough to bring it in. This is, after all, what mediums in the Western tradition have been doing for centuries. It is your choice whether you want actually to embody the spirit and let it speak through you or simply to converse with it while you are in a trance. It is believed that ancestral *suld* souls remain in close contact with their descendants for eight generations and can be called in fairly easily. Thus, if you are the relative of the person being invoked or if a relative of the spirit being called is in the ritual space, you should have no trouble bringing it to you.

Sometimes your shamanic spirits will advise you to go to the *suns* of the person you need to contact rather than to the *suld*. This could be because the information you need is something that requires the collective knowledge of the reincarnation lineage of the spirit. In such cases you must journey to the lower world to find the *suns*, or you may be surprised to find that it is here in the middle world, inhabiting a new body. Each situation is unique, so follow the advice of the spirits as to where to find it. I have not heard of journeying to the upper world to consult an *ami* soul, but it probably is possible. If you do need to contact a *suns*, be sure to go to it rather than drawing it back into the middle world; free *suns* spirits can inadvertently cause disease in humans who are non-shamans. If a *suns* spirit comes to you, be sure to send it back to where it belongs.

Sending the *suns* to the lower world is referred to in Western traditions as psychopomp work. The phrase comes from the Greek term for "leading the spirit." In most cases a *suns* soul can find its own way to the lower world, but you may be required to conduct it there. The most common reason is that the person who has died is close to one or several people and it continues to hang around its former home or loved ones. This is the chief cause of hauntings and poltergeist phenomena. The people the *suns* was close to may actually feel its presence or some kind of psychic contact with the dead person. Although this is comforting to many bereaved people, a lingering presence of the dead person's *suns* will ultimately be disruptive and result in psychological or physical disease or even soul loss. Sometimes a *suns* will loiter around a place even when its family has left, or it may hang around the place where it has died, especially if the death was sudden or violent. In any event, whether the spirit is benevolent or hostile, the solution is the same.

When you are required to return a *suns* to the lower world, interact with the spirit as if it were still a human being—after all, spirits have the same emotions and personalities as the living, and this needs to be acknowledged. Therefore, when you begin this work, invoke the spirit or address it directly if it is already present and visible to you. The spirit may not appear in human form, of course; it may appear as a shadow or a light, or it may be physically palpable to you. It may even manifest in the form of an animal. Each one will be different. When you converse with it, you may use trance, depending on the situation.

Sometime during the procedure, offer the *suns* soul some of the food or drink that you set out in your ritual space. Once you start conversing with it you will get a good idea as to why it is lingering rather than returning to the lower world. It may be attached to a person or place, hostile or vengeful, or simply confused and lost. Address it kindly and compassionately and tell it that it needs to go on to the lower world, that its time on earth is finished for now. Tell it that its continuing presence is disruptive, even if it means no harm. Assure it that you will respectfully bring it to the lower world so that it can go into a better future and eventually live again as a human being. Tell it to release its attachments to the middle world and release any hostility it may bear against any human beings. A good share of *suns* souls will agree to go with you once they realize that they can cause harm to the ones they care about. Those that have gotten lost on their way will be more than happy to follow you on the journey to the lower world.

There are some spirits that will be less willing to depart. Persuasion and bribery with food offerings may be enough to change their minds. The least cooperative, however, need to be confronted and struggled with. In such cases, use the techniques described on pages 103–105 for subduing intruder spirits. In this situation you can settle the spirit temporarily into an *ongon* made out of grass or some other flammable material or into a shaman mirror. Ask one of your helper spirits to hold it while you prepare for your lower-world journey. If it is especially difficult, invoke the assistance of Erleg Khan, for this is within the area of his responsibility.

Lower-world journeying for returning a *suns* is almost the same as for a soul retrieval, except that you will be leaving the *suns* there rather than bringing it back to this world. While you journey, a cooperative *suns* will fly with you and your spirits; if it has not agreed to go freely, you carry it or have your spirits carry it for you until you reach the lower world. Leave the soul at the entrance to the lower world or travel farther in, depending on what you desire or feel is appropriate. If you settled a spirit into a temporary *ongon*, be sure to either burn it or throw it away in a natural place after you have returned from your journey. If you have asked Erleg Khan for help, show your appreciation by pouring a cup or two of some delicious beverage on the ground outside while thanking him (he especially likes beer).

The presence of a free *suns* soul is polluting to people and places. You will need to do *ariulga* on the people and objects that were affected by the spirit you sent away. You also must do an *ariulga* of the place where it had been lingering; this type of *ariulga* is discussed more in the next chapter.

USING DIVINATION FOR SHAMANIC DIAGNOSIS

As I will describe in the next chapter, divination (fortune-telling) is an important part of a shaman's everyday work. Much of what the shaman uses fortune-telling for is to answer general questions about family, love, money, and luck. In Mongolian shamanism there are a few divination techniques that are not used for fortune-telling but, rather, as tools for shamanic diagnosis. Employing these techniques, the spiritual and physical causes of disease and spiritual problems will be revealed, and many of these techniques will also include "prescriptions" for the patient's condition. This information may include which spirit to invoke or placate and what kind of ritual or ceremony is needed for the healing. As some of you may know, I have presented several types of general fortune-telling techniques in my book *Riding Windhorses* (see the bibliography). The techniques below are specific for diagnosis.

The tools for these divination techniques are quite simple. I still marvel that Mongolian and Siberian shamans have been able to achieve effective results with everyday objects. The techniques I present here use pebbles, coins, and beads—common objects that are easy to find anywhere. You may wish to get your own set of these things. Most shamans do, but they can also improvise with whatever is on hand if necessary.

In doing this kind of divination, there are four important points to keep in mind:

1. Call spirits either silently or aloud for their help in giving a truthful and accurate reading.

2.   Do not repeat a reading by the same method twice within twenty-four hours or the second reading will be inaccurate. Remember that you should have asked the spirits for a true answer and remained focused on what you were doing. Regardless of whether or not you like the answer, a second reading is not going to alter the message.

3.   Do a reading seriously if you want serious answers.

4.   A bad omen can be corrected or averted if an appropriate ritual is done to restore balance as soon as possible.

Most important, remember that divination, like any other shamanic activity, is not to be taken lightly.

Pebble Divination: Six-Fields Divination

Gently drop a small pebble, about the size of a pea, from the height of about one foot onto a paper on which six lines have been drawn radiating out from a center point (see the illustration below). The six fields are numbered clockwise from the upper right. The meaning of the divination is determined by which field the pebble comes to rest on.

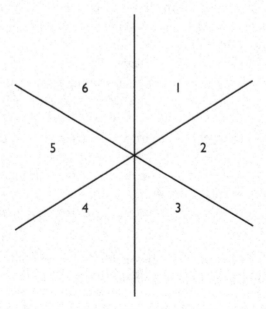

1.   Very good omen. The spirits will help, enemies will be defeated. Going to the city will be lucky. Marriage will increase blessing. Victory in any competition. Guests will arrive without problems. Illness will be healed quickly. If you are sick, it is because you ate bad food at the home of an elderly relative. If there has been a birth, there should be a ritual to honor the spirits. There will be news about something that was lost. Stolen things will be found after a short time of worry. The spirits will show favor. That which is desired will be accomplished. It is a good time to start building. Burn thirteen sticks of incense.

2.   Neither good nor bad. One normally calm spirit has been offended. It would be unlucky to meet with an enemy or to enter a competition. Not a good time to start building or a new project. Guests will be cause of worry. If a person is sick, recovery will be slow. The bad luck is from the offended spirit. Bad luck from water spirits and guests. Problems with newborn child. Bad news about lost things; stolen things will not be found. Do a ritual to calm the angry spirit. Do actions to bring *buyan*. Do a ritual to banish bad luck into *tsats*. Do *dallaga* (gather in spiritual power). A guest has offended the spirit. Do ritual for water spirits.

3.   Windhorse is abundant; that which is desired will be accomplished. Victory over enemies. Prosperity, increase in material goods. Marriage will be harmonious. Reconciliation with someone with whom there was conflict. Guests will be peaceful. Illness is not serious. Lost or stolen things will be found. If a child is born, it will have a blessed life. Burn incense or light candles to show thanks to the spirits. If you are sick, these is no need for a doctor; a little rest will bring recovery. Illness was the result of either spoiled food, defiled clothing, or fright.

4.   Do a ritual to call help from the water spirits as soon as possible. Loss of food and money. Many worries. If there is illness, it will be serious. You are under attack from *chotgor;* a ritual will send it away and bad things will end. Conflicts bring worry. Lost things will not be found. Much worry over something that was stolen. News about stolen item will come only after a long time. Anything that you plan to do will have problems. It is a dangerous time to move. *Chotgor* came from something that you found.

5.   This is a bad omen for any question. The spirits have abandoned you and there is danger of a life-threatening illness. There is the possibility of being killed. Danger of bankruptcy. Marriage may end in divorce. If you go on a trip, it will be worrisome or disastrous. If a person is ill, it is from impure food or from contact with the clothing a person was wearing when he died. Birth will have complications. Lost or stolen things will not be found. Burn thirteen sticks of incense several times to calm the spirits. Do a ritual to restore the spirits' favor. Do *ariulga*. Do a ritual to banish bad luck into *tsats*. Do a ritual for Bayan Hangai and nature spirits.

6.   The spirits will help in anything you want to do. Abundance of food and material goods. Everything will be successful. Marriage will be happy. No enemies. If you are sick, recovery will be easy. The illness is the result of a bad dream. Victory in any contest. Birth will be lucky. It is a good time to move. Do a ritual to show thanks to the nature and water spirits for their help. Burn incense and candles.

Divination of the Eight Petals of Heaven's Door

Gently drop a pea-sized pebble from the height of about one foot onto a drawing with a circle in the center surrounded by eight fields (see the illustration that follows) representing the directions north,

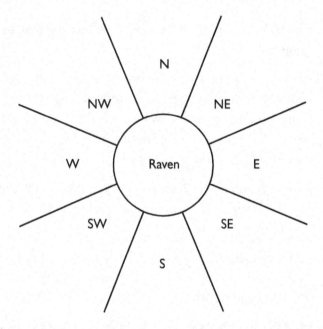

northeast, east, southeast, south, southwest, west, and northwest. The center circle is called Raven.

Raven: Desired thing will happen quickly. If a person is sick, it is from contact with an infected object or clothing. Do a healing ritual to banish illness into an *ongon* or animal, then recovery will be quick. In an argument, you will be right. Do *ariulga* for personal protection. Travel, whether near or far, will be successful. News of what has been lost will come from a red-faced person living fourteen kilometers to the north.

North: Desired thing will not be accomplished. There is great danger. In a conflict, you will be wrong. What has been lost is far away and cannot be recovered. Illness will be serious. A strong ritual is needed to restore luck.

Northeast: Neither good nor bad. Guests will cause problems. If things are borrowed, they will not be returned. A ritual will bring success in a contest. Illness will not go away. If an animal has been lost, it has been found by someone to the southeast.

East: Everything will be accomplished. Prosperity. If there is illness, it is the result of contact with a *chotgor*. A lost animal will return on its own. Guests will come to stay overnight in twenty-one or twenty-two days. If you are ill, do a ritual to send away *chotgor*.

Southeast: Very bad omen. Loss, deprivation. What is the cause of this bad fortune? Use appropriate ritual to do *zasal* (repairs).

South: Fairly good omen. Lost things will be recovered quickly. A lost animal has been found by someone to the south. Illness is the result of bad food and an offense to the spirits. Do a ritual to calm spirits.

Southwest: Very good omen for any question. A lost animal will return today on its own. Illness will go away within the month without any help. Conflict will be averted.

West: Success in one's own private affairs, but a bad omen for any business involving other people. Illness is due to contact with an evil spirit or undead being. A ritual to cleanse the person of this defilement is necessary.

Northwest: What is desired will come in abundance. Rain will come if there is drought. Food will be abundant. A good omen for any question. Peace, safety, happiness. Lost animals will be found.

Forty-one-Pebbles Divination

This technique is somewhat more intuitive than are the other pebble-divination techniques. Although this can be done with pebbles collected on the occasion of the reading, more commonly the shaman has his own collection to be used specifically for this reading. These pebbles are usually colored semiprecious stones or beach pebbles collected from places like Lake Baikal, where there is an abundance of pretty-colored stones. Tumbled crystals and semiprecious stones such as those found at rock shows and "new age" stores are ideal for this technique. Perfectly round pebbles are not necessary; in fact, having a few oddly shaped pebbles (oblong, pear-shaped, square, triangular, pointy) will add to the imagery manifested in the pattern of the final reading. Your collection should include at least a few red, yellow, black, and white stones, but the more colors and varieties of minerals you have, the better. Shamans usually keep these pebbles in their own special bag or box. The number of pebbles traditionally is forty-one, although if you have a few more or a few less it will not really matter, as not all will be used anyway.

The forty-one-pebbles reading is one of the most popular reading techniques in Siberia and Mongolia and is far more widespread than either coin or card reading. As is true for all divination techniques, however, the pebbles are only a tool for the intuition that the spirits give you. What is important in learning the pebbles technique is to practice a lot so you can have some idea of what the symbolism is—for like dream symbolism, it can vary somewhat from person to person.

When you are ready to do a reading, dump out all the pebbles in a pile in front of you.

Think carefully for a minute with the pebbles under the palms of your hands. Using one or both hands, start pushing the pebbles around with your fingers without paying attention to the color or shape of the stones. Push them around under your palm, and you will start to get the sensation that certain pebbles want to stay in the center and some want to be taken out. Do not have any expectation as to how few or how many pebbles get taken out—usually half of them are discarded, but it could be more or less.

When you feel that you have taken out all the pebbles that are to be discarded, push the remaining ones into a circular pile, still without paying much attention to the color or shapes of the stones. Once again, move them around until they are spread out in a circle four to six inches across. Take your left and right index fingers and use them to separate the pebbles into three groups. With your hands, arrange each set of pebbles so that they become three vertical parallel oblong piles.

Now use your index finger to divide each of these piles into three sections. These represent "head," "body," and "legs."

You are now ready to start interpreting the arrangements of the three rows of pebbles. Generally, the center pile represents the spiritual being of the person being read, the left pile the person's physical being, and the right pile either a person or a spirit that is strongly affecting the person's life or health. As you study these piles, you may sense that additional pebbles can be discarded, as they seem to have no meaning and are superfluous. This is normal. Once you feel that all the pebbles left in front of you are significant for the reading, start studying the colors and shapes of the remaining stones. The designation of the three divisions of each pile of stones is literal: A big black stone on the head or body of the pile representing the physical body may very well represent some kind of illness. Red and white stones clearly represent energy. Buff or brown represents flesh or skin. Blue and crystal also have special meanings that you will learn with experience. The pebbles in the row representing the spiritual body can indicate sites of intrusion, pollution, and so on. What does it mean if the middle row has a lot of black or dark stones? Do another divination technique or reading of the person's spiritual body to check for soul loss. Pay close attention to the right row to see what kind of external entity is affecting the person being read. Matching colors between it and the other two piles may offer important clues as to the nature of the effect.

Another application of the forty-one-pebbles technique is for relationship readings. When the reading of the pebbles is done for this purpose, the left and center piles represent the two people in the couple; the left pile usually represents the person whom the reader knows better (or the reader herself if the reader is doing a reading for herself). The right pile represents external influences such as parents, friends, and former lovers. Using the pebbles in this manner can be a fun way to practice pebble reading for the more serious business of shamanic diagnosis.

Reading with Five Coins

Coin reading has always been a popular divination technique, especially among Mongols. The reading with nine coins is described in *Riding Windhorses* (see the bibliography); the five-coin technique is less complicated but has many more interpretations. When employing this reading technique, either flip one coin five times or flip five coins and line them up in a row from left to right. In Mongolia the coins most commonly used are antique Manchu (Chin dynasty) brass coins with a hole in the center such as can be bought inexpensively in Chinese gift shops. If you do not have any such coins, pennies or other copper or brass coins will work just as well. (If you do use antique Manchu coins, the side with the squiggly Manchu script is heads and the side with Chinese writing is tails.) The interpretations are as follows:

All heads: *Shiljih deed tulge*
The best omen. That which is desired will happen. Everything will be good. Profits will be great, travel will be safe, very little trouble. If something has been lost or stolen, it will soon be recovered.

1 head 4 tails: *Huvilah deed tuvshin*
Matters will be resolved only after a long time. Profit will be small and difficult to obtain. Every matter will go slowly. Querent will go on a business trip. Private matters are fine; any questions with regard to home or family will be resolved without trouble. Lost or stolen things will be found.

1 tail, 1 head, 3 tails: *Gendeliig tailah tuvshin*
Worries about health and home. If querent is going on a trip, it will take longer than expected. Items querent is selling will get the desired price. Illness will be difficult to treat.

2 tails, 1 head, 2 tails: *Hishig soyorholiin dund tuvshin*
Blessing will increase and everything will turn out well at the end. Lost or stolen items are near and will be found soon. Travel will be safe. Good health, moderate profits. If the querent is attacked, he will win the fight.

3 tails, 1 head, 1 tail: *Gal deerh doord tulge*
No disease or suffering. Travel will take longer than expected. In doing business, the merchandise needed will be hard to find.

4 tails, 1 head: *Taria elbegshih dund*
Trouble with all things. Situation at home is bad. Lost or stolen things will not be found. Delays in business. If a person is ill, a ritual for Father Heaven is necessary!

2 heads, 3 tails: *Enerel buteh deed*
This is a good omen for any question. Much blessing, long life. Old age will be easy. Do deeds to increase *buyan*. Business will be profitable. A person with whom there was an argument will come back and be reconciled with the querent in two days. Victory in any contest.

1 head, 1 tail, 1 head, 2 tails: *Erdemiin sang oloh sain*
Good omen for any question. Good luck. Quick and big profit; business affairs will go as planned. There will be peace of mind. A person who went on a business trip will return soon. In the future, however, a woman will cause problems.

1 head, 3 tails, 1 head: *Amgalan dund tulge*
If the querent is planning to buy something, the desired item will be hard to find or too expensive. In business, profit will be small. If the person is ill, he or she must see a doctor immediately. A person who went on a trip will return in a day or two. The querent will have a guest who is going to cause trouble.

1 head, 2 tails, 1 head, 1 tail: *Setgelhlen buteh dund*

All affairs at home will go well. Profit will be great. Business is good. If the querent is in a lawsuit, he will win. A person who is traveling will come home. There is danger of serious, possibly life-threatening illness. Someone will find something that was lost or stolen and bring it back.

1 tail, 2 heads, 2 tails: *Gamshig arilah sain*

This omen signifies good luck for all questions. At home, every-thing is fine. In business, profit will be great but business matters will be completed slowly. A traveler will come home quickly. If the querent is ill, do a ritual to call the spirits to bring quick healing.

1 tail, 1 head, 1 tail, 1 head, 1 tail: *Husel buteh dund*

If married, the querent will soon have a child or grandchild. There are constant worries, however. Profit in business will not be greater than 10 percent. If there is illness, do a ritual to get help from the spirits for healing. If a lost or stolen item is not found within three days, it will probably not be found. A traveler will be home in five days. Things will be completed after some time, not quickly.

1 tail, 1 head, 2 tails, 1 head: *Saadtai muu tulge*

A very bad sign. When the querent looks in the mirror, he will look bad, worse than he really is. Profits are small. Querent will become sick. There is discord at home. Travel will be unprofitable.

2 tails, 2 heads, 1 tail: *Amar door tulge*

Many things that the querent wants to do cannot be accomplished. There will be trouble with paperwork for government such as tax forms, permits, or licenses. Mental confusion. No peace at home. Lost things will not be found. Travelers will be delayed. Find out the cause of the bad luck! If a person is ill, a ritual for Father Heaven and the spirits is needed.

2 tails, 1 head, 1 tail, 1 head: *Saad ihtei muu*

What is desired cannot happen. Travel is difficult. No profit. Heal-ing of illness will be complicated. Difficulty with any matter. A shaman must do *zasal* immediately!

3 tails, 2 heads: *Gamshig arilah dund*
At home all matters are well. A lawsuit will be won in querent's favor. Illness will be easy to treat. Everything will go as planned. Profit in business will be great. Traveler will come home immediately. Lost item will be found.

3 heads, 2 tails: *Bayar boloh dund*
This omen is good for all questions. Everything will be completed as planned.

2 heads, 1 tail, 1 head, 1 tail: *Amin hamgaalah doord*
Worries at home. A minor quarrel will not be resolved. There is danger of being a victim of violence. Do deeds to increase *buyan.* Perform a ritual for protection. Travelers will return slowly.

2 heads, 2 tails, 1 head: *Gal shinjtei doord*
This is a fearful omen. Possessions or money will be lost. An old lover or relative will become an enemy. Business will decline. Querent will become sick suddenly. Querent will lose lawsuit. No profit. Have shaman do *serjim* for protection and restoration of luck before it is too late! (See "*Serjim:* Spells of Scattering and Pouring" in chapter 9.)

1 head, 1 tail, 2 heads, 1 tail: *Suuj elbeg dund*
At home things are neither good nor bad. Peace of mind. Querent will win a lawsuit. If a person is ill, do a ritual for Father Heaven. Business is good.

1 head, 1 tail, 1 head, 1 tail, 1 head: *Hishig nemeh sain*
A good omen for any question. Fame and happiness. Things will be accomplished as planned. At home, all is happy and peaceful. If someone is ill, it is not serious. Victory in any contest. Lost or stolen things will be found. Big profit in business. A traveler will return in three days. Burn thirteen sticks of incense to thank the spirits.

1 head, 2 tails, 2 heads: *Setgelhlen buten dund*
This omen is like the light of the moon at night. Peace reigns at home. Quick recovery from illness. A person who will bring a lot of luck will be coming soon. Victory for querent in a lawsuit. All matters will be completed as intended.

1 tail, 3 heads, 1 tail: *Buyan hishigiin dund*
Power is sent down from heaven. Fame and happiness. Blessings will be great. Lost things will be found. There will be victory in any contest. Quick recovery from illness. Burn thirteen sticks of incense to thank the spirits.

1 tail, 2 heads, 1 tail, 1 head: *Saad hiigeed shinjiltei doord*
This omen indicates failure and is generally bad. Work or business will be unsuccessful. Bad luck. Querent will lose lawsuit. There is a possibility that an enemy has had a shaman or other spiritual practitioner invoke the spirits to cause problems for the querent. Have shaman do *zasal* to restore luck.

1 tail, 1 head, 1 tail, 2 heads: *Ilerch nevtreh sain*
Family will prosper. Quick recovery from illness. Good luck, success in business. Victory for querent in a lawsuit. Profit will be good but less than expected.

2 tails, 3 heads: *Buyan zuzaarah deed*
Lost things will be found. Recovery from illness. Success in finding money brings happiness to the family. A person who has traveled from far away is responsible for this good fortune. Everything is good. Victory in contest or lawsuit.

1 tail, 4 heads: *Saijrah deed tulge*
This omen is like the effect of rain on plants. Everything is about to get better in all aspects of life. Great happiness will come for a long time. Lost things will be found. Victory in lawsuit. A traveler will come home safely. Burn thirteen sticks of incense to thank the spirits.

2 heads, 1 tail, 2 heads: *Delgereh tuvshin tulge*
Success and prosperity. Events that should be unlucky turn out to be harmless. People are ready to do business with the querent. Victory in a lawsuit.

4 heads, 1 tail: *Buyan hishigiin sain*
This indicates fame for the querent. Good for business. Lawsuit will be settled out of court to the querent's advantage. If there is illness, a doctor will be necessary. Happiness in family. A traveler will return. Lost things will be found.

1 head, 1 tail, 3 heads: *Etses sainii tuvshin tulge*

This sign is like standing on ice with thin shoes. At home, neither good nor bad. Travelers will return slowly with delays. Lost things will be found only after a long time. With any question, things will turn out as intended but only after several delays.

3 heads, 1 tail, 1 head: *Ayagui muu tulge*

Travelers will have too little money and no one to turn to for help. Any kind of business will decline. Any business proposition will turn out less productive than expected. Travelers will not come home. Lost things will not be found. What is the source of the bad luck? Find out and do *zasal* as soon as possible.

5 tails: *Toogui muu tulge*

Worst omen of all. No peace at home, failure in business, death. Illness cannot be healed. Failure in lawsuit or in any other kind of contest. Travelers will not come home. Lost things will not be found. Shamanic emergency!

Bead Divination

In Mongolia and Siberia bead divination is a popular divination technique used by shamans and laypeople alike. While doing bead divination, many shamans wear an *erih* (Tibetan rosary, also known as a *mala*), not for use in prayer, but for use as a divination tool. Any kind of necklace can be used, as long as it has a pendant or clasp that interrupts the series of beads. A necklace that has all identical beads and no clasp would not be useful, but any necklace that has an "end" or "tail" would be appropriate. The currently popular Chinese power bracelet is appropriate for use in bead divination, because like the Tibetan *mala* it has a tail bead with a tassel.

Bead divination, like the forty-one-pebbles divination, requires a certain amount of intuition. When you do the divination you close your eyes and hold the strand of beads in your hands, running your fingers along the beads until the spirits prompt you to focus on a certain one. Grasp that bead between your left thumb and index finger and open your eyes. How far are you from the nearest end, tail, or pendant? Count off beads in groups of six in the direction of the closest end, tail bead, or pendant. When there are too few beads left to count off another group of six, note how many beads are left (there should be one to five, or perhaps none at all if you counted out all the way to the end) and refer to the interpretations below:

1 bead

This is a very good omen. There may be a family problem, but the spirits are ready to help with any question. Health is strong. Lost things will be recovered easily. A good omen for traveling. Show gratitude to the spirits by burning thirteen sticks of incense and giving to charity in order to increase *buyan*.

2 beads

There are many difficulties, probably because of interference by a hostile spirit. Threat of scandal. Illness is dangerous. A ritual should be done to banish evil spirit into a *tsats (zolig)*. The sick person is not getting a correct diagnosis and needs to see a different doctor. Defeat in conflicts. Lost things will not be found.

3 beads

Generally good but there are family problems. What querent wants will be partially fulfilled. Material goods will increase. If someone is sick, there should be a ritual to banish the disease spirit. Do a ritual to call back what has been lost. If a person is going on a trip, there is danger of robbery. Burn incense and do *serjim* to invoke the protection of the spirits.

4 beads

There are many difficulties but there is peace at home. There is very little free time or freedom of choice. The spirits cannot help the querent do what he wants. Do a ritual to restore a good relationship with the spirits. If not, the querent will lose any dispute. What has been lost will not be found but will be replaced with something of equivalent value. Neither a good nor a bad omen for travel. Some spirit has been offended and needs to be propitiated in order to restore luck.

5 beads

A fortunate omen. A ritual for the *sahius* spirits will bring even greater happiness to the family. A friend may prove unreliable. Prosperity in material goods. Illness will not be serious. The querent's life will be long because his or her body is strong. However, if the person is ill, some sort of medical test should be performed by a doctor. In a conflict, the querent will win but the defeated person may try to get even. Good omen for finding lost things or traveling.

6 beads (0 beads)

The most difficult omen. The spirits do not favor what the querent wants. Possible divorce or separation. Loss of money over long period of time. Business failure. Do a ritual to restore luck and make a contribution to charity. To preserve peace in the family, do *dallaga*, and cleanse the home in order to expel a hostile spirit. Interference by this hostile spirit is the reason for illness and the sick person cannot be cured until a ritual is done to remove the spirit. Avoid conflict until balance has been restored. Lost things will not be found. New enemies. Bad omen for travel.

EIGHT

Healing of the Earth, Blessing, and Protection

Between two worlds I travel,
And I understand more clearly those who have gone.
And I value the living more strongly.
Life—I love.
And if I am happy, I know
It is by your bidding.
And by your bidding I wish the best
For my friend, for the land, for the century.

—BAYAR DUGAROV, *SAGAAN DALI*
TRANSLATED BY LAURIE DANIELS[1]

HEALING PLACES, HEALING THE EARTH

Just as people need healing, sometimes a place will need to be healed. A very important element of Buryat shamanism is the idea of *ezed*, or spirits of place. Animals are alive and people are alive, but rocks, mountains, fields, and even cities also have their own consciousness; indeed the whole world is vibrant with life and consciousness.

If people truly understood this, I believe the abuse of the environment on both a physical and spiritual level would decline. Many human beings today view the seemingly inanimate world as being dead and therefore not to be respected. How wrong they are! Because the world itself is full of consciousness, a shaman's work will necessarily include the healing of places as well as of the earth itself.

The most common problem a shaman encounters in this kind of work is pollution. The world been polluted physically, and violence, hatred, abuse, and war have polluted it spiritually. Although there will be times when even a shaman may have to resort to physical violence in mundane life in order to protect himself or his community, shamans recognize the polluting effect that violence can have on a place. Houses that are haunted by a discarnate *suns* spirit are also polluted. Dealing with hauntings is such an important part of shamanic work that I will discuss it first.

A place—usually a house, a building, or sometimes even a place in the natural world—may sometimes become the haunt of a free *suns* spirit or of a nature spirit that is hostile to human beings. Its effects on people who live at or frequent a place will be a good indication of the general personality of the spirit that haunts it. It should be understood that haunting spirits are of a different class from the *suld* souls that settle and become *ezen* of places. *Suld* souls generally have little effect on the living unless there are many of them who died violently in a certain area (such as on battlefields or in crime-ridden neighborhoods). The issue of calming *suld* souls will be discussed later in this section. If people frequenting a certain place become violently ill, experience soul loss, feel unreasonable fear, or see frightening manifestations, it is likely that the spirit haunting the place is of a hostile nature. If people have fleeting psychic contact with a spirit, see harmless manifestations, or have milder cases of mental disorder or disease, the haunting entity is probably benign or confused. Knowing the general disposition of the spirit is important in figuring out how to deal with it.

If the haunting spirit is generally benign, you can send it fairly easily to the lower world and it will not give any further trouble. If it is a nature spirit that is cooperative, you can send it to another place in the middle world and it will not return once you have done *ariulga*. You do *ariulga* of a place by smudging with sacred smoke, then spraying the area lightly with *arshaan*. Strew the perimeter of the place (inside and out if it is a building) with salt; salt is known in many traditions as being effective for confining or repelling spirits.

If the haunting spirit is hostile, you will have to struggle with it and keep it under control until you either expel it or send it to the lower world. If you can see it, grab it and confine it in an *ongon* or have your helper spirits hold it (you may also invoke the help of Erleg Khan, as described in the previous chapter). Many times, however, the spirit may try to hide or run away from you. In this case begin doing *ariulga* at the perimeter, starting with natural entrances and exits such as windows and doors. Smudge around the perimeter and then strew salt all the way around so that the spirit is confined within the place and cannot run away. Continue to do *ariulga* with smudge and salt room by room, finishing each room by salting in front of the door. Soon you will reduce the space in which the spirit can wander. In my experience the spirit becomes more agitated, even knocking things over, as it becomes trapped. Once you have confined it in a small space, it will be easy to overcome the spirit and then you can either eject it or send it off to the lower world. In any case, it will be necessary to smudge one more time and spray the area with *arshaan*.

Ariulga is used in places for other purposes as well. When a place has been the site of murder, battle, rape, abuse, or another violent act causing suffering for humans or animals, the spiritual pollution of the place will lower the spiritual power and health of all things that live in or frequent it. The pollution is cleansed by smudging; spraying of *arshaan;* and the strewing of salt, sand, and seeds. Note that the amount of the substances being strewed does not have to be so excessive that it creates a mess or causes harm to plants. The strewing should be light but thorough.

The Peace Tree ritual, described in my book *Riding Windhorses*, is a special ritual for calming the *suld* spirits that have settled in places. This ritual combines the *ariulga*, the invocation of the spirits, and the creation of a *barisaa* tree as a location for the ongoing channeling of spiritual energy for blessing and inspiration. It honors the spirit of the tree and the *suld* spirits that inhabit the area.

A Buryat elder prays and ties on a ribbon at a sacred tree (barisaa).

This ritual is especially necessary in places where there has been a lot of violence, such as inner-city neighborhoods, sites of extremely violent crimes or genocide, and battlefields. As the twentieth century has been a time of mass violence unparalleled in human history, this ceremony is particularly important in healing the spiritual atmosphere of the world so that the cycle of violence can finally be stopped and the earth can be cleansed for the new millennium. The massive amount of violent human deaths created a large number of nature spirits that are angry, hurt, and resentful, and even though they do not affect humans as much as *suns* souls do, in hauntings they collectively tinge the atmosphere of many places with feelings of panic, anger, confusion, and desire for revenge. This is why inner-city crime, feuds, and guerrilla wars are so difficult to stop once they start.

The Peace Tree ritual starts with an *ariulga* directed outward in all directions from a tree that will be the focus of the ceremony. After doing the *ariulga,* the shaman invokes the *suld* souls that have settled in the area around the tree. This area is circular, a kilometer or more from the tree in each direction. The *ariulga* is directed outward, so by intention the shaman's act includes this entire large area. The nature spirits within the area included in the ritual are asked to turn their thoughts away from violence and instead toward working to bring peace and inspiration into people's thoughts. Offerings of food and drink are made, then the drink is ritually tossed out to the spirits and given to the tree spirit as well. The tree is consecrated as an *oboo,* a place of connection between heaven and earth and a source of spiritual power and blessing. The participants tie strips of cloth to the branches in honor of the spirit of the tree and then partake of the ritual food and drink in a gesture of honoring and sharing with the spirits invoked in the ceremony.

The Peace Tree is one way in which the shaman can work to heal the earth and convert the character of the nature spirits from negative to positive. The shaman staff, or *horiboo,* once it has been fully empowered, has the ability to do this by touching the ground or water while making the proper invocations. It is said that in ancient times Abai Geser did battle with four powerful nature spirits known as the four enemies of peace. He journeyed to his father-in-law, Uha Loson Khan, chief of the water spirits, and received a powerful metal shaman staff (the attribute of a Buryat shaman of high degree). He went to the places where these spirits resided and said the magical phrase *"Hoyor sagai negende!"* while touching the shaman staff to the ground. Like the *barisaa,* which is a living magical link to the *gol,* Abai Geser's use of the *horiboo* with this phrase, which invokes the power of the *gol,* provided the ability to transmute malevolent nature spirits into benign nature spirits. Abai Geser's career is a reminder that one of the most important aspects of the shaman calling is to serve the community as a whole, above and beyond serving individual clients. Be sure to ask your spirits how you can use intention and shamanic ritual to help heal the earth in order to bring a better future for all.

PROTECTION

Protection can be viewed as a type of preemptive shamanism. Protection is usually invoked when a person or place is likely to be attacked either spiritually or physically. Protection from physical dangers is necessary when a person is traveling or being exposed to epidemic disease, war, or the risk of being a victim of a crime. A shaman invokes protection from spiritual forces for a person who is especially vulnerable, such as a child, or when a person has a known enemy that may be capable of having spiritual forces invoked to bring harm. Throughout the world, unfortunately,there are unethical spiritual practitioners who will use their abilities to channel spiritual energy for destructive purposes.

Invocation for spiritual protection is similar to that for physical protection; remember, the spiritual world mirrors and influences the physical world. For general protection a shaman can invoke the helper spirits as well as some of the more powerful entities such as the *tenger* and *zayaans* to augment the power of the protection. In other cases you may create an *ongon* or talisman to give to the

Ongons, representing a moose, birds, and two warriors bearing spears, protecting a shaman's tent

person for whom protection is being invoked so that he can keep it on his person as a reminder of the spirit that has been invoked specifically for the purpose of protection. Creating an *ongon* for protection and imbuing it with a spirit for that purpose will keep the protection strong for as long as the spirit occupies the *ongon*. *Ongons* are especially good for protection during travel and exposure to physical danger. *Ongons* to protect cars from accidents and theft are common in Mongolia and Siberia. They are easy to make and quite effective.

In Buryat tradition, shamans were sometimes requested to become a *naija*, "spiritual friend," for a child. The shaman would create an *ongon* or give a talisman to the child to protect him during his very young years, when he was especially vulnerable to spiritual attack and soul loss. Once the child grew older and his spiritual body became stable and "hard," the *ongon* or talisman would be returned to the shaman along with gifts of gratitude for the protection work.

You may, of course, create strong protection for yourself when you feel endangered. When you are exposed to contagious illness, imagine your spirits creating an impenetrable barrier around you in order to repel infection. If you leave a house, car, or other valuable item unattended, call down spiritual protection on it with the intention of creating fear and confusion in potential thieves so that they are discouraged from stealing. When you go alone to a dangerous place, visualize your helper spirits in a frightening and warlike aspect so that they will create fear in any potential attackers.

BLESSING

Blessing can be invoked for individuals, businesses, projects, even for large groups of people. In Mongolia and Siberia it is fairly common for a shaman to be asked to do a blessing ritual at the beginning of a project, to improve business, or to ensure the health and fertility of livestock. You too can invoke the spirits to grant power, blessing, and protection in cases of new enterprises or businesses or to bring fertility for someone wanting children. For most situations in which you will be asked to do blessings, you can do the *serjim* (see chapter 9) or the *dallaga*. This is a simple but effective ceremony in which the people desiring blessing prepare plates of food and money (coins) and burn incense. You will make your invocation and when you state your intentions of blessing, you will follow each sentence with the magical phrase *Hurai, hurai, hurai* (see the description of its use in the "Magical Phrases" section of the glossary). Afterward, the participants share the food and money, for they have been imbued with the energy invoked for the blessing.

A shaman may journey to the spirits in the upper world to present the petition of the people involved to the *tenger* and other high-ranking spirits. Study the descriptions of the spirits of Buryat

Oboo sacred to the thirty-three warriors of the Sayan Mountains.
The mounted warrior is Abai Geser.

The tamkhinii bariaasha *is an altar for tobacco
offerings to the mountain spirits.*

shamanic practice in appendix 2 to determine which spirits may be
helpful for the issue at hand (shamans in our tradition keep lists of
shamanic helper spirits for this purpose), and ask your helper spirits to guide you to the entities that would be most helpful for the
problem for which you are journeying. In *Riding Windhorses* (see
the bibliography) I describe the journey to the mountain spirits, a
journey for the bringing of blessing for a specific purpose.

WEATHER AND HUNTING MAGIC

Shamans have traditionally done work to make changes in the weather. Understandably, this is done in moderation; stopping or bringing rain may bring adverse effects if done too often. The *tenger* and other upper-world spirits are generally considered to be the controllers of weather, so they are invoked in weather work (once again, consult appendix 2 to see which *tenger* control the various types of weather). When appealing for rain, it is usual to shamanize by an *oboo, turge* tree, or other representation of the *gol.* The most common way of bringing rain is to do an invocation at such a location, throwing water with a ceremonial wooden spoon toward the *oboo* or other representation of the world center (the Geser invocation in appendix 4 is especially effective when used in this ritual). If there has been a severe drought, an upper-world journey may be more powerful.

Stopping storms is usually accomplished by invocation, and you do not necessarily have to do this in a ceremonial space. Drumming and incorporating the spirits will stop even the wildest storm fairly quickly. I have found that invoking Tatai, the *tenger* of storms, will stop rain or severe storms almost at once, especially if accompanied by drumming. If you have them, *zadai* stones, stones that have great magical power for stopping storms or bringing rain (see the section on magical stones on pages 178–81, should be placed with the *ongons* in weather-related ceremonies.

In Siberia, hunting is an important part of daily life, and shamans will journey to the master spirits of the animals, the most important of whom is Bayan Hangai (Bayan Ahaa), master of the forest. In undertaking this journey, the shaman asks the masters of the game to bring hunting success for his community. These rituals are done only for subsistence hunting, however, and not for recreational hunting, and the shaman usually does not participate in the hunt personally. An invocation of Bayan Hangai is therefore appropriate on behalf of hunters if you know they are hunting in order to obtain food and not for sport.

DIVINATION

Seeing the future is part of a shaman's work the world over. The techniques vary from shaman to shaman, depending on which work best for the individual shaman. Some shamans use mirror gazing, gazing into unopened bottles of vodka, bones, rocks, cards, beads, and coins. Others can do psychic readings, using information passed from the helper spirits. When you do divination, use whatever technique you prefer. What distinguishes readings by shamans from those of other people is that shamans customarily ask the spirits to assist in the reading so that the best and most accurate information comes through. In addition to the divination techniques described in this book, learn those presented in *Riding Windhorses* if doing readings is an important part of your shamanic work.

TRADITIONAL FESTIVALS

In the tradition in which I was trained there are certain festivals highlighting important times of the year. You are free to choose whether you want to observe them; you may prefer to observe festivals out of other traditions that you feel more connected with.[2]

In Siberia and Mongolia the White Moon Festival *(Sagaalgan)*, held in mid-February, marks the beginning of spring. It starts with the new moon of that month and usually falls close to the beginning of Lent in the Western calendar (there is a joke here in Siberia that when the Russians have to start fasting, we are feasting). The White Moon is the festival of the return of the spirits. It is believed that all the shamanic and nature spirits go to the upper world for cleansing and return at sunrise on the morning of the White Moon. The spirits are welcomed with fire, sacred smoke, and offerings of food and drink, and it is customary to avoid any conflict or hostility until the moon becomes full. Thus the White Moon season is a time of forgiveness and reconciliation.

On April 20–21, when the migratory birds have arrived and mushrooms start to appear, the Great Spring Ceremony welcomes the birds and celebrates spring. A shamanic journey may be done to invoke blessing for the community and to ask for fertility of the

The oboo *to the ancestors of the Hongoodor tribe in Akha aimag, Siberia.*
In the foreground wood and food offerings are prepared
for the shamanic fire ritual.

people, the livestock, and the earth. Offerings of food, predominantly milk and other dairy products, are made.

The Great Summer Ceremony, honoring Mother Earth, is held around June 5 or June 6.

The summer solstice, known as Ulaan Tergel (Red Round) or Naran Butsah Odor (Day of the Sun's Return), is commemorated with a ceremony at an *oboo* or similar sacred place. One or more shamans will drum and incorporate the spirits in succession with the purpose of bringing blessings on the people assembled there. It is believed that the summer solstice starts a time when the amount of spiritual help available to the shaman is at its peak, and this period lasts for three months. Some groups throw water on the *oboo* and on each other to ensure rain and fertility. Another custom is to cut up the food offerings after the ceremony and throw them to the children, who scramble to grab up as many morsels and pieces of candy as possible.[3]

July 3 or July 4 is the day usually dedicated to shamanic rituals in honor of the water spirits and the spirits of the lower world.

On September 11 or 12 there are rituals to honor the upper-world spirits and the master spirits of sacred places, the *tenger* and the *khans*.

The Harvest Festival, held at the fall equinox, ends the peak period of spiritual activity and is a time of thanking the spirits for the bounty of the summer. Food offerings and feasting are a major component of this festival. In the shamanic ritual calendar, this is the new year and it was the original Sagaan Sar (White Moon) festival. Outside of the hunting ritual of the following moon cycle, shamanic activity is limited to small-scale rituals until the Great Spring Ceremony of the following year. This is because many of the spirits are much less active between the autumn and spring equinoxes.

On October 16 or 17 Buryat shamans honor Bayan Hangai, the spirit of the forests and natural world. This marks the beginning of the hunting season and establishes a good relationship between the community and the provider of game animals. This also marks the advent of winter, for this is about the time when the first snow will fall in Siberia.

SERVING ONE'S COMMUNITY

The central idea expressed in the festivals mentioned above is that the shaman serves his community. In your practice you may create your own community out of the clients whom you serve or acquaintances who do shamanic work with you. Doing shamanic work for the community as a whole brings great blessing and increases your windhorse even more than shamanizing for a single person does. In

Buryat tradition the shaman serves the community and helps to per-petuate the knowledge passed down from the ancestors. In your own small community you can serve as both a healer and a teacher of shamanic customs and ways of understanding the world.

Just as a shaman is capable of performing a healing for a person who is not present, it is also possible to perform work to benefit groups not even aware that you are doing so. You can do shamanic work to bring blessing or protection to the city where you live or to your country, and you can even do work to help heal the earth. Knowledge of your work by the people it benefits is not necessary; the spirits will respond to your invocations and intentions just the same. If you hear about disasters or disease in a foreign country, you can create *buyan* by invoking healing and protection for the people who are suffering. I have proposed a worldwide network of shamans who can coordinate their work in times of disaster, dis-ease, or epidemic. I hope this will eventually come about.

The Clean Tent ritual, which concludes this chapter, is tradi-tionally performed for the collective protection and blessing of a community.

May the spirits continue to inspire you and guide you to work for the healing of self, community, and the earth!

The Clean Tent Ritual

The Clean Tent ritual is done among the Samoyed peoples of north-ern Siberia, the Ostyak, Nenets, and Yukaghir. It is a group ritual invoking blessing and protection for each of the participants, traditionally all of the inhabitants of a camp or village. This cer-emony, presided over by one or more shamans, would normally be done during or shortly after the White Moon. It is called the Clean Tent Ceremony because traditionally a special tepee is erected spe-cifically for the ritual. In some cases this ritual is performed outside using a stone circle to enclose the ritual space in lieu of the tent.[4]

This ritual complements the idea that the White Moon is a time of spiritual cleansing, forgiveness, and reconciliation. The forces that bring bad luck and illness are ritually bound up and the shaman makes an upper-world journey in order to ask the spirits about the welfare of the community over the coming year. The participants join to dispel negative and destructive influences from their community with their collective intention. In this section I will present an abbreviated version of the Clean Tent ritual that can be done by shamanic practitioners either indoors in a ritual space simulating the ceremonial tepee or outside in a natural place using the stone circle.

The ideal time to perform this ceremony is in the early spring, on or during the White Moon (mid-February to mid-March). It will be effective almost any time of the year , however, with the exception of Bituun (the waning moon preceding the beginning of the White Moon). Bituun is considered to be a low-energy period that is not good for any kind of shamanic work, and major ceremonies should be postponed, if possible, until it is over.

In describing this ritual I will focus on the items that are specifically necessary for it. The ritual space should be large enough for all participants to be able to sit in a circle comfortably and to dance around the circle without having any impediments to their movement. (See appendix 1 for the details of how to set up a shamanic ritual space.)

If you plan to go the upper world as a group journey, there should be enough room in the ritual space for people to lie down or sit on the floor comfortably during the journey. Every participant will need five strips of rawhide or ribbon, each about two inches long, and a piece of red ribbon about three inches long. These will be used for the binding part of the ceremony. These strips and ribbons should be kept on the person of each participant so that they will be handy when it is time to use them. At the center of the space, place either a smudge that will stay lit during the ceremony or incense sticks, to represent fire. If the ceremony is done outside, a real fire can be made.

In the outdoor version of this ceremony, a large amount of fist-size rocks are used to make the circle. At least two rather large rocks should mark the "gate," the entrance on the southern side of the ritual circle. The shaman or all the participants collectively can place the rocks. Each person can take a few rocks while walking sunwise around the circle, placing the rocks until the distinct outline of a circle is visible. Because the traditional number of poles used in the ritual tepee was twenty-one or a multiple thereof, the number of rocks ideally should also be twenty-one or a multiple. The presiding shaman is responsible for placing the gate stones; this should be done last. If you are going to use a fire, make sure you have a designated fire keeper and adequate firewood inside the circle, as no one should leave the circle during the ritual except for the two people leading the shaman when he enters the circle for the second part of the ceremony. Although more than one or all of the participants in the ceremony will be shamans, one is designated the *ahanad*, the leader of the ritual. Traditionally this is the oldest or most experienced shaman.

If this ritual is done inside, the circle should be created with smaller rocks, either gathered by the participants and collected in a basket or provided by the *ahanad*. Once again they can be placed by the presiding shaman or by the participants, and the gate on the southern side should be clearly marked. Because you are creating a virtual version of the ceremonial tepee, try to use twenty-one or forty-two small rocks for the circle. Be sure to place them far enough at the edge of the ritual space that they will not be in danger of being kicked when people are dancing around.

The chief elements of the imagery used in the Clean Tent ritual are the *gol*, the *turge* (World Tree), the gate, and the Altan Hadaas (polestar). The gate is the customary entrance for all shamanic ritual spaces, and some representation of the *gol* is always present. In the second part of the Clean Tent ritual the shaman will be led in through the gate to his seat inside the circle. In the upper-world journey, which is the climax of the ritual, the shaman climbs the nine steps of the *turge* tree to the upper world. The smoke hole of the heavens, the entrance to the upper world, is marked by the polestar.

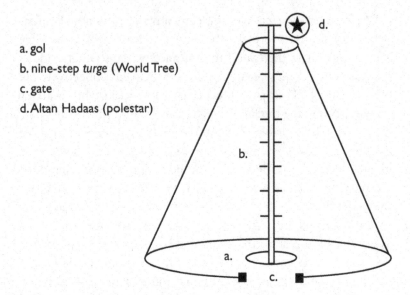

a. gol
b. nine-step *turge* (World Tree)
c. gate
d. Altan Hadaas (polestar)

Consecrating the Circle

Once you have set up the ritual space, all of the participants may drum together, or the *ahanad* drums alone, in order to call in the helper spirits to bring power to the work that is about to be done. This drumming is done according to what feels right and can be long or short. The most important purpose of the drumming is to bring the collective attention of all of the participants into sharp focus so that intention can be directed as a group.

You can instruct the participants in the meaning of the clean tent, that this place will be cleansed by the spirits of all negative thoughts and influences. Tell them to visualize that the sound of the drumming is driving away all bad things that may have come with them into the circle. In the first part of the ritual, the *ahanad* does not normally wear his ritual clothing; the ritual clothing should be placed nearby, outside of the circle, so that the *ahanad* can put it on later.

The Binding

In this part of the ceremony, each of the participants should take out his strips and red ribbons. The strips represent potential diseases that people could suffer over the next year: headache, colds, blood diseases (leukemia; blood poisoning; heart, liver, and kidney disease; and diabetes, for example), arthritis, and epidemic diseases (for instance, flu, AIDS, hepatitis, and cholera).

The red of the binding ribbon is a power color and represents the power of the spirits being invoked to bind up these diseases. Each person should take the ribbon and tie up the five strips with three knots. The tying up of the strips is done solemnly and meditatively, each person thinking carefully about the symbolism of the action and imagining himself as being in perfect health. You may want to drum softly and slowly while this is being done in order to keep the participants silent and in a state of contemplation. Once the little bundles have been made, they are placed at the center of the circle, near the fire or whatever you have placed to represent the *gol*.

Entrance of the Shaman, Stomp Dance

The *ahanad* shaman now exits the circle through the gate. Two people should be designated leaders for the shaman. The *ahanad* puts on the ritual clothing, takes up his drum, and drums until the two leaders come out. The *ahanad* will be blindfolded or keeps his eyes closed. The two leaders grasp the shoulders of the shaman to guide him through the gate.

When you enter the circle, the other participants who have drums will follow the rhythm of your drumming. The two leaders will lead you sunwise around the circle three times, bringing you back to your seat. While you are going around the circle without being able to see your surroundings, imagine that you are indeed inside a tepee. Bring yourself back to the time of the ancestors, smell the smoke of the fire, allow the drums to drive your shamanic vision. When you open your eyes after being led to your seat, or when your two leaders take off the blindfold, allow the image of the tepee to remain with you as you proceed with the ritual.

Stand up and approach the fire, then make an invocation to the spirits to bring their power into the binding of the diseases. Ask them to help as you and all the participants dance around the circle to drive away bad things from your lives. When the invocation is finished, return to your place in the circle but remain standing. With a prearranged signal, have the rest of the participants stand and drum with you as you all do the stomp dance.

The stomp dance is quite simple. It is actually not a dance but a walking about the circle with exaggerated stomps. The sound of the stomps drives away all bad things from the lives of the people who are dancing. Everyone should visualize the stomping as driving away any problems, bad influences, and dangers. The stomp dance goes around the circle sunwise three times three (nine) times. Everybody sits down when it is done. If you use a ceremonial pipe, pass it around the circle before going on to the next part of the ritual. In Buryat tradition, a pipe was smoked as a way of commemorating victory over evil forces. Give smoke to Father Heaven and Mother Earth and the ancestors in three exhales. In Siberian rituals, pipe smoking usually is done between sections of a major ritual.

Upper-World Journey

This is the most powerful part of the Clean Tent Ceremony, and it can be done in two ways. In the first, the *ahanad* drums alone and makes the upper-world journey on behalf of the entire group. In the second, if all of the participants are shamanic practitioners, the *ahanad* can do the upper-world journey as a guided visualization in which he describes the ascent of the World Tree so that everyone can participate in the journey with him. In this case the drumming at first is soft and then becomes forceful when the upper world is reached. The *ahanad* stops speaking when he reaches the upper world so that each person's journey can take its own course. Because most of you will probably be doing this ritual with other shamanic practitioners, I will describe the second method more fully.

Make sure that all people who are doing the journey are either lying down or otherwise comfortable so that there is nothing to distract from the journey experience. Only you as the *ahanad* will be drumming, so all drums besides your own should be put aside. While you are speaking, be sure not to drum so loudly that people cannot hear you clearly: you may want only to tap along the edge or stop altogether if you find it distracting. Let your spirits guide you to use the most powerful and evocative words as you talk.

Describe an image of the shaman's tent as it would be in the traditional ceremony. Tell participants to imagine that each is a shaman working on behalf of the tribe, going to the upper world to bring blessing for all in the community. What kind of shaman costume are they wearing? Can they feel the warmth of the ceremonial fire and smell its smoke? Imagine the smoke drifting upward, toward the smoke hole at the top of the tepee. Use images from your vision when you walked blindly around the circle. Suddenly a tree emerges from the place of the fire, tall and magnificent, reaching toward the sky. It is so tall that it reaches the heavens; however, it has nine branches like steps that will bring you to its very top when you climb it (imagine a pine tree, with its steplike layers of branches). In the ascent you will describe each branch and how you perceive it. As you ascend you will feel the heaviness of physical existence fall away; you will feel ever lighter and more ecstatic with each level. If you are leading a group, you may want to do a short burst of drumming as you and the people sharing the vision climb from branch to branch.

When you step up to the first branch, you step out of present reality. You are in the time of the ancestors, following in the footsteps of the ancient shamans. You become one with all shamans who have come before. You realize you are traveling with great power as all of the helper spirits cluster like birds in the branches around you.

When you ascend to the second branch, you are liberated from all concerns, all worries, all regrets, for now and from this time onward as long as you work as a shaman. Your mind becomes more and more focused.

When you reach the third branch, your mind becomes like a point, directed toward the intention with which you make the journey. You may experience a sudden flash of insight about what your life purpose is, about why you were called to be a shaman. Pause here for a couple of minutes (of journey time, not real time). Feel the roughness of the bark under your fingers, smell the fragrance of the forest, feel the pulsing of life through the trunk as you wrap your arms around it.

The fourth branch brings greater lightness and ecstasy. Visualize peace and happiness in your life, in your community, in the entire world.

On the fifth branch all fear, illness, and danger are swept away for you and for all who travel with you. All these things have been sent far away or bound up for an entire year by the power of Mother Earth, Father Heaven, and the spirits. You suddenly notice that your helper spirits are singing like birds.

On the sixth branch, all illusion of time, distance, and separation disappears. The tree you are climbing is the *gol*, the center of all existence. Indeed, from here you can go to any time or place or potential reality. Your sense of being in a physical body seems to fall away and you are incredibly light and luminous. Listen to the rustle of the wind through the branches of the tree, and suddenly you hear a flock of geese flying by, honking, as they seem to be flying upward, leading the way.

On the seventh branch the foliage is thinner and you can look outward to the sky. The heavens seem to slope steeply upward toward a hole above you, like the walls of the tepee. You feel as if you are a bird, and you spread your wings and hop lightly upward to the eighth branch.

When you reach the eighth branch you see a great light in the sky, large as a full moon. It illuminates the branches of the tree with a silvery light. This is the Altan Hadaas, the polestar, the stake of heaven. You fly past it, reaching the ninth branch at the top of the tree.

Here you are in a fully ecstatic state. You and your spirits are clustered together and some have come into your body. When you are on the ninth branch you realize that you have reached the hole in the sky, the gate to the upper world. It is like the smoke hole of the tepee. Stand up and look through the hole to the place beyond the heavens. Is it day or night? Is it clear or cloudy? (The condition of the weather when you first enter the upper world is an omen for the condition of the coming year.)

It is now time to travel to the upper-world spirits and ask blessing for the community. Each person who has been journeying with you will now journey individually. Resume drumming at a rate that is most suitable to drive your vision. Go on your own journey and follow as long as it leads you; your drumming will help drive the visions of the other participants in the ritual as well. Once you have completed your journey and returned to ordinary reality, slow down your drumming gradually so that the other participants in the journey can start coming back. Stopping suddenly is not a good idea; a person's *suns* soul is out of the body during the journey and an abrupt return might result in soul loss, or at least temporary confusion of the *suns* that will leave the journeyer disoriented.

It is customary to share the experiences of the journey after it is finished. Once everyone who has journeyed has shared his vision, each person takes the bundle that was created earlier in the ritual. The bundles should be kept in a secure place. Their effectiveness is good for one year. Doing a Clean Tent ritual again a year later can renew them. Be sure to thank the spirits in some way before breaking the circle at the close of the ceremony.

NINE

Shamanic Tools and Magic

Who is with a drum,
He has one bottom.
Who prays to the land,
Has one head.

Who is with orba,
He has one road.
Who prays to the Universe,
He has one head.

—Song of the shaman Chylym-Kham,
in Mongush Kenin-Lopsan,
Shamanic Songs and Myths of Tuva[1]

In this final chapter I will acquaint you with the tools you need in order to perform useful and effective shamanic actions. These tools include the usual attributes of the Siberian shaman such as drum, rattle, and staff as well as magical actions known as *serjim* and *dom*, which are used as parts of rituals or by themselves for various purposes. As you become familiar with these tools, remember that the uses described here are only a starting point for incorporating these tools into your work. Be open to the communications of your shamanic spirits, because they will familiarize you with certain uses of these tools that will be unique for you. In my experience with various shamanic teachers, I have noticed that they have all developed their own variations of shamanic techniques that reflect their individual spiritual heritage.

TONOG: SHAMANIC EQUIPMENT

The equipment of a shaman, known as *tonog* ("tools"), has both a physical and a spiritual component. In the unity of time within the *gol*, the time of the creation of the object destined to be used by a shaman and the time when a shaman starts to use it are not separate. Each piece of a shaman's equipment is said to be *amitai* ("alive") or *ezetei* ("having its own master spirit"), which means that it has a master spirit that entered into it at the moment of its creation. When a shaman begins to use a certain piece of equipment, he needs to contact and interact with its master spirit so that it can be used most effectively, for the *ezen* of a shaman's tool will add its own spiritual power to that of the shaman. Once the shaman has bonded with the spirits of his tools, other people are not normally allowed to touch them unless the *ezen* of his tools allow it. This does not preclude the giving of shamanic tools as gifts to other shamans or students—this is actually quite common, but the spirits of the tools will let a shaman know when something can be given away and tell him who is destined to have it. For example, I have given away many shamanic tools, especially mirrors, to other shamans—usually students or beginning shamans, but also to advanced shamans who were teachers. It is also common practice to keep shamanic tools out of sight or wrapped in a cloth when they are not being used, as this will prevent careless handling of them or accidental disrespecting of the spirits of the tools by people ignorant of shamanism.

Drums: The Magical Steeds

The drum *(hese, hengereg)* is the most famous attribute of shamans, for its sound drives the shamanic journey and its rhythm represents the hoofbeats of the shaman's magical mount. Siberian drums tend to be relatively large, twelve to twenty inches in diameter on average. A shaman will decorate the inside and outside of the drumhead in a way that has spiritual significance for him; he may draw certain spirits, heavenly bodies, or animals on the drum. It is customary among Mongolian and Siberian shamans to attach bells to the inside of the drum so that the drum can be shaken as well as struck. Shamans recognize certain parts of the drum as being the top, bottom, left, and right sides. Ribbons and *hadags* are tied to the top, left, and right sides of the drum to represent the crown and ears of the drum.

In addition to being a musical instrument, the drum has other abilities. It can hold spiritual energy and carry souls inside it during soul retrievals. The drum is rubbed against the shaman's chest to pick up windhorse and then laid on a person to transfer the windhorse energy from the drum into that person's body. During a soul retrieval or during a journey to bring a spirit back to the lower world, a soul can be carried inside the drum until the shaman reaches the place where the soul needs to be placed (into a body or somewhere in the lower world).

The drumstick, or *orba,* is also a significant tool. In fact, it has certain uses independent of the drum. A Siberian or Mongolian drumstick usually is rather spoon shaped. It is six inches to a foot long, with a distinct front and back side. Fur or soft leather covers the striking side, while the back side has rings attached that jingle with the motion of the drumstick. Usually the rings are strung on a wire, but they may be stapled to the drumstick in a way that allows them to jingle against each other. Thus the drumstick can also function as a type of rattle, and a shaman will use the drumstick as a rattle without using the drum. The drumstick is also usually decorated with streamers to match the drum's.

Shaman Staffs

Staffs, another attribute of shamans, can take many forms. They are usually made of wood, but some shamans use staffs made of iron. They are usually referred to as *horiboo* or *tayag,* both words meaning "cane." In many Siberian tribes the use of the staff precedes the use of the drum and the shaman learns to journey without the ben-

A horse-headed wooden shaman staff.

efit of the drumbeat. Most shaman staffs are adorned with *hanhinuur* ("jingle cones"), so that the staff can be used as a type of rattle during journeying.

Most shaman staffs are either forked or adorned with animal heads. In Buryat tradition the most common type of shaman staff has a horse head carved at the top, and sometimes a staff will be adorned with a double horse head. This staff is decorated with a miniature halter and reins as well as bunches of jingle cones. A forked shaman staff has a wire strung between the two forked ends on which many jingle cones and bells are threaded so that the staff will jingle when it is shaken. Shaman staffs of either type are decorated with *hadags* and streamers.[2]

Abai Geser used a special staff, the *ilbete zandan modon,* which was made out of sandalwood. This staff had the ability to induce trance or sleep in a person when it was touched to the crown of the head. He also used his *horiboo* to magically transform harmful things into beneficial things during the course of his journey (see page 136).

Rattles

Rattles, or *shigshuur,* have a much more limited use in Siberian and Mongolian shamanism than in Native American tradition. Many types of shamanic instruments, such as the drum, drumstick, and staff, are decorated with bells and jingles so they can function as rattles on their own. There is a special kind of rattle, however, that is believed to have magical powers. This is the raven rattle. It is made out of a cow horn, with the tip carved to look like a raven's head. It is not normally used as an instrument to drive the shamanic trance; rather, it is a tool to direct spiritual-magical energy in a specific direction. The rattle is shaken in the direction toward which the energy is to go, with the movement imitating pecking *(tonshoho)*. The energy then flows out through the raven's beak. The power of the raven rattle is usually directed toward sources of negative energy or harmful spirits.

Shaman's Robe

Shamans commonly wear two kinds of costumes, depending on what kind of work they are doing. For work that does not involve journeying, shamans may wear the traditional costume of their people — in Siberia and Mongolia, this is usually a silk robe that buttons on the right side or a knee-length silk vest or coat that buttons in front. The shaman wears this over his ordinary street clothes. The silk robe is an indication that the wearer is acting in the role of shaman and is a reminder of the role of the shaman as a preserver of traditions.

Front view of shaman costume, showing symbol of the nine-branched World Tree on chest. Note the face covering made of ribbons.

The costume that is worn by shamans specifically for journeying work is made of leather and can be in the form of either a robe or a *dudig*, a piece of leather with a hole in the middle for the head that is worn over other clothing like a poncho. The shaman robe usually is tied in the back; the *dudig* is secured with ties at both sides. The shaman costume is sometimes called a *boo huyag* ("shaman armor") because it is believed to possess magic powers that protect the shaman during his work. The shaman costume is thought to have its own *ezen* spirit, but it also is like an *ongon* for the shamanic helper spirits when the shaman merges consciousness with them.

Shaman costumes are usually elaborately decorated with things that represent the powers of the shaman and his spirits, the shamanic universe, and the tribal affiliation of the shaman. The costume may be decorated with a representation of the World Tree, sun, moon, stars, and various animal helpers. Among the Buryats, the costume has decorations made from rabbit, sable, squirrel, ermine, or weasel skin, depending on the tribal heritage of the shaman. Miniature

Back side of shaman costume showing masks of ongon spirits, bundles of "snake" tassels representing wings, bells, and deer-hoof pendants

weapons including a bow and arrow, a knife, or an ax may be sewn on as pendants. Feathers may be attached on the back below the shoulders to represent wings for shamanic flight, and long buckskin fringe on the hem and sleeves also represents the shaman's birdlike aspect while journeying. Bunches of round tassels called snakes are usually attached at the shoulders in front and back. These represent wings but are also a reminder of the shaman's ability to use a snake as a magic steed while journeying. Pieces of fur of various animal helpers may also be attached to the costume; in Mongolia, many shamans use a bear paw with claws. An important part of the shaman costume—which also makes it quite heavy—is the *hanhinuur*, or jingle cones, that are traditionally attached to it. Because today they are difficult to obtain, some shaman costumes do not have the traditional complement of ninety-nine jingle cones. These cones are attached to the costume in bunches of three, at the wrists and elbows and in rows across the chest and back. In lieu of jingle cones, many modern costumes use jingle bells, small cowbells, and tiger bells (Chinese brass bells rather similar to jingle bells). The jingle cones and bells serve the purpose of making noise while the shaman moves and dances. The noise of the costume itself helps to induce the state of consciousness the shaman needs for merging with the spirits.

In addition to the costumes mentioned above, many shamans, especially female shamans, carry a piece of jewelry or a scarf in a purse or shoulder bag to serve as a sort of abbreviated costume for those times when shamanic work needs to be done and the shaman does not have time to go home to collect her tools. These "substitute costumes" will have been specifically empowered for this function at some previous time.

Hats (*Malgai*)

Shamans traditionally keep their heads covered while working with the spirits. In low-level work a conventional hat is sufficient, but work involving merging with the spirits requires a special hat. Shamans' hats are of two forms, and many shamans possess both. The first type is a traditional Mongolian- or Siberian-style hat that is either rounded or pointed at the top, but because it is used as a shamanic attribute, it is decorated more elaborately. The brim will have fur and jingle cones or bells attached to it. The hat usually has two or more foxtails attached at the sides or rear.

The second type of shaman hat is a feathered headdress, somewhat like that worn by some Native American groups. The headdress consists of a band of leather or cloth three to four inches wide that is long enough to go around the head and be tied in back. The bottom of it may be trimmed with fur. The band itself is decorated with a small copper mask or with beads and or cowrie shells to represent a mouth, nose, eyes, and ears. This decoration represents the senses of the shamanic spirits merged with the shaman. Eagle and owl feathers are stuck into the top of the headband. Sometimes feathers of other birds will be added as well, depending on which birds the shaman associates with. Eagle, Owl, and Raven are associated with all shamans, so these are the most commonly used feathers in shaman costumes.

The shaman wears a headband that is tied on before putting on the hat. This headband has a fringe of silk threads, horsehair, or ribbons that are long enough to cover most of the face. This headband is not worn at all times; it is used only when the shaman is going to merge with the spirits. The fringe will not completely blind the shaman, but it will help him to dissociate with reality when he enters a trance. It is also like a mask: I call it a "mask of a thousand faces," for it becomes a mask for whatever spirits the shaman merges consciousness with. In many cultures, shamans will put on certain masks representing various spirits; however, this custom is relatively rare in Siberia. The only mask that is commonly used is the copper Avgaldai mask, which shamans hardly wear at all. It is actually more like an *ongon* than a mask.

Crown

The shaman crown is the badge of the advanced shaman among the Mongolian peoples. Some ethnic groups, in particular the Evenk/Tungus peoples and the Yakut, use the shaman crown more generally. The shaman crown consists of an iron band to which are welded two arched crosspieces, one going from the right side to the left and the other from front to back. The crown is adorned with either metal or actual deer antlers. This headgear is worn over a skullcap that is large enough that the iron bands do not chafe the head. Blue and white silk scarves may be tied to the antlers as a gesture of honor to the shaman spirits. In the traditional Buryat system of nine degrees of initiation (see appendix 3), the crown *(maihabsha)* is conferred on the shaman when he achieves the seventh degree — *Tengeriin orgoito boo* ("shaman with heaven's costume"), which can be done only fourteen years after the original shamanic initiation. Other Siberian peoples are not quite so strict about the use of the crown.[3]

Whip

The whip, called a *minaa* or *tashuur,* is used to urge on the shamanic steed during the journey, but it is also an offensive weapon against

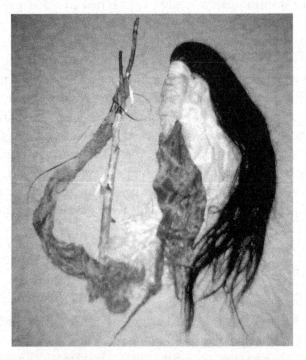

Left: Shaman staff made from branch of lightning-struck birch
Right: Shaman's horsetail whip (minaa)

negative energy and harmful spirits. The whip is visualized as smashing or disintegrating negative energy and then sweeping it away. A common form of the *minaa* is the horsetail whip, made out of horsetail hairs, attached to a wooden handle. When it is used to clear a body of intrusions, the shaman will lightly swat the whip along the length of the body in front and back. It is commonly believed that horsehair has a repelling effect on evil spirits and negative energy (see "The Legend of Abai Geser" on page 193 for teachings about the use of the *minaa*). The other form of the whip imitates the common horseman's whip, *tashuur,* and is a long stick or bone with a lash made out of two strips of leather on one end and a lanyard that secures it to the shaman's wrist on the other. The shaft of the whip (if it is wood) is usually painted red or orange.

A closely related shamanic tool is the *dalbuur,* the shaman fan. The spirit fan can be made of feathers or from a three-branched stick with horsehair tied to the ends. The healing ritual using the *dalbuur* is described at length in *Riding Windhorses* (see the bibliography).

Mirrors

I call the mirror, or *toli,* the "Swiss Army knife of Mongolian shamanism." It is the most versatile of the shaman's tools, serving a variety of purposes, and it is small enough to carry on one's person or keep in a purse or shoulder bag (most shamans carry a small shoulder bag containing small tools and commonly used herbs). Mirrors range in size from as small as an inch across to as large as eight inches in diameter (the power of mirrors is not proportional to size; in fact, the little ones tend to be the most highly prized). They are round and made of brass, silver, iron, or nephrite. They usually have a loop welded on the back for a string or ribbon to be passed through so the mirror can be worn around the shaman's neck. The back side of the *toli* may be plain or decorated with animal figures.

Mirrors made in China that are adorned with the characters representing the "four happinesses" are especially prized. As far as I know, new mirrors are not being made and all shaman mirrors are antiques. They are usually passed down from shaman to shaman. In Mongolia and Siberia, shaman mirrors that are thousands of years old have been found at archaeological sites, and I have seen and held a shaman mirror that was made by the Huns almost two thousand years ago! In Siberian mythology, when the spirits called the first two shamans in a dream, they awakened to find a tree growing outside their house. It was the World Tree, and its leaves were shaman mirrors. Knowledge of metalworking arrived in Siberia remarkably early. According to legend, smiths came down from the upper world and taught their craft to shaman-smiths, and the lineages they established endure to this day (in fact, in the Terte clan we have one smith, my relative Dorjo Frolov, because shaman lineages produce both shamans and smiths). This is important to note in discussing shaman mirrors because many were forged by shaman-smiths who created them in the context of shamanic ritual, and they therefore were endowed with magical power from their inception. If you want a shaman mirror, they are rather easy to obtain in Mongolia from the Ministry of Culture store in Ulaanbaatar; getting one through official channels will prevent any possibility of confiscation (Mongolia is very strict about exportation of antique shamanic objects). Mirrors also can be found in some antique stores in Inner Mongolia. In Siberia they tend to be much more difficult to find.[4]

Shamans try to collect as many mirrors as they can because they have tremendous protective and energizing power. These mirrors will be attached to the shaman costume, with at least one on the chest and one on the back. Shamans also commonly wear a mirror on a string or ribbon either over or under their clothing at all times. The reason is that mirrors have the property of pulling in and accumulating energy in all frequencies at all times, and wearing a mirror over the chest channels energy into the *setgel* (the *gol* of one's being). This keeps a shaman energized and ready to do his work at any time, and the *toli* will be available if the shaman suddenly needs to do some kind of healing work. Furthermore, the mirror is a badge of a shaman's office and people recognize the wearer as being a shaman. When I went to Severobaikalsk in 1997, as I walked through the metal detector at the Ulan-Ude airport the alarm kept going off. I removed all my jewelry and emptied my pockets, but to no avail. Suddenly I remembered my *toli* (mirrors tend to stay very warm and they can be easily forgotten if worn next to the body). I pulled it out and laid it on the tray holding my jewelry. The security guard was astonished, and all of the Buryats smiled, saying, "Look, she's a shaman!"

Shamans also wear mirrors because they have strong protective properties. Not only do mirrors absorb energy, but they radiate it as well. When shamans put on the mirror, they do so with the intention that if they encounter hostile people, dangerous spirits, or negative energy, the mirror will radiate sufficient energy outward to neutralize any danger. For this reason, mirrors are especially good to keep on your person while traveling. Mirrors link into the *gol* and can pull in and channel incredible amounts of energy. People who have handled shaman mirrors often remark that they experience an electrical or burning sensation when touching them. During shamanic work, shamans can direct energy through the mirror into an area of a patient's body that has been spiritually or physically injured, or they can use the mirror aggressively against a harmful spirit, directly beaming energy at the spirit.

The absorbing and radiating capabilities of a mirror come in handy for removal of intrusions and for soul retrieval. In the removal of intrusions, the intruding spirit can be sucked up into a mirror and then expelled into the earth by placing the mirror on the ground facedown. This is helpful because the shaman will have no direct contact with the spirit and there is no risk of accidentally absorbing it into his own spiritual body. In a journey for soul retrieval, the mirror can hold the soul when it has been found. Then the mirror can be touched to the chest of the person being healed so that it enters the *setgel* and reincorporates into the body. In healing, a bowl of water, vodka, or milk can be placed on top of a mirror to instantly convert it into *arshaan*. In the final phase of a healing, a shaman may also place two or three mirrors along the body axis of the patient (as he is lying down) and allow him to rest with the mirrors on him for five to ten minutes. The mirrors will adjust and strengthen the energy flow in his spiritual body. In healing work, mirrors are cleansed afterward by washing them with alcohol, passing them over a juniper smudge nine times, or by holding them in sunlight.

Mirrors are also used for clairvoyance, much like crystal balls in European magical tradition. Even though they are called mirrors, they are not mirrors in a literal sense because they tend to be cloudy enough that you cannot see clearly in them. This same cloudiness, however, is helpful in visualization, and shamans can do readings with them. In Inner Mongolia there is a divination technique in which an egg is placed on a mirror and the shaman watches which way the egg rolls off (the interpretation is similar to that of the pebble divination described on pages 116–17. In addition, a shaman can often see intrusions and illness in a person by looking at the reflection of the patient in the mirror.[5]

Another use of mirrors is for *dom* (shamanic magic). There is a magical spell known as *toli erguulehe*, "spinning the mirror." The meaning is understandable when you remember that the mirror is a direct connection with *gol* and the spinning evokes its vortexlike nature. The shaman takes the mirror he wears around his neck, twists it around on its string until it is fully wound up, and then allows the mirror to spin while he states his intention. This technique is so powerful that once it is done, reversal of the spell is extremely difficult. Unfortunately, this is often used for black magic, which I will not discuss.

As we have seen, the *toli* combines the functions of many other shamanic tools and is essential in shamanic practice. It is my hope that perhaps some of you who are following the shamanic path have skill in metalworking. It is very important that the technique of making shaman mirrors be revived, as they are powerful spiritual devices that could do a lot of good for people throughout the world. If you are interested, contact me and I will impart the teachings needed to create them in the proper ritual context.

Musical Instruments

Shamans use a great variety of musical instruments in their work, including bells, cymbals, the Tibetan *tingsha*, the Jew's harp, the two-stringed *morin huur* (horsehead fiddle), the four-stringed Chinese violin, and the *tobshuur,* a ukulele-like two-stringed instrument with a head carved like a swan. Musical instruments are referred to as *huur.* What is significant about them is not what they are but how the shaman relates to them and is able to produce sounds that boost him toward the ecstatic state he needs to merge with the spirits.

Theoretically any musical instrument—guitars, horns, and synthesizers, for example—can be used in this way. It has been noted that certain musicians, such as some jazz artists and rock guitarists, seem to reach a quasi-shamanic state of exaltation while improvising. It is certainly possible that some great musicians may be coming in touch with shamanic abilities that the spirits have given them even though they have not consciously realized their calling. In Mongolia and Siberia, the performance of epic songs called *uliger* was traditionally done by a shaman, and the performer would go into shamanic ecstasy while playing. This kind of singing was often accompanied by throat singing *(hoomei)*, a type of singing that has much magical power when used by a shaman and can quickly produce a state of being *ongod orood*. *Uliger* have great healing and protective power and are sung in times of disease and danger, similar to the performance of the Blessingway by the Navajo *hataali*. These songs are also important because they are a vehicle for transmitting knowledge of shamanic techniques and beliefs from generation to generation. This again reminds us that shamans play a vital role in passing down the traditions as well as in being teachers and practitioners of many varieties of artistic expression. Therefore, if you are a musician or other kind of artist, do not forget that you can use your creative abilities to enhance your communication with the shamanic spirits.

Percussion instruments such as bells, cymbals, and the *tingsha* may be used in lieu of the drum in certain ceremonies. Any kind of instrument is satisfactory for journeying if the shaman has developed a rapport with the *ezen* of the instrument so that it will allow itself to become the steed of the shaman during the journey. Small percussion instruments appear to have become popular in more recent times, since the persecution of shamans by Tibetan Buddhists and then by the Communists, for they are much quieter than the drum and are more easily carried from place to place. My teacher Sanjai *zaarin* uses a bell almost exclusively in his work, a Tibetan bell used with a piece of brass representing lightning called an *ochir* or *dorji*. While ringing the bell with one hand he holds the *ochir* upright, allowing energy to be channeled through it.

The symbolism of the horse-headed fiddle and *tobshuur* is apparent. The adornment of these instruments with horse and bird heads represents their becoming magical steeds for the shaman when he uses them in singing *uliger* or *hoomei*.

The Jew's harp *(hel huur)* is a popular shamanic instrument throughout Mongolia and Siberia. In Russia it is considered equal to the drum as the classic shamanic instrument. Some Jew's harps are made in the shape of a bird, usually a swan, again symbolizing the animal as a shamanic mount. Jew's harps, like the shaman costume, are usually decorated with "snake" tassels, colorful ribbons, and sometimes jingle cones. As with *hoomei,* the playing of the Jew's harp sets up a vibration in the head and throat that helps to induce an altered state of consciousness. I watched my Mongolian teacher Byambadorj *zaarin* use the Jew's harp several times in healing. He would play it, sing shamanic invocations, and then gently slap the patient's body with the tassels hanging from the instrument.

Knives, Swords, and Other Magical Weapons

A shaman usually possesses a traditional knife or sword, called the *boogiin helme* ("shaman sword"), which has many ritual uses. The most straightforward is that of menacing enemies and hostile spirits during a ritual. When the sword is drawn, its physical size is not important: the shaman's power upon merging with that of the spirits becomes as large and powerful as it needs to be for its ritual use (in the spiritual world). Some shamans use the sword as they would the staff, as a steed for shamanic journeying. The shaman focuses on the sword in order to induce the state of mind needed for journeying and merging with his spirits.

Shamans may have other types of full-size or miniature weapons for ritual use. The most common ones are bow and arrows, spears, and axes. The miniature bow and arrow is quite common. In the story of Abai Geser, the hero used a "bow made from a twig and an arrow made from a splinter" (see "The Legend of Abai Geser" on page 193. In spiritual reality they became a giant bow and black arrow that struck the demon Abarga Sesen with the force of lightning after Geser had spoken an invocation over the arrow.

In Manchu shamanism, which is derived from the Evenk tradition of Siberian shamanism, the shaman had a variety of miniature spears and axes that could be transformed to gigantic size in spiritual reality. These can be seen at the Manchu shamanist Temple of Heaven (Tian Tan) in Beijing, and reproductions are available to buy—I use a Manchu bronze spear and ax in my work. When I went to the United States in 1998, my teacher gave me a protective amulet for my travels that was a miniature iron ax. The use of these miniature weapons is a reminder that in Siberian shamanist tradition it is easy to change the size of things in the spiritual realm, making the small large and the large small.

As is shown in the following example, the shaman can obtain powerful results with simple objects. Just as the size of shamanic weapons can be changed, they can also be transformed—when Geser fought the monster Sherem Minaata, all of his weapons were unable to defeat the monster. He journeyed to the upper world to meet the mother goddess Manzan Gurme Toodei, who gave a him a stick. When he once more faced his enemy, the stick became a fearsome weapon that smashed Sherem Minaata to bits. In the same way, if you engage in battle with a hostile spirit, it is possible to use a stick to beat on it if no other ritual weapon is available: with the proper invocations and merging with the spirits, any weapon will become a manifestation of the spirits' power.

Pipe *(Gaahan)*

Mongols and Siberians use pipes quite frequently during the process of shamanic rituals, although their pipes are not as large as the ones used by Native Americans. The Mongolian long pipe can be eighteen inches in length but is usually less than a foot long. Mongolian and Siberian pipes have a bowl made of silver, a stem made of wood, and a mouthpiece made also of wood or of stone, usually agate, onyx, or nephrite. All three parts are detachable to facilitate cleaning. Tobacco, as in Native American tradition, is believed to be an excellent smoke offering to the spirits, especially at sacred sites (until five hundred years ago, the ritual herb was *Cannabis sativa*, as is confirmed by the remains found in burial sites of Siberian shamans). In Tunkhen there is a special shrine for the spirits of the Sayan Mountains that features a giant pipe about six feet long called the Tamhinii Bariaasha. The bowl itself is almost a foot in diameter! In this shrine tobacco offerings are made to the spirits.

In a ritual, the pipe is passed around at certain intervals, usually at the beginning, after the invocation, before the shaman starts the journey, and at the end. In addition, the shaman may ask to be given the pipe while he is *ongod orood* so that the spirits can enjoy the smoke more directly (at which point the spirits will cry out, *"Ikra!"* or "Give me a puff!"). The most traditional way to light the pipe is to use the *hete*, the flint and steel that, along with the pipe, is an attribute of the shaman. In the Geser epic (see page 193) the ceremony of the pipe smoking is described as "taking a pipe out as long as his forearm, taking out a tobacco pouch of black fleece as large as a sleeve, he packed a moose ear [broken off piece of twisted tobacco] into the silver bowl. Striking flint and steel like lightning his breath whistled like the wind and the smoke was like a campfire." When it is described in this manner, the smoking is in the context of the conclusion of the journey. It was not surprising that when I brought a Native American pipe to Siberia, the shamans knew exactly how to use it ceremonially. And when I brought a Buryat from a shamanic lineage to America, the customs of the Native American elders he smoked with were practically the same as his own.

Altar *(Sheree)*

In Mongolia and Siberia it is traditional for a shaman to make or acquire a wooden trunk in which to store his shamanic implements until he needs them. This kind of trunk has a flat top and can be used as a ceremonial table or altar, as its name shows (*sheree* means "table" or "altar"). It is usually decorated with sacred symbols and placed in the *hoimor* (sacred place) of the household. The use of the *sheree* for storage of the shamanic tools prevents non-shamans from offending the spirits by carelessly handling them. The fourth degree of Buryat shamanism *(shereetei boo)* denotes that the *sheree* is formally dedicated during this stage of initiation, even though shamans of a lower degree might already use one.[6]

PREPARING SHAMANIC TOOLS

Mongolian and Siberian shamanic traditions have certain tools that almost all shamans use, but shamans are also quite flexible in using things from other cultures as their spirits direct them—they will even use certain natural artifacts such as antlers, sticks, rocks, and shells if the spirits direct them to do so. Shamans have readily adapted Tibetan bells and cymbals, Russian cowbells, and—now that there is some contact between America and Siberia—certain Native American attributes such as rattles, prayer sticks, and dream catchers, although the meaning of these things to a Siberian shaman may very well differ from their significance in the culture they came from. Thus, if you have shamanic equipment that is not part of the traditional attributes of Mongolian and Siberian shamans, you can still use them in the context of rituals and magical actions of those traditions according to how your shamanic spirits advise you.

Intention and communication with the spirits play significant roles in preparing shamanic tools for use. In the nine-degree system of Buryat initiation, in some ways reminiscent of Freemasonry, each degree has certain shamanic tools or attributes specific to it. Even though the shaman may make use of these things before he is initiated into the degree to which they belong, the initiation, among other things, will entail making contact with the *ezen* spirits of the tools specific to the degree and gaining deeper knowledge of their nature and magical uses. Even if you do not follow this tradition, the essential teaching in this practice is still useful. First, when you start using a shamanic tool, that which makes it effective is your intention, united with the intention and power of your helper spirits. Results are often quite dramatic. The next step, which is addressed in the initiation rituals, is to journey or otherwise find a way to meet the *ezen* spirit of each of your shamanic tools so that you will know their character and allow them to teach you how to use them more effectively. For instance, the awakening of the drum ritual (described on pages 191–93) will dramatically increase the power of a drum; such a ritual may be done for every one of your shamanic tools. This is just another reflection of true shamanic power as directly related to the shaman's ability to communicate with the various spirits with which he needs to interact in certain situations. The spirits will tell you how to use them; do not be limited by what I or anybody else says about how your shamanic equipment will bring the most power and blessing to your work!

SHAMANIC MAGIC

In the Western tradition it is common for people to distinguish between shamans and magicians. This distinction does not apply in the Siberian and Mongolian tradition. Indeed, there are various types of supernatural practitioners—healers, psychics, magicians, bards (specialists in invocations and reciting *uliger*), as well as shamans—in our tradition, but shamans are considered to be different in that they master the abilities of all of the above-mentioned practitioners.

Shamanic power outside of magical applications is usually referred to as *erdem* ("knowledge" or "science"), and the energy itself is referred to as *tsog* or *huch*. Magical power is referred to by the term *id shid*, *ilbe*, or *aba*. *Id shid* is closest to what would be called "magic," *ilbe* is the ability to induce hypnotic trance, and *aba* is probably best described as psi or paranormal abilities. Like other shamanic abilities, magic employs *tsog* and windhorse and taps into the powers of the *gol*. The main difference is that magical acts are more formalized, while the other shamanic techniques mentioned above involve improvisation as the shamanic ritual evolves at the prompting of the spirits. Why, then, do Siberian shamans use magic? Because as all magical practitioners know, certain types of magical/ritual actions have a unique power that has been learned through centuries of tradition. Magical acts may be performed in order to influence people or spirits, in the context of shamanic rituals or journeys, or on their own for specific purposes.

In Buryat tradition we speak of our shaman heroes Abai Geser and Alma Mergen:

> Arban hoyor abaya
> Aligan deeree guilgeje
> Horin gurban abaya
> Hurgan deeree hatargaba

("Gathering up twelve magicks on the palms / Making twenty-three magicks dance on the fingers")

The Buryat shamanic teacher Boris Bazarov defines five different types of magic in Siberian shamanism: contact magic, addressed magic, imitational magic, cleansing magic, and verbal magic. *Contact magic* is the ability to exert magical forces through something that is somehow associated with the object of the magic, such as hair or clothing. The use of a piece of clothing belonging to a patient in cases of remote healing (as described in chapter 6) is a typical example of contact magic. *Addressed magic* uses information about the person who is the object of the magic in order to form a connection between the shaman producing the intention and the person being influenced. For instance, the full name, birthday, astrological sign, birthplace, and other detailed information about a person is given to the shaman in order for him to more easily make contact and exert magical forces. *Imitational magic* involves the imitation of certain actions by the shaman in order to manifest particular forces in the spiritual realm, such as the acting out of drawing and releasing a bow when shooting magical arrows against an enemy. I have already presented some forms of *cleansing magic* in my discussions about the making of *arshaan* and the cleansing of pollution. I will present more examples of cleansing spells in this chapter. *Verbal magic* is the manifesting of magical forces through the speaking of certain invocations and intentions, particularly when doing *serjim* spells (see page 184)[7]

The Buryat teacher Bazarov *zaarin* also groups magic into five categories based on the intentions of the magical actions:

1. Healing and protective magic

2. Business and prosperity magic

3. Romantic (sexual) and family magic

4. War and strategy magic

5. Punitive-destructive magic[8]

Most shamans today do not engage in the last two types of magic. These were most commonly used in earlier times, when shamans played an important role in the protection of the tribe or clan against hostile tribes or bands of raiders. The literature about Siberian shamanism is full of stories about battles between shamans of enemy tribes or clans. Contemporary Siberian shamans have knowledge of these techniques in a theoretical way but do not engage in them because the current climate in Siberian society does not offer many situations in which they are needed. Occasionally a shaman may be requested to take action when a person has committed a crime against an individual or family and has not been caught and punished by civil authorities. Remember that aggressive and destructive magical acts can throw the world as well as yourself out of balance and can have negative effects on your *zayaa* (karma). For this reason, I will not present all of the spells I know—some of them can be too easily abused.

The majority of Mongolian and Siberian magic spells are concerned with the more common problems in life: protection, prosperity, romance, other relationships. Please heed this advice seriously: *When you do magical actions to change reality in some dramatic way, especially if it involves changing a person's attitude or resistance toward what the magic is supposed to manifest, always ask the spirits to manifest the intention in a way that brings greater happiness and blessing to all who are involved.* In this way you preserve the integrity of your own karma as well as ensure that however the magic finally manifests its results, you will not be placed in a situation in which you create enemies for yourself or for the people on whose behalf you did magic. Furthermore, there will not be a disruption of spiritual balance.

MONGOLIAN SPELLS: *DOM*

The word *dom* in Mongolian and in other Siberian languages comes closest to the European concept of "magic spell." When an object is said to be *domtoi,* it means that the object has been imbued with magical power. This is in contrast to the concept of *ezetei* (see page 155), in which an object has been possessed by a master spirit (such as is the case with shaman drums, *ongons,* and other shamanic attributes). A *domtoi* object has been imbued with power by the spirits through invocation or by focused but silent intention by the shaman. *Domtoi* objects are usually not dangerous to handle, as some *ezetei* objects may be. The exception is if the object is empowered with a protection spell and the spirits providing the protection believe that the person handling the object presents danger to the person on whose behalf the protection was invoked.

Thread *Dom*

One of the most common types of *dom* uses red or sky blue threads for protection or healing. When you visit Mongolia or Siberia, it is not unusual to see people wearing these threads around their necks because they have recently visited a shaman and had such a spell done. Red and sky blue are power colors in Mongolian and Siberian shamanism. Red is used for physical healing and protection; blue, for spiritual healing and protection. These threads are not the thin threads used for sewing but, rather, thicker yarn or embroidery thread made of cotton, wool, or silk (silk is preferred). The shaman cuts the thread and then places it on his palm, brings it close to his face, and prays to the spirits to imbue the thread with the power needed for the healing or protection. The shaman merges consciousness with the spirits and blows on the thread three times to convey their energy through the breath. He then ties the thread with a triple knot. The client wears it around the neck until it falls off. In some cases, threads are tied around other parts of the body in order to address specific injuries, such as around an injured arm or leg. The shaman may tie on a thread in advance of a more powerful healing ritual in order to prevent a condition from worsening, or he may tie it on after he does his *zasal* in order to prolong the effects of a healing once it has been done.

Magically Empowered Jewelry

It is very common for certain items of jewelry to be made *domtoi* for various purposes. In fact, much of the jewelry that Mongolian and Siberian shamans wear is magically empowered in this way. For instance, many shamans wear a gold ring on the left hand and a silver ring on the right, representing the balance between the female side (the gold) and the male side (the silver). A non-shaman can have a ring or necklace empowered for various purposes: protection, romance, or prosperity, for example. The shaman speaks over the piece of jewelry and blows on it in the same way that a thread is empowered as described above. The jewelry is worn as long as its magical effect is desired. This can also be done for a piece of jewelry (or even clothing) that is to be given to someone in order to convey spiritual power to a person for some specific intention (such as a favorable attitude toward the person giving it).

Bear Claws and Porcupine Quills

Bear claws are displayed for protection of the household, usually next to the entrance to a home or apartment. The spirit of Bear is believed to be a strong protector if invoked by prayer and strong intention by the shaman at the time when the claws are hung up. Porcupine quills have a similar function but are more specifically used for protection when a person or household is believed to be under spiritual attack or in danger. Bundles of porcupine quills are taped to doorways and windowsills to discourage the entrance of hostile spirits or negative energies. The porcupine is a manifestation of Zar Zargaach, who represents wisdom and justice for mankind.

Please note that my mention of the use of bear claws and porcupine quills does not encourage poaching. *If you use animal parts that were taken from an animal killed in an improper or illegal manner, the circumstances of the animal's death will negate the magical powers of its body parts!*

Triangular Pouches *(Gurbaljin Dom)*

Triangular pouches filled with wool, herbs, and sometimes horsehair are used for *dom* for the protection of fetuses and children, as well as for adults in certain situations. The pouches are in the shape of an isosceles triangle—that is, with two sides of equal length and then a third, longer side. When a woman is pregnant, a shaman will make a *dom* made out of three triangular pouches strung together and decorated with beads and tassels, the colors of the pouches being blue on top, green in the middle, and red on the bottom (blue is for the upper world, green for the earth, and red for the lower world). The spirits are invoked to empower the pouches with energy to protect the fetus, and they are hung from the belt of the mother's clothing until the child is born. The pouches are then hung over the child's crib. If the child is a girl, a yellow pouch (representing fire and Golomt Eej/Ut in her aspect as mother goddess and patron of all females) is added on the bottom (see page 229 for more about Golomt Eej). In former times the *dom* hanging over a child's cradleboard told visitors whether the baby was a boy or a girl.

Similar *dom* made from three pouches have other purposes, such as protection of a person during travel, protection of a household, and protection of a relationship. In these cases, a *dom* should hang in a place of honor in the house or from the rearview mirror of a car.

The triangles of this *dom* are hung with the long side on top and one angle pointing downward. This shape gathers and directs energy from Father Heaven. The points on each side are like branches on which beneficial spirits can perch.

Sharp Objects

A pouch stuck full of needles may be empowered as a *dom* for the protection of a person or household. Such a pouch hangs near the entrance of a household to protect against evil spirits and people with evil thoughts. A miniature bow and arrow may be made for a similar purpose. Another variation is the placement of sharp objects, such as knives, nails, broken glass, and needles, outside the building with their points facing outward. Still another variation is to make a crude carving of a person out of wood and place a miniature spear or knife in its hand so that the weapon points outward toward potential trouble. Or you could empower an image of a warrior (of clay, wood, metal, or even plastic) with the purpose of protection and place it outside the home, again with its weapons pointing outward. In Ulan-Ude I saw a shaman's tepee that was surrounded by dozens of crudely carved warriors holding spears. The most unusual of this type of *dom* was one in Mongolia made to scare away a troublesome female spirit—it was carved in the shape of a huge erect penis![9]

Nail Clippings, Hair, and Clothing

Because something that was in contact with somebody provides a channel for the directing of energy between that person and the person working magic, Mongols are very careful about the disposal of their nail clippings, hair, clothing, and other personal items. They can be used for both negative and positive magic. Stepping on and defiling these objects, if done under the proper circumstances, can cause spiritual injury and pollution of the person they belonged to. On the other hand, these items can be useful in directing energy for healing and influencing emotion, especially in attracting a person of the opposite sex. For this last purpose, the hair of the two intended partners may be tangled and rolled together, cleansed, and then put with objects of shamanic power.

Clothing can be an effective way to connect magically with a person in order to do remote healing. Hats and belts are considered to have great power in contact magic because of their connection with the *zulai* (crown chakra) and *setgel,* and they are carefully protected against being lost or given to other people because of their potential power. On the other hand, they are the most effective objects for doing remote healing of the person they belong to.

Certain types of clothing, however, are used for black magic. Menstrually soiled clothing and dirty socks are believed to have the ability to defile and weaken an opponent and were once used in shamanic battles when shamans feuded among each other. The sorcerer Lobsogoldoi was able to subdue and enchant Abai Geser by putting a dirty sock on his head (on the *zulai*). Of course, this does not mean that you have to be afraid of such clothing; it is magically dangerous only when employed in connection with the invocation of the spirits with the intent to do harm.

Other dangerous apparel is the clothing of people who have died. The disease spirits of these people sometimes linger in items of clothing or other possessions, then go on to harass the next owner. In order to avoid this danger, shamans are careful to smudge any objects they obtain that belonged to people who have since died.

Magic Stones

The use of stones with magical power is widespread in Mongolian and Siberian shamanism. The three kinds of power stones are the meteorite, the quartz crystal point, and the *zadai.* All three are believed to be *buumal*—that is, sent down from the sky for use by shamans. Therefore (with the exception of the quartz crystal point), what the actual mineral a *buumal* stone is made of is less important than the fact that as *buumal* it will have power perceptible by shamans. I should mention that ancient arrowheads and stone blades (not the imitations sold in souvenir shops) are believed to be *buumal* stones as well. They are highly prized by shamans and are sewn onto the shaman costume to add to its power.

A few years ago, when I was visiting the Khangalov Museum in Ulan-Ude, Siberia, I had an interesting experience with a *buumal* stone. A curator was showing me various *ongons* and other shamanic objects and she handed me a *buumal* stone wrapped in birch bark. Seemingly by accident (but the spirits probably made it happen), the rock fell out of its bark container into my palm. I saw it was a black stone with a white quartz vein in it that looked like a bolt of lightning. When it touched my hand, its energy was like an electric shock, but because my spirits liked it, it then felt warm and comfortable in my palm. I felt honored to handle such an old Buryat shamans' tool but had no idea then what it would do. That night, when I fell asleep, I had many hours of visions about various ancient shaman rituals and woke myself up singing shaman songs I had never heard before. This is the special power of the *buumal* stones: they are believed to channel shamanic knowledge from the patron spirits of shamanic practice to shamans.[10]

Meteorites are thought to be the carriers of new *udha* spirits into the world. If a non-shaman steeps a meteorite (tektite) in liquor and then drinks the liquor, the *udha* spirit will enter the person through the liquid and the person will be able to become a true shaman. These powerful stones are a gift from the great patron spirits of shamans, Shargai Noyon Baabai, Buumal Sagaan Tenger, and Buuluur Sagaan Tenger. Meteorites aid shamans in communicating with the spirits of the heavens and have great magical powers for healing and increasing psychic abilities. I recommend that you obtain a piece of moldavite, a tektite, or another type of meteorite and commune with its *buumal* spirit.

Quartz crystal points used by Siberian and Mongolian shamans come most frequently from the Sayan Mountains. This is significant because these mountains are the sacred dwelling place of the patron

spirits of shamanic practice and of the spirits of the greatest shamans of the past, who help, protect, and shape the destiny of all
shamans. In healing, quartz crystal points three to four inches long
(7–10 cm) are used to manipulate the energy of the human spiritual
body. They are used in combination with two carved pieces of wood
four to five inches long to readjust the energy flow in the central
axis of the body. One piece of wood is pointed on one end (imitating the ceremonial *serge* post), and represents the male principle;
the other is blunt on both ends and represents the female principle.
While the patient is lying down facing up, the pointed piece is placed
on the chest and the blunt piece is placed on the belly. Both pieces
must lie parallel with the axis of energy flow within the body. The
shaman grasps the crystal with the point facing down toward the
patient and passes the crystal over the axis of the patient's body
from head to foot and then up again. This is repeated several times
(usually three to nine times) until the shaman is satisfied that the
power of the crystal has restored the energy flow and soul movement to a normal state within the spiritual body of the patient.
Afterward the shaman may blow three times briskly on the crown
of the head to make sure it is completely clear. The pieces of wood
are smudged after each use and the crystal is cleansed in alcohol
(vodka is preferable to denatured alcohol because the denaturation
will damage the spiritual effectiveness of the alcohol). The liquid is
then thrown outside.

Zadai stones tend to vary in appearance from region to region—
some are red and others are black, and some are *bezoar* stones
(stones that have been swallowed by animals). There is no rule
about how they should appear or even how they should be obtained, yet each shaman will recognize a *zadai* when it comes into
his possession because of the intense energy of the stone. The
zadai have many uses, most of which fall into the realm of weather
magic, but they are also used for awakening sexual passion in an
indifferent lover or in a partner that a shaman or a client desires.
When the *zadai* stone is used, the shaman bites the stone and spits
three times, then spits the stone out.

When *zadai* stones are used in weather magic, they can stop
storms, bring hot or cold weather, or cause rain to fall. Do not

underestimate the power of these stones. When I used a *zadai* in the case of a drought in the spring of 2000, it brought a foot of snow! You may have to use your stone again to moderate its effects—the magic is so powerful that it can bring extreme results. Abai Geser had a powerful *zadai* known as the "*zadai* to stop a thousand storms." (See "The Legend of Abai Geser" on p. 193) One of the most dramatic powers of the *zadai* is its ability to stop severe storms and tornadoes. The *zadai* is bitten and the shaman spits at the storm, then addresses the sky spirits of the western direction. The effect will often manifest as a splitting of the clouds so that blue sky is revealed, usually starting in the northwest. When the *zadai* is used to bring rain, the biting and spitting may be followed by an invocation to Abai Geser, accompanied by throwing spoonfuls of water toward the sky.

When the *zadai* is used to awaken sexual passion, the shaman bites and spits three times and then asks the spirits to kindle love and desire between a certain man and woman. This may be combined with a "cold" *serjim* of vodka (see page 185). There must be an invocation of Eriin Tenger (the deity of male romantic love) and of Hani Tenger (the deity of female romantic love). The shaman needs to exercise caution, of course, so that balance is maintained and there are no negative karmic consequences.

Uses of Salt

Salt plays several roles in Mongolian and Siberian shamanism, chiefly for protection and cleansing. Salt is thrown for cleansing. This is an important part of the Peace Tree ritual, for the throwing of salt to the disturbed nature spirits has the power of transforming them from hostile entities into benevolent and helpful spirits. Salt is a barrier to evil spirits and enemies. When a house cleansing is done, a shaman strews salt throughout the home in the process of dispelling the *chotgor* that is haunting the place. A shaman will usually keep the threshold of his household well salted in order to keep out hostile spirits as well as unpleasant people.

Salt mixed with water has its own special properties. A shaman will measure out a certain amount of salt (three or four large spoonfuls) in response to a request by a client. This salt can be empowered by the spirits for healing, protection, harmony in rela-tionships, or safety during travel. The shaman invokes the spirits and states the intention, speaking in a low voice into the salt. When he is done, the salt is wrapped up into a small bundle. The person or people for whom this *dom* has been done then dissolve the salt in cool water and wash their hands and face with that water. The salty water removes any potential for danger, illness, or disharmony. Once this has been done, the rest of the water is poured outside (not down the toilet!). See the salt *serjim* (page 190) for more magical uses of salt.

Uses of Water

Water is used in certain types of *dom* as a way to remove negative energy from objects or hands. In all cases the water is cold. If there is a place where something objectionable, spiritually defiling, or violent has happened, a shaman may invoke the spirits and throw cold water on the spot where it occurred. Although smudging will remove spiritual entities that may be lingering, a splash of cold water quickly removes any negative energy. If a shaman has touched some-thing that was spiritually polluting, he will wash his hands in cold water, then throw the water off the hands rather than drying them with a towel. Water is also used for washing the threshold of a household for blessing and protection. It is important to remember that the excess water should not be dumped down a toilet—this is believed to negate the spiritual use of the water.

Sucking and Spitting

In the performance of a healing or in the removal of negative en-ergy from people or objects, a shaman may suck negative energy into his mouth. When this is done, it is important to spit out a door or window so that the negative energy will be completely removed from the household. Follow this by rinsing out the mouth with cold water and likewise spitting outside.

Spitting is also used in a type of *ariulga*. This is most commonly done at the end of a shamanic ceremony when the shaman does quick healing work on several of the participants. The shaman, who is still partly merged with the spirits at this point, will be able to impart the spirits' magical power into liquids he takes into his mouth. The shaman normally uses vodka that was turned into *arshaan* during the ceremony, taking it into his mouth and then spitting it onto the head and body of several people, one after another. The shock of being hit with the liquid immediately dissolves any negative energies and repels disease spirits. A shaman must be careful, however, not to swallow the liquid, because at a large ceremony in which fourteen or more people may be getting healings the shaman could get drunk if he swallowed too much of the alcohol (even though it is *arshaan* and the conversion of vodka into *arshaan* usually reduces its alcohol content because the spirits consume it).

Uses of Fire (Matches)

Shamans generally keep packs of matches with them in order to have fire readily available for cleansing *dom*. Fire can be jabbed at intrusions in a person, as mentioned previously, but this is only part of the magical use of fire. When lighting the matches (wooden matches are always used), the shaman invokes the spirits and gestures with the matches toward Father Sky and Mother Earth to gather energy to the matches. Matches are usually lit in groups of three. Matches are good for on-the-spot cleansing of objects. They are lit and then passed around the object three times or, if it is large, jabbed at the object three times. The smoke is allowed to smolder until it goes out by itself.

The brightness with which the matches burn is a reflection of how strong the cleansing energy is. If the item being cleansed is quite polluted, the shaman will light three times three (nine matches), three at a time. When the matches go out, they are thrown down with disgust, as an expression of the belief that the essence of the pollution has become embodied in the burnt matches. The matches are carefully gathered up, broken, and thrown outside when the fire *dom* is finished.

Gestures to Manipulate Energy

Certain gestures will expel negative energy and place protective energy within things. Some shamans open the door of their house, turn so that their back is to the door, and make a motion of waving or shoving out negative energy. This cleansing practice is usually done once at night and again in the morning in order to keep their household free and clean of negative and disruptive energies. This same throwing-backward or shoving-backward motion is used during many kinds of shamanic work when negative energy is removed. Negative energy is also believed to be dispelled by clapping the hands three times while invoking the spirits.

In order to place protective energy into a place or thing, a shaman raises his hands toward the sky to gather in energy, brings his hands together in front of him, and directs the energy toward the thing through his fingers.

SERJIM: SPELLS OF SCATTERING AND POURING

There are many types of spells known as *serjim*. The materials they employ will vary greatly—and they can be solid as well as liquid—but what all types of *serjim* have in common is that each entails scattering or pouring. A *serjim* is actually a type of sacrifice in which the shaman offers the essence of a substance to the spirit in exchange for its applying its powers toward what is intended. This is not to be confused with *tsatsah (sasali bariha)*, in which liquids are scattered to the spirits by shamans and laypeople alike as a gesture of honor. The *serjim* may resemble *tsatsah*, but a *serjim* is directed toward certain spirits with a specific statement of intentions, during which the shaman may go into a semi-trancelike state. In actual shamanic practice in Mongolia and Siberia, as much as half of a shaman's everyday work entails making different kinds of *serjim*, for *serjim* will harness tremendous amounts of magical power without the shaman having to journey or merge consciousness with the spirits. The invocation of the spirits and the offerings made to them are enough to solve most common spiritual problems a shaman will face. View it as a delegation of the work that needs to be done so that the spirits a shaman invokes can fix what is wrong without his having to be personally involved. After all, the volume of work most shamans face today is so large that it is physically impossible to do lengthy rituals to handle every problem, and *serjim* will accomplish what is needed by the power of the helpful spirits.

Liquor *Serjim:* Hot and Cold

Serjim are usually called *haluun serjim* ("hot" *serjim*) or *huiten serjim* ("cold" *serjim*), depending on whether fire is used in the course of the ritual. *Haluun serjim* is one of the most powerful magical instruments in the Mongolian shaman's repertoire, for it taps directly into the power of the *gol* by using fire in the invocation. The use of liquor in Mongolian and Siberian shamanism tends to be poorly understood by outsiders. In the past, the only liquor used in ritual was *arza*, which was distilled from fermented milk (*kumiss* or *airag*). This sacred drink was termed the "essence of the herds" and was considered to be the perfect substance to offer to the spirits. With the decline of the nomadic lifestyle under Russian rule, *arza* has become too rare to be available to most shamans, except for those living in remote rural areas. As a result, vodka is the substitute of choice in Mongolia and Siberia, for it is clear like *arza* and therefore retains the symbolism of the purity and clarity that make it pleasing to the spirits. In no case is a colored drink such as wine or whiskey used in *serjim;* it would probably be considered an insult to the spirits and would negate the effects of the *serjim* as well as be potentially dangerous to the shaman who made the mistake.

When a shaman's clients come to visit, they normally bring a bottle of vodka that will be used for *serjim, arshaan,* or both. The shaman will look into the unopened bottle, using it like a crystal ball for divination. Once he is done, he opens the bottle. He lights one or three matches and quickly sticks them into the top of the bottle, allowing them to sputter out and fill the neck of the bottle with smoke. The smoke's roiling patterns contain important information about the spiritual situation of the person who brought the bottle (or the person on whose behalf the shaman is being consulted). One safety tip: Stick the matches in the top of the bottle immediately after opening. If the bottle is left open too long before the matches are introduced, the alcohol fumes will mix with the fresh air and when you stick in the matches a big blue flame will erupt and burn your fingers!

Following this, the metal or plastic ring that detached from the lid when the bottle was opened (if there is one) should be cut or broken in order to ritually kill the bottle. Now smudge the bottle with juniper or fir. Once the shaman has consulted with the spirits by looking into the bottle and by asking further questions in a short prayer, he will know what kind of *serjim* needs to be performed.

If a *haluun serjim* (hot *serjim* with fire) is required, the shaman takes out a shallow bowl or metal tray and pours a little vodka into it, enough to cover the bottom. More vodka, usually about half the bottle, will be poured into a ceremonial silver cup or Chinese-style teacup. A shaman will have a special small teaspoon, usually made out of silver, for doing *serjim,* but sometimes regular tablespoons are used. The shaman invokes the spirits and lights the matches in a ceremonial manner (see "Uses of Fire" on page 183). He will touch the matches carefully to the surface of the liquid in the tray so that it blazes into a large, brilliant blue flame. The shaman then starts invoking the spirits and spoons vodka into the tray in order to feed the fire. After the spirits have been invoked, the shaman states the intentions of the ritual. If the bowl is emptied of vodka, it is refilled until the shaman has stated all the intentions and invoked all of the spirits he deems helpful for the purpose of the *serjim.* The shaman may repeat the intentions in order to add more energy to them. When the invocations and stating of the intentions are accomplished, the shaman carefully pours whatever vodka remains in the bowl into the tray so that the fire will not go out but not so much that the tray overflows. (Exercise caution in this ritual because a dangerous fire can start very quickly if the tray overflows.) The shaman and the client watch the fire prayerfully until the alcohol is depleted and the fire goes out. The remaining liquid should be thrown out the nearest window or door leading to outside. When you dispose of the liquid, be sure the fire is out. A shaman friend in Ulan-Ude set afire the bushes outside her window when she threw out the liquid prematurely!

When you do the *serjim* with fire, focus on the blue fire in the tray in front of you. It is a true manifestation of the energy of the *gol*, and if you comprehend this, you will understand that you have vast amounts of magical power available to you. It is advisable to have an idea which spirits you want to invoke before you start and, naturally, a clear idea of how to state your intentions. When you do a liquor *serjim*, whether hot or cold, try to keep the remainder of the liquor to use as a ceremonial drink or for making *tsatsah* offerings to the spirits, as the liquid has now been imbued with the power invoked during the *serjim*. It is also customary to offer a drink from the remaining liquid to the client and for the shaman to take a little as well, but this is the choice of the people involved in the ritual.

The cold-liquor *serjim* involves two ceremonial bowls about the same size, usually either silver or copper bowls or Chinese-style teacups. The vodka bottle is opened with the same kinds of divination and ceremony as in the case of the fire *serjim*, but the vodka is poured into one bowl and then spooned into the other bowl while the shaman invokes the spirits and states the intentions. When the shaman is finished speaking to the spirits, any vodka remaining in the first bowl is poured into the second bowl. The vodka is then thrown out the nearest window or outside door.

It is customary for the shaman, in lieu of throwing the liquid outside, to throw the liquid onto a wall or ceiling in order to see the pattern the splash makes. The shaman throws the vodka while shouting the magic word *Tooreg!* The pattern of the splash has specific divinatory meanings (according to the knowledge of the individual shaman) with regard to the outcome of the *serjim*. If you are concerned about the alcohol marring the paint of a wall, you may throw the liquid against a window pane instead. In doing the cold *serjim*, it is important to note patterns created by any drips or dribbles on the table left over from the spooning of the liquid from one cup to another—this is also believed to have divinatory meaning.

Tea *Serjim*

The tea *serjim* is different from the vodka *serjim* in that the liquid is not scattered by the shaman; rather, the tea is prepared magically by the shaman and then brewed later by the client for whom it was made. The tea *serjim* is for cases of healing and protection, often as a follow-up to a cold-vodka *serjim*, during the course of which the shaman has discovered through divination the cause of the client's trouble. The shaman takes a new package of loose tea provided by the client and opens the box, invoking the spirits and speaking intentions into it. If a certain disease or hostile spirits are causing problems for the client, the shaman may take a knife and stab it into the tea, invoking the shamanic helper spirits to attack and defeat the trouble-causing spirit. Once the invocation and statements of intention are over, the shaman returns the package of tea, usually keeping a portion as a gift to the spirits (to be used by the shaman in future rituals). The client will take the tea home, brew the tea himself, sprinkle some of the tea for the spirits, then drink the rest so that the magical power imbued in the tea can take effect.

Serjim of the Three Ritual Liquids

A special mixed *serjim* is done to remove danger and illness from a family or community. The three ceremonial liquids of Mongolian and Siberian shamanism are used: vodka, tea, and milk. The power of the three liquids is connected with their symbolism:

Vodka	Father Heaven	Spiritual Being
Tea	Lower World	Wisdom of Ancestors
Milk	Mother Earth	Physical Being

The liquids are placed in three bowls in front of the shaman. An additional empty bowl is also directly in front of the shaman. Each bowl has its own spoon so that when the shaman spoons the liquids into the empty bowl the liquids will not mix together and become impure. This *serjim* is more "shamanic" in nature than are the other types of *serjim* because the shaman uses a bell or rattle to induce a light trance. The trance enables him to communicate with the spirits and determine the course of the *serjim*, and to know which spirits need to be invoked, which spirits are causing trouble, and in which direction the liquid should be thrown to restore balance between the empowering and trouble-causing spirits.

The shaman starts by ringing a bell or rattling in order to connect with the spirits and retrieve information about the course the ritual should take. The shaman usually stays in a semi-trancelike state for the duration of the ritual. As he calls the spirits and communicates with them, he will pour spoonfuls of the three ceremonial liquids into the empty bowl as he is prompted by them. When the bowl is full, he will call the main client or head of the family or community on whose behalf he is doing the ceremony to take the bowl and tell him in which direction the mixed liquid should be thrown. On the instruction of the shaman, the person who takes the bowl goes outside and reverently pours out the contents of the bowl, knowing that the liquid contains the power of the spirits invoked and the magic to neutralize the spirits bringing trouble and danger. This process may be repeated two or three times. At the end of the *serjim*, the participants follow the custom of *joroo*, the passing around and sipping of the three ceremonial liquids, for the liquids have become magically energized *arshaan* that will bring blessing with their consumption. At the last, the shaman finishes off what remains of the liquids. Often there is a dinner afterward to honor the shaman and the work he has done.

Serjim with Salt, Sand, and Rice

These three substances, when thrown, each in turn, have great power for spiritual cleansing and transmuting of negative spiritual beings into positive ones. This is most commonly done when a person is under spiritual attack either from hostile spirits or from a curse. The shaman or the affected person throws these three substances around where he or she stands. The procedure is to turn around three times throwing salt, three times throwing sand, and three times throwing rice (uncooked). Seeds other than rice can be used; the important thing is that a grain or seed be used in the ceremony. Perhaps this represents a three-step process of the transmutation of negative energy or spiritual beings, for this same action is done in the Peace Tree ritual. Salt has the most power to bar and dispel negativity; sand seems to have a neutralizing effect; and the seeds seem to effect the final step of transformation from negative to positive (perhaps because they contain the sacred essence of life).

It is interesting to note that in the magical act of *serjim*, these are used together and not separately (with the exception of salt, as shown below).

Salt Serjim

The use of salt in *serjim* is not much different from its use in *dom*. Salt has the powerful effect of repelling negative energies and spirits. When used in *serjim*, it is mixed with other substances and prayed over by the shaman. Either the shaman or the client (or both) then scatters the mix. Salt is mixed with herbs (juniper or fir) for most purposes, combining cleansing with repelling. When the shaman has determined his client's problem, he will invoke the spirits and speak intentions into some salt (usually a few spoonfuls), then he throws the salt in the direction of the cause of the client's problems while continuing to speak with the spirit. The client then takes the remaining salt to sprinkle when he feels in danger. Shamans also keep such salt on hand to scatter where they sit when in an unknown place or where they feel under spiritual threat. A special type of salt *serjim* is made in which a few grains of dirt from a grave have been mixed in. This is a very strong *serjim*, often used for types of black magic better not discussed in detail. It is most commonly used to break up destructive relationships.

Juniper Serjim

As in the case of the tea *serjim*, the shaman prepares the juniper *serjim* for someone else to use. In Mongolia and Siberia, the sacred smoke *arsa* (juniper) is kept on hand in large quantity because a shaman will often be required to prepare such a *serjim*, either by itself or in addition to other types of *serjim*. When the shaman prepares this *serjim*, he speaks over a few spoonfuls of ground juniper to invoke the spirits and ask them to empower the juniper for a particular intention. The shaman then wraps up the juniper into a little paper bundle. The client will burn a bit of it every day until it is gone in order to continue to energize the intention that has been introduced into the juniper.

Money *Serjim*

This involves the scattering of coins at a sacred place (such as an *oboo* or sacred tree) with the aim of gaining the spirits' favor for a certain intention. This may be combined with the leaving of tobacco offerings.

Food *Serjim*

This is usually done in preparation for rituals in which the nature spirits will be invoked at a place out in nature. This *serjim* gets their attention so they will be more responsive in the ritual that follows. The food *serjim* consists of crumbled biscuits, nuts, and candy. In reality it raises windhorse by providing food for small animals and birds, and the generosity toward the animals of nature wins the favor of the nature spirits. Some shamans leave out bread and seeds for birds for the same purpose.

Awakening of the Drum Ritual
(Hese amiluulah)

I present this ritual here as a good example of how shamans connect with the spirits of their instruments so that they can be used more effectively. Most of you are probably using or will be using drums in your shamanic work, so this should be especially relevant for you. Once you become familiar with this procedure, you can adapt it easily for the awakening *(amiluulah)* of other shamanic implements, such as rattles, staffs, and ritual weapons. Remember, the chief aim of awakening rituals is for the shaman to connect with the *ezen* of the object being awakened so that it will become a helper spirit.

In this section I will also briefly describe the legend that accompanies the awakening of the drum, for it is one of the great shamanic teaching stories—evocative of the meaning of the drum as the magical steed of the shaman during the journey.

Before you awaken of the drum, spend some time meditating on the drum and where it came from. What is the head made out of? Is it artificial or is it skin? If it is skin, what kind is it? What kind of wood is it made out of? Do you know where it was made? If the drum has a head or rim made of plastic, consider how plastic comes from petroleum, which is the essence of many animals and plants that lived in ancient times. After all, unless your drum is made out of metal, its parts all come from things that were alive at one time. An important part of this ceremony will be the visualization of the living things from which the drum was made, so thinking about it beforehand will make this part of the awakening of the drum much easier. As I mentioned above, the *ezen* of the drum enters at the time of its making. It is especially magical if it happens that you made the drum yourself, for the *ezen* would have passed through your hands into the drum as you made it: two times being as one—the time of creation and the time of awakening are one even if they seem separated in our perception of linear time.

In Siberia it is traditional for a drum to be given to a shaman rather than for a shaman to buy it, although there are exceptions. A drum is usually given to a shaman by clients or family members in honor of and gratitude for the work he is doing. Indeed, a drum that is gifted is a great blessing, for it is a sign that the spirits have selected a specific drum for a shaman and brought it into his possession. It is not unusual for a shaman to have multiple drums; after all, with the passage of time drums become worn out and need to be replaced with something that has a better sound and a tighter head. If you bought your drum, this does not lessen the effectiveness and power of this ritual—outside Siberia, shamans tend to serve much smaller groups of people and are not often compensated for their work with shamanic instruments, as is the custom among Buryat shamanists. Also, it is customary to paint the head after the awakening of the drum, but if your drum has already been painted, do not worry about it.

Another interesting custom is to have children play with the drum before its awakening. The spirit of the drum seems to enjoy being played with by people other than the shaman before the awak-ening ritual. When I do the drum awakening in workshops, I fulfill this custom by allowing the participants to pass their drums around the ritual circle. Everyone drums on each of the drums a little be-fore passing it on to the next person. It is fun, and the joy of the drum spirits in being handled in this way is great—the energy is palpable as the drums go around the circle. The playing with the drum or drums is the first part of the ritual. If you have children, let them play with the drum a little, then let others who will be in the ritual circle play. Apparently the happiness that comes out of play is stimulating to drum spirits. Incidentally, this ritual action is not done in the awakening of other shamanic instruments, although it could probably be done with rattles or bells (it would be unthink-able, after all, to have a child play with ritual weapons!).

The Legend of Abai Geser

After the passing around of the drums, the students receive their own drums back and remain sitting in the ritual circle while I tell the story of Abai Geser. Recounting the legend is an important part of the ritual because it gives the students a better understanding of the role of the shaman and his steed in serving the spirits for the benefit of the community and the world. This is the most sacred teaching story of southern Siberian shamanism, and for this reason I will recount part of it here. The story of Abai Geser's initiation imparts several important lessons about shamanic work and will be helpful when you do your shamanic journey as part of the drum awakening. I have translated the entire legend into English and plan to publish it in the near future.[11]

In the *galab* time, in the most ancient of times, when mankind was new on the earth and the trees of the taiga were but seedlings, the sky spirits lived in balance with each other and mankind and other living things lived in peace and happiness. At that time the brothers Han Hormasta and Atai Ulaan, who represented the cre-ative and destructive forces of the universe, had a dispute over who would be more dominant in the world. In the center, in neither the western skies ruled by Han Hormasta nor the eastern skies ruled by

Atai Ulaan, there lived Segeen Sebdeg Tenger, the god of winter, who had sent the white-headed eagle to earth as the first shaman in even earlier times. He refused to become the ally of either brother, which is a reminder to us shamans who follow the tradition started by Eagle that we should be in balance. Atai Ulaan Tenger, believing that he should be dominant, made thirteen magicks dance on his palms and twenty-three magicks dance on his fingers and sent sickness into the sun goddess Naran Goohon, so that the sun became dim and the world was filled with fear and terror.

Bukhe Beligte Tenger, the heavenly incarnation of Abai Geser, went to the great mother Manzan Gurme Toodei and asked her what to do. She told him that if Naran Goohon died, the powers of destruction would prevail and death and suffering would overcome all living things. There was only one being that could save her—the great white skylark of the heavens, the magical shaman bird, with magic words written in gold on its back and magic words written in silver on its chest, that flew at the edge of day and night singing its words of power. If this bird were brought to Naran Goohon, it would heal her and good and happiness would prevail for all time.[12]

Bukhe Beligte mounted his magical flying horse, Beligen, whose bones were full of wisdom (this is the symbol of his shaman drum), traveled up to the sky where day and night came together, and retrieved the magic lark. When Manzan Gurme Toodei touched the lark to the sun goddess, she was restored to health and the great mother allowed the magical bird to return to the sky with her blessing.

This having happened, Atai Ulaan Tenger was greatly enraged. One day, when he went to visit Segeen Sebdeg in order to try to win him over to his faction of the sky spirits, he encountered Han Hormasta and they quarreled. As their fury increased they began to fight, and Han Hormasta's son Bukhe Beligte, knowing that his father could be killed, journeyed to Manzan Gurme Toodei and asked her how Atai Ulaan could be defeated. She told him, "He has hidden his souls in the big toe of his right foot." Bukhe Beligte then rode his flying horse back to the scene of the battle. Atai Ulaan, having summoned great and terrible magic powers, was about to kill Han Hormasta. Bukhe Beligte threw a great black spear that smashed the big toe of Atai Ulaan's right foot. His souls now knocked out of his body, Atai Ulaan lay helpless. Han Hormasta, overcome with the passion of battle, hacked his enemy's body into pieces and threw them out of the heavens. Where the pieces fell they exuded great poisonous fogs, diseases, and heat that dried up plants and springs. Mankind and other living things immediately started becoming mortally sick from the pollution. Malevolent disease spirits came out of the remains of Atai Ulaan and tormented humans and animals alike.

At that time mankind was ruled by three *khans*, Sargal Noyon, Hara Zutan, and Sengelen Noyon (probably early incarnations of Shargai Noyon, Elbite Hara/Buhe Noyon Baabai, and Ulaan Zalaa, the patrons of shamanism). The suffering people and animals came to them and asked what they should do, and so they assembled for a shaman ritual. The old shamaness Sharnaihan Shara *odigon* did a *tuksavi* ritual, the throwing of a message to the heavens. When the *ongon* spirits came into her, she took a *tsatsal* filled with the tears of suffering of humans and other living things and threw it up into the sky. It landed on the table of Manzan Gurme Toodei. When the mother goddess saw the tears spilled on her table, she took out her two shaman mirrors *(toli)*; looking in the larger mirror she saw all was peaceful in the skies, but when she looked into the little mirror she saw destruction and suffering on earth. She cried out in rage, she tore her scarf in half, in anger she struck the ground so hard with her staff that it almost broke. With a face like a stormy sky she went to the home of Esege Malaan *Tenger*, chief of the sky spirits, and told him, "This is your responsibility. Do something about it!"

Esege Malaan Tenger called a meeting in the Pleiades and on the moon and told the sky spirits what was happening on earth. He quickly determined that Han Hormasta was the cause of the problems and told him he must repair the damage. As the princes of the skies argued among themselves, Han Hormasta's son Bukhe Beligte stood up in the assembly of the *tenger* and declared that he would go, for his father's work in the heavens was too important and should not be interrupted. He said he would go on certain conditions, to which the *tenger* agreed. He would be able to have his flying horse Beligen, he would have the *zadai* stone that stopped a thousand storms, he would have the two shaman staffs that could still the

waters (in Buryat shamanic initiation, the shaman ultimately receives three staffs), he would have the healing sandalwood staff
that put people into a trance when it was touched to their heads, he
would have a magical snare that could catch seventy animals, the
sun goddess Naran Goohon would incarnate as a human to become
his mother, and his three sisters and elder brother from his heavenly family would be his protectors while he was on earth. This
having been agreed to, Bukhe Beligte turned into an eagle and flew
around the earth to see what had happened. Esege Malaan Tenger
would take care of his *tonog* (shamanic tools) until the time of his
initiation.

Sargal Noyon had a dream in which he saw the great skylark of
the heavens flying at the edge of day and night, and the spirits told
him that if this lark was brought down to earth, it would be the
salvation of all living things. When he awoke, he went out and beat
on his golden drum to call people from the north and on his silver
drum to call people from the south. When his subjects arrived, he
told them about the dream and asked if anyone knew how to find
this magical bird. His brother Hara Zutan answered, "I can do it!"
and took out a great black arrow, spoke invocations on the arrow-
head, spoke invocations on the shaft, spoke invocations on the feathers, and shot up into the sky (this is the custom when using the
shaman's bow and arrow). A giant white lark came fluttering down.
When it landed it turned into an astonishingly beautiful woman—it
was the sun goddess Naran Goohon. The spirits told Sargal Noyon
that in order for her to be the mother of the savior of living things
she must learn their suffering. He commanded that one of her eyes
be blinded, that one arm and one leg be broken, and that she be
married to his brother Sengelen Noyon. He furthermore commanded
that they live in a grass-roofed tepee deep in the forest and that
they survive by digging roots, catching minnows in the stream, catching rabbits and rodents in snares, and eating out of cracked pots. As
he commanded, so it was done.

The poor couple lived a long time in great hardship until one
night Naran Goohon awoke to find an invisible man in bed with
her. When he realized she had awakened, he threw back the blan-
kets and ran out of the tepee. Suddenly she realized that her eye,

arm, and leg were healed and her beauty was restored. Greatly astonished, she hurried outside and saw strange, large, square footprints in the snow. Following the tracks she came to a cave in the mountains. When she entered she found a man sleeping, a "man from the sky" (alien) who had a light in the middle of his forehead that glowed even while he was asleep. Frightened, she ran back to her tepee.

In only a few days it became obvious that she was pregnant. After only nine days she gave birth to a very strange-looking red boy (this symbolizes the fact that shamans are chosen by the spirits from birth and are innately different). He had one arm raised as if to strike and one leg bent as if to kick. One eye looked straight ahead and the other squinted. Suddenly he spoke from the cradle, saying "I raise my hand to strike my brave enemies and bend my leg to kick my cowardly enemies. With one eye I see the way I must go and with the other I see through illusion."

The boy grew rapidly but because of his unusual behavior his parents placed him on a hilltop at night while he slept. The first night that he slept there the spirits who were the enemies of living things sent two giant rats to chew him up. The boy Abai Geser put out his magic shaman's snare and the rats were caught. Taking out his *minaa* (shaman whip) he said, "From this time onward, two times being as one, you will be only small!" When he smashed them they became a swarm of rats and mice, and from that time rats and mice are small. The next night the evil spirits sent two ravens with iron beaks and iron talons to attack him. He grabbed them and ripped out the iron, saying, "From this time onward, two times being as one, you will have beaks and claws made of horn!" And so ravens do to this day. The third night the evil spirits sent a mosquito as big as a horse to suck out all of his blood. When it came the boy took out his shaman's whip and smashed the mosquito so that it became a swarm of tiny mosquitoes and gnats, saying, "From this time onward, two times being as one, you will cling to blades of grass and go about hungry!" (This part of the story illustrates the use of the *minaa* and the use of the phrase *hoyor sagai negende* [see the "Magic Phrases" section of the glossary], one of the most powerful magical phrases in our tradition because it harnesses the power of the *gol*.)

On the fourth day the leader of the evil spirits turned himself into a black shaman and came to the tepee where the baby Geser and his parents lived. When he came he said, "I am a shaman who becomes *naija* to little boys and girls and protects them until they are old enough to dance the *yohor* dance. I hear that you have a son: Let me become his protector." Sengelen Noyon and Naran Goohon believed him and put on their best clothing for the shaman ritual. Geser started crying as he lay on his cradleboard and the false shaman said, "What is the matter? Does he have colic? Let me see him!" As he approached the baby he turned into an ugly monster and shouted, "I will cut off your *ami* and *suld!*" The little boy grabbed the head of the black shaman and kicked him in the chest so that the shaman's *zuld* (head, throat, heart, and lungs) was torn out and he died. (In this part of the story we see how shamans become shamanic godparents of children, *naija;* the significant idea of loss of *ami* and *suld;* and the relationship of these souls to the *zuld,* for death is instantaneous if the *zuld* is separated from the body.)

The next three nights the baby Geser, who took on the form of the full-grown Bukhe Beligte on his journeys, traveled to the yellow, blue, and black lakes where nine hundred disease spirits congregated every night. Making himself look like them, with a small pointed beard and a hat trimmed with squirrel fur, he won their confidence. He deceived them into going swimming in the lakes and when they did so he stirred up the waters with his shaman's whip so that they were buried in the mud at the bottom of the lake. He said to them, "From this time onward, two times being as one, you will no longer trouble mankind!" He then put his shaman staff into the water and the water once more became pure and clear. After that he took a large reed and sucked up all of the pollution and disease in the world and spat it out into the Arctic Ocean. (In this section we see the use of the shaman staff as a tool for transformation and the use of sucking and spitting in the process of healing.)

The boy Bukhe Beligte/Geser has several more adventures but I will shorten the story here because they are not as instructive as the parts I just related.

When he became a young man, he had great magical powers

but still he had not had his initiatory experience. At this time he was what would be called a *butur* or *huurai boo* ("dry shaman" or "uninitiated shaman"). While he was still quite young, Bukhe Beligte (who was not yet known as Geser) won for himself two wives, but he never slept with them because at night he was mentally disturbed and would wander about the forest until dawn. (This is a common manifestation of the mental illness that sometimes accompanies the shaman calling.) His wives decided to find out what he did at night and followed him secretly during his wanderings.

As they followed him, he suddenly turned into an eagle and flew up the slopes of the World Mountain Humber Uula (a symbol for the *gol*) until he reached its summit, the gateway between the middle and upper worlds. He kindled a fire and offered a ram to the *tenger*, doing a *tailgan* (shaman ceremony). Suddenly his body was transformed, and where once there stood a boy there now stood a man with a mighty and heroic body, with *tsog* energy like lightning sparkling in his eyes! He had a red face and hair hanging down his back an ell long, and he stood there singing his shaman songs and asking Esege Malaan Tenger to send down his shaman tools so he could start his work of cleansing the earth of the harmful things that troubled humans and animals.

He called the spirits and they listened, for the time of his initiation had come! Esege Malaan Tenger and all of the *tenger*, hearing his invocations and smelling the sacred smoke that rose to the sky, met at once. They sent down Beligen Heer Morin, Bukhe Beligte's magic steed, the symbol of the shaman drum, who bore the tools that Abai Geser would use on his beautiful back. When he alighted on the mountain his hooves struck sparks as he walked. He said, "What power do you have to call me? I can fly three times around the world without eating even a handful of hay!"

Having been initiated, Bukhe Beligte had become Abai Geser, and Abai Geser replied to the horse, "If the world had a handle I could turn it around!"

The horse Beligen replied, "Then let us work together!"

Abai Geser put his foot into the silver stirrup, grabbed the beautiful red reins, and swung into the saddle. As they leaped from the mountain they flew like eagles at the edge of the middle and upper worlds. Sometimes if they went too low they trod on treetops or struck sparks off the peaks of mountains. Three times they flew around the earth. As they came around the world the last time, the skies were filled with shouts of joy. The thirty-three warriors of the Sayan Mountains came riding on their flying horses and followed Abai Geser, shouting, "Our Abai Geser, Abai Geser of great magical power!" and they returned to Abai Geser's homeland to become his assistants and protectors in his work. Sargal Noyon beat his golden and silver drums, assembling the people of the world. They did *dallaga* and honored the *tenger,* for the time of the healing of the earth had come.

This legend reminds us that the shaman drum comes to us by the destiny of the spirits, just as Esege Malaan Tenger sent down Abai Geser's magic steed at the time when he was ready. It is no coincidence that many Mongolian and Siberian shamans decorate their drums with miniature representations of a harness and that *hadags* are tied on to represent the horse's head and ears. As you see in the legend of Abai Geser, he already was doing shamanic work before he contacted the spirit Beligen Heer Morin, the horse spirit of his drum, but contact with this spirit was transforming and a type of initiation. As you will see below, the Buryat system of shamanic initiations brings the shaman into greater levels of power as the shaman awakens his various instruments in profound and powerful visions. The nine parts (*halaa,* or "branches") of the full legend of Abai Geser as well as the nine degrees of shamanic initiation represent the nine branches of the *turge,* the World Tree, and so the teaching story of Abai Geser teaches these nine levels of shamanic accomplishment. Of these, I believe the awakening of the drum is the most essential for all shamanic practitioners.

I hope that before you do the ritual to awaken the drum, you will read and contemplate this story a few times, for it is very instructive and can be of great help in guiding the vision you will have on your journey. When I do this ceremony in workshops, I tell the legend to my students and illustrate the story by showing the various shamanic instruments that Abai Geser used.

The Awakening Ceremony

To prepare for this ceremony, meditate on the drum and on the legend I described above. Have someone else play the drum before you do the journey. Needless to say, this should be done in a ritual space indoors or outdoors—I sometimes do this ceremony by a campfire, combining it with the Mongolian fire ritual (described in *Riding Windhorses;* see the bibliography). Once you have made invocations to the spirits you normally honor in your work, be sure to make an invocation to the drum spirit and ask it to come to you and become your ally. Now, if you have not had the drum played with in advance, have somebody else play your drum before it becomes bonded with you.

When you awaken the drum you should play alone, or if you are doing this with other people, you set the speed and rhythm of the drumming. As you become more focused, ask the drum spirit to show you the place where the animals who provided the skins lived, what they looked like, how old they were when they were taken. Ask the drum spirit to show you the tree from which its wood was cut. If you have plastic parts to your drum, ask the drum spirit to show you what kinds of animals provided the essence for the chemicals that the plastic is made of. If the drum has metal parts, imagine the place from which the metal was mined and smelted. Close your eyes. Imagine yourself on a mountaintop, waiting for the drum spirit to come to you. Allow the rhythm of the drum to become as natural as your breath, your heartbeat. Allow the drum spirit to merge with you so that the speed and rhythm of your drumming will be controlled by it as you become *ongod orood.*

Do not be surprised by the appearance of the spirit of the drum. Perhaps it will appear as a heroic steed, as in the vision of Abai Geser, but remember, the shamanic mount can manifest itself as any kind of natural or fantastic creature. Let it show you the places where its components came from, what forest the wood came from, what kinds of animals gave themselves to the making of the drum. You may even have a vision of when the drum was being made and the spirit entered into it. The spirit may teach you some special ways you can use the drum for your shamanic work that you did not know before—your drum spirit and your *udha* together are instructing you in powerful ancient shamanic knowledge when this happens!

As you continue to drum, you will become more ecstatic and the spirits will create new rhythms and perhaps cause you to sing. You are now stepping into a higher level of shamanic consciousness and skill. At some point in your journey, you—like Abai Geser and other mighty shamans of the past—will realize that all your helper spirits and power animals are traveling at your side and rejoicing that you have merged with the spirit of the drum. Now you have obtained the power to do much greater things than you were able to do before. You will not realize the full magnitude of this change until a few days or even a couple of weeks afterward.

This kind of initiatory ceremony is called *shanar* (best translated as "increase in ability"), and it is a time of great celebration. When this is performed as a ritual with many participants, the ceremony is followed by a festive meal in which the shaman or shamans are honored and the people rejoice that the spirits have brought the blessing of greater power to the shamans for the benefit of the community and of mankind.

APPENDIX I

Setting Up
a Ritual Space

In various procedures described in this book, I speak of creating a ritual space. Although a shaman may indeed do his work wherever he goes, it is preferable to work in a ritual space. A ritual space helps set the state of mind for the shaman and for the people for whom shamanic work is being done. Just as the donning of ritual clothing helps the shaman to induce the state of mind that allows the spirits to work through him, so the creation of a ritual space has the same effect. When creating the ritual space, remember that no matter where you create it, the sacred circle is actually the same place. The reason is that the *gol* is the center of your space, and the *gol* is everywhere and anywhere. In this way you have continuity in your work: you are working within the same sacred circle. It is a good idea to try to arrange things the same way wherever you set up your ritual space.

In Mongolia and Siberia the creation of a ritual space is customary in shamanic work, as it is pleasing to the spirits and gives them a specific place in which to perform their tasks. The placements of food and drink offerings, the arrangement of the *ongons* on an altar or sacred place, setting the shamanic implements where they are convenient to the shaman—all are ritual actions that show respect to the spirits and to the shaman who is doing the work. The creation of the sacred space can be done by the shaman or by all the people involved in the ritual.

Because all rituals use sacred smoke, fire, or both, designate someone to be responsible for the fire if you are not working alone. The fire keeper is responsible for ensuring that the fire and other burning materials do not accidentally burn anything around them. This person will make sure the smudges and incense stay lit and that the fire, if a fire is being used, is stocked with wood. It is most important that burning materials do not go out, for that is a bad omen for the success of the ritual. The vigor, or lack of vigor, with which the fire and the sacred smoke burn is considered to be a reflection of the amount of windhorse being raised during the procedure. I often see fires suddenly start burning very fast and hot when the *ongon* spirits come into the shaman or shamans working in a ritual, a sign of the great spiritual power at work.

A ritual space should be oriented to the four directions. The back side of the sacred circle should be on the north; if that is not possible, make the back side of the circle opposite the entrance of the room in which the ritual is being done. In arranging the rest of

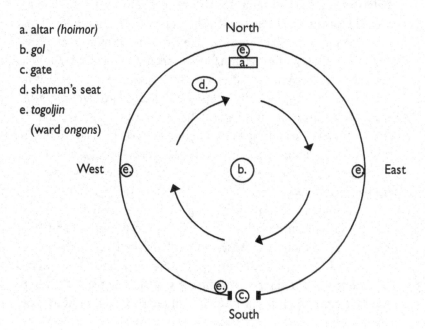

a. altar *(hoimor)*
b. *gol*
c. gate
d. shaman's seat
e. *togoljin*
 (ward *ongons*)

North
West
East
South

the elements of the sacred space, place them as if the back side of the circle is the north.

The first important element of a ritual space is the *hoimor*, the most sacred part of the circle. Most shamans use a small, low table as an altar in the *hoimor*. The altar is usually covered with a nice cloth and the shaman's *ongons* are spread on part of it. The rest of the table will be occupied with food and drink offerings. The custom is that the people for whom the ritual is being done provide these offerings. The food offerings may be fruit, candy, baked goods, nuts, cheese, and cooked meat or sausage. The drink offerings are milk, tea, and vodka or beer. If several people are participating in the ritual, only small token parts of the food are set on the altar; the rest is eaten in the meal that follows most major rituals. If the group of participants is large, the meal will be quite a feast!

Usually the shaman has his own cups for liquids that will be thrown during the ritual (one each for the milk, tea, and vodka). A wooden spoon for tossing liquids should be placed conveniently next to the cups of liquids that will be used in the libations. The *ongons* and food and drink should be arranged in an artistic manner. The shaman is responsible for the arrangement of the *ongons* and the ritual liquids, but the people for whom the ritual is being done are responsible for the arrangement of the food offerings.

The second important element of the ritual space is the representation of the *gol*. If the ritual is done outside, an *oboo*, ritual tree, or fire will represent the *gol*. If the ritual is performed inside, a small temporary *oboo*, a small fire (if it is possible), or a placement of incense sticks can represent the *gol*. If the room where you are doing the ritual has a fireplace or wood-burning stove, you may also kindle a fire there and use that even if it has to be at the edge of the circle rather than in the center. The most important thing is that the representation of the *gol* is a focus of movement and the starting point for journeying.

The third important element of the ritual space is the perimeter of the circle and the gate, customarily located on the south side. When you create the circle, you will start at the gate and move around sunwise, placing small rocks to describe the circle if you wish to do so. Otherwise, visualize the space that the circle encompasses while you are doing your work. Although you may want to create a well-defined circle within your own home for personal work, it may not be feasible to create one when you are away from home. If it is not too cumbersome, carry a small bag of stones for that purpose when you go out to do work away from home.

The shaman's seat is usually located at the northern side of the circle by the altar, positioned in such a way that your back will not be turned to the *ongons* on the altar. In Siberia the shaman may sit on an animal skin during a ritual, but you may use a blanket or cushion, depending on what is comfortable for you. It is customary for the elders of the family to sit closest to the shaman, but this is not necessary.

At each of the four directions are four ward *ongons* called *togoljin*. They may be created specifically for the ritual or you may decide to create a set that you carry with you from place to place. They are made from sticks and have human faces carved into them. They act as guardians of the circle during the ritual.

Another element you may want for your ritual space, especially in creating one for yourself, is darkness. Because darkness helps in going into a trance, a dark room is much better for shamanic work than a brightly lit one. Turn off the lights and work by natural light or by candlelight, if possible.

Consecrating the Circle

Once all the elements of the circle have been assembled, you will smudge the entire area with juniper, sage, thyme, or incense. The purpose is to dispel any negative influences within the ritual space and energize it for the work you will do.

After completing the cleansing of the circle, place three sticks of incense in a holder in the center of the circle. This represents the place of the fire *(gal golomt)*. If you have juniper, light it and place it in a burner. If you have thyme, burn it with the juniper in the same burner. Pass it around yourself three times; if a group is participating, walk around the group clockwise three times holding the burner. You, or each participant in the shamanic work you are doing, should wave smoke into each person's face. Sacred smoke opens the spirit channels of the body and raises windhorse. If you are not using juniper and thyme, do this with the incense. Once this is done, bow to the sacred smoke and say:

> *Golden-edged Golomto, daughter of Father Heaven,*
> *We thank you and ask your blessing.*

Taking the three incense sticks, wave them in a circular motion while saying *"Hurai, hurai, hurai,"* completing three circles.

Wave the sticks in the direction of the altar nine times, then replace them in their holder. If the sticks burn down during the ritual, replace them before they go out.

The Ritual of the Four Directions

Walk up to the altar and pick up the bowl containing the liquor or milk. Dip your right ring finger into the liquid and flick it three times over the altar. Then take your drum (or bell or rattle), hit it three times, and say:

> *Father Heaven, Mother Earth*
> *Spirits of the ancestors*
> *Spirits of the animals*
> *Spirits of the mountains, forests, and waters*
> Tenger *of the four directions*
> *Han Hormasta, Erleg Khan, Bayan Hangai, Umai*
> *Nature spirits of this place*
> *Raise our windhorse*
> *Bring us blessing,* hurai, hurai, hurai.

(Wave the drum clockwise three times; the other participants should wave their hands.)

If you have any power animals or other spirit guides, mention their names in this prayer as well (see "The Structure of the Mongolian

Shamanist Pantheon" in appendix 2 for proper pronunciation of the names of the spirits).

Walk around the circle to the rock marking the southern point, all the time drumming (or rattling or ringing). You then say:

> Ninety-nine tenger *of the red southern direction*
> *Usan Khan, lord of the waters*
> *Direction of the upper world*
> *Source of our body souls*
> *Raise our windhorse*
> *Bring us blessing,* hurai, hurai, hurai *[circular motion]*.

Continue drumming, walk around to the western point of the circle, and say:

> Fifty-five tenger *of the white western direction*
> *Who sent us Eagle, the first shaman,*
> *Raise our windhorse*
> *Bring us blessing,* hurai, hurai, hurai *[repeat circular motion]*.

Resume drumming, walk back to the altar, and say:

> Seventy-seven tenger *of the black northern direction*
> *Tatai Tenger, bringer of lightning,*
> *Direction of the lower world*
> *Raise our windhorse*
> *Bring us blessing,* hurai, hurai, hurai *[repeat circular motion]*.

Walk around to the eastern point of the circle and say:

> Forty-four tenger *of the blue eastern direction*
> *Thirteen Asarangi Tenger*
> *Raise our windhorse*
> *Bring us blessing,* hurai, hurai, hurai *[repeat circular motion]*.

Walk back to the rock marking the southern direction to complete the circle, then walk around the circle two more times, drumming continuously. All those walking the circle will raise their windhorse. At no time in this ritual should anyone walk in a counterclockwise direction. After walking around a total of three times, the circle has been consecrated. You or any other participants can stomp the floor or ground to drive far away any evil influences in the vicinity of the circle.

To raise extra windhorse, walk around the circle six more times to make a total of nine revolutions. This ritual is useful for raising windhorse and bringing down blessing. It is also a preparation for the more advanced shamanic work you will be doing inside the circle after it has been established. On the conclusion of the ritual, extinguish all of the candles and other burning materials, then pick up the first stone toward the direction in which you will be leaving. Then pick up the other stones while walking sunwise around the circle. If this ritual is being done in preparation for other shamanist rituals, leave the rocks in place but exit the circle through the southern, front end if possible.

APPENDIX 2

The Origins of the Mongolian Shamanic Tradition and the Shamanic Pantheon

THE ORIGIN OF THE SHAMANIC HELPER SPIRITS

In Mongolia and Siberia the most spiritually powerful place is the area of the Sayan-Altai Mountains. Most Siberian nationalities as well as the ancient Mongols lived in that region during some part of their history and the most famous and powerful shamanic traditions come from there—Tuvan shamanism, the Hongoodor shamanic tradition, and Huvsgul Mongol shamanism. Why is that area so important? Why are the Sayan Mountains like the Olympus of shamanic tradition? For the answer, you must go back to the legends about the early history of mankind. These tell how the sky spirits looked after mankind after humans had been placed on the earth by the sky spirits living in the Pleiades and on the moon. (It should be noted that even today, UFO sightings are quite common in Mongolia and in the Sayan Mountains.)[1]

It is said that in the *galab* time, thousands and thousands of years ago, when humans were first placed on earth, people lived in perfect harmony with the earth, prospering and without illness. The eastern sky spirits, who in our tradition represent the forces of destruction, realized that mankind would quickly overrun the earth and that something needed to be done to control the human population. Remember that the "black" spirits of the east and the "white" spirits of the west do not represent good and evil but, rather, the two balanced principles of creation and destruction, as essential to each other as the two sides of a coin. Only when they are in balance will the earth prosper; if more were created than could be destroyed, our universe would be overcome with an excess of old and superfluous things. On the other hand, if destruction is greater than creation, the beauty and richness of our lives will also be lost.

When illness was introduced into the human population in order to protect balance, the effects were too drastic (let me remind you that the eastern *tenger* are controllers of destructive forces and magic, not intrinsically hostile to life). This having happened, the sky spirits met in the Pleiades in order to determine what to do about the future of mankind because people were dying off too quickly. They decided to send Eagle down to earth to become the first shaman, but when he arrived he could not communicate with humans because he could not speak man's language. He then found a Buryat girl sleeping under a tree. He mated with her and she became pregnant. Like all offspring of the sky spirits, their child grew up unusually quickly and became the self-taught shaman Mergen Hara, the first black shaman (it is generally believed that the black tradition is older than the white tradition). He was so powerful that he could bring the dead back to life. The sky spirits punished him because his powers were too great and he abused them.

Later in the very ancient history of mankind, another catastrophe took place (I will summarize here because it is explained in more detail in the legend of the awakening of the drum). The sky spirits of the east and west, who were related to each other and who had lived in balance, got into a war with each other. The result of this war was that extremely poisonous and dangerous things fell down to earth (this reminds me of nuclear winter) and turned the sky dark; made the air poisonous; dried up or polluted all of the water; and caused the plants, animals, and humans to die off to the point of extinction. When the sky spirits sent Abai Geser to earth, at the time of his initiation he summoned thirty-three sons of the sky spirits as his warriors to aid him in cleansing the earth of the contamination that threatened living things. When his work was done, he returned to the sky. The thirty-three warriors, however, settled into the Sayan Mountains to be protectors of living things and helpers of shamans. In my own lineage we work with these spirits, and I have seen these awesome beings with my own eyes. This set the precedent for the relationship between the sky and the Sayan Mountains.

Somewhat later in history, probably about six thousand years ago, the sky spirits saw that the shamanic traditions were being forgotten and that humans lived very difficult lives. They had forgotten the technology they had known before, were grubbing in the ground with sticks, and using spears, arrows, and knives made out of stone. (Buryats believe that humans had advanced technology in the time of Abai Geser but then reverted to a "stone-age" lifestyle.) Seeing this, they sent the brother of Esege Malaan Tenger, Khan Shargai Noyon, who came down from the sky and taught shamanism and the use of metals to mankind. He met eighty-eight of the Zaarin clan (ancestors of our Terte clan) and ninety-nine of the Shoshoolog clan (the most ancient clan in the Sayan Mountains and the most honored shamanic lineage). He initiated thirty-three of them (the same number as the warriors living in the mountains) as shamans and seventy-three as shaman-smiths. The shamans beat their drums and the smiths pounded their metals so as to shake the earth. Soon afterward, brother Ulaan Zalaa (he of the red shaman badge) also came down to earth, to become the protector spirit of young boys.

Elbite Hara, who was one of the eastern sky spirits, was curious about the sudden surge of spiritual activity and technology on earth and came to see what was happening. He was jealous of what Shargai Noyon was doing. He shot a magic arrow that killed him and scared the shamans and smiths so terribly that they ran out of the Sayan Mountains. When the western sky spirits discovered this, they sent down Shargai Noyon's brother, who did an *ariulga* over him and restored him to life. Afterward, Shargai Noyon had certain adventures with Elbite Hara that converted him into a patron of shamanism, at which time he settled in the Sayan Mountains with a human wife and took the name Buhe Noyon Baabai. He is worshiped by almost all shamans and is believed to be an ancestor of at least two tribes.

As a result of these events, Shargai Noyon Baabai, Ulaan Zalaa, and Buhe Noyon Baabai are the three chief patrons of shamanism. They are believed to reside (spiritually) in the Sayan Mountains and monitor the activities of shamans throughout the world. They have selected certain great shamans to join them and there are now ninety-nine great shaman spirits living in those mountains. These spirits not only determine the inheritance of *udha* spirits (within their original lineages or among other unrelated shamans) but also allow new *udha* spirits to call more shamans and create new lineages. All of our shamanic callings are in some way connected with their activities.

Shargai Noyon Baabai is personally responsible for the safety of all shamans. A story is told that once many years ago there was a Russian soldier who murdered a shamaness because she refused to tell him where a certain fugitive was hiding. As he was riding home, he passed an old Buryat man riding a decrepit nag and was astonished to see that his own head was hanging from the man's saddle. When he got home he learned that he had seen Shargai Noyon Baabai and a premonition of the revenge the protector of all shamans would have on him for his crime, whereupon the soldier fell dead. My shaman colleagues, do not ever be afraid of the evil and harmful things in the world, for Shargai Noyon Baabai knows everything and personally punishes all wrongs done to shamans!

From the time when Shargai Noyon Baabai came down to earth and established the shamanic tradition, it is very easy to see how the Mongolian-Siberian tradition has developed, for the pattern of shamanic traditions is amazingly uniform over an area of our world that is larger than that of the United States and Canada combined. Furthermore, those of you who have studied other shamanic traditions such as those of Native Americans or ancient Europeans

214 ORIGINS OF THE MONGOLIAN SHAMANIC TRADITION

will notice the strong similarities between those traditions and those of the Buryat Mongols. Furthermore, the dozens of Shoshoolog shamans who were trained by Shargai Noyon Baabai, and their descendants, spread these teachings throughout the world as they migrated outward from the Sayan Mountains region, bringing a message of shamanic revival and wisdom to all peoples. Eventually these teachings spread to all humans everywhere, which is why there are certain beliefs and techniques that are universal to all shamanic traditions. The teachings passed down from Shargai Noyon Baabai's time constitute the true "core shamanism."

Remember, the influence of the patron spirits of shamanism is universal; it's just that other cultures know them by different names. In Siberia, people remember how the ninety-nine great shaman spirits and their leaders, Shargai Noyon Baabai, Ulaan Zalaa, and Buhe Noyon Baabai, have on occasion intervened to revive the shamanic traditions when they were threatened or corrupted.

The first great revival movement in the southern Siberian tradition probably happened about two thousand years ago when the shaman Ergil Buga, known as the "crazy one of Tunkhen" (Tunkhenei Galzuu) or Holongoto Ubgen (Sable Man), was born. He is so significant in the history of Siberian shamanism that one man told the American anthropologist Jeremiah Curtin that he is as important to the shamanist religion as Jesus is to the Christian religion. This is perhaps an exaggeration, but he established the tradition of the nine degrees of shamanism (connected with the mystical nine branches of the World Tree) and in his time was responsible for the crowning of ninety-nine shamans and ninety-nine shamanesses with the *orgoi* crown of the advanced shaman; after their death, all of their spirits joined him in the Sayan Mountains as patrons and protectors of all shamans. His *ongon* is made of skunk skin and is a precious connection with this significant moment in history. It is said that he was the son of a virgin birth: his mother ate a hailstone that contained the semen of one of the sky spirits, which resulted in his conception. Furthermore, his name Tunkhenei Galzuu is a reminder of the important connection between the Tunkhen valley and Shargai Noyon Baabai and the other shaman spirits that inhabit the Sayan Mountains on its northern side. The region where the mountains and the Tunkhen valley come together is called Hoimor, "the holy place."[2]

The most recent revival movement in Mongolian shamanism was about 350 years ago among the Shoshoolog clan, who were descendants of the shamans initiated by Shargai Noyon Baabai in ancient times. It is interesting that in the invocations of Mongolian shamanism, we speak of the "ninety-nine Shoshoolog" in remembrance of these events. This revival was started by the shamaness Khan Hemekshen Toodei. As a child she lived in a camp where the spirits constantly attacked the people, and they were helpless because they had forgotten their old traditions. This was when Mongolian shamanism was under attack from Tibetan Buddhism on one side and Russian Orthodox missionaries on the other. The girl was a shepherdess, and she was astonished to see that an eagle came again and again to steal sheep from her herd. She suddenly realized that the eagle was a manifestation *(hubilgaan)* of an *udha* spirit from her Shoshoolog ancestors and that it was telling her to become a shaman. She followed the calling of the spirits and expelled the spirits that harassed her community so that it prospered, and by the guidance of the ancestors she revived the traditions that the foreigners had tried to destroy. Like the great shaman Ergil Buga of ancient times, she initiated and crowned ninety-nine shamans and ninety-nine shamanesses during her career and ensured the survival of the shamanic traditions to the present time. Once again, in the story of Khan Hemekshen Toodei, we can see that Shargai Noyon and the other Sayan Mountain spirits intervened to preserve shamanic knowledge through the Shoshoolog lineage, which has carried the traditions for thousands of years.

The Buryat scholar Dorji Banzarov, who was the first Buryat educated in a European university, wrote a valuable account of these traditions. He was educated in the Western way of knowledge, but he never lost the mystical spirit inherited from the ancestors. He commented in the early 1850s, shortly before his premature death, "I see a very dark time coming over the western nations. Will Abai Geser and his thirty-three warriors call our people again to cleanse the world from evil and save mankind?" These words were prophetic. Starting with the American Civil War, the wars of colonial conquest, two world wars, and the Cold War, the Western world has been forever changed by evil and greed unequaled since the wars between the sky spirits in incredibly ancient times. Where is the fulfillment of the other part of this prophecy? I and other people here in Siberia believe that the revival of shamanism in practically every part of the world at this time is the fulfillment of what Dorji Banzarov had seen. Abai Geser and Shargai Noyon Baabai, knowing the suffering of living things, are calling shamans from throughout the world in order to heal mankind, heal the world, and restore balance. We are all part of this! We are not limited by the bounds of one tradition or another: as shamans we are all spiritually the children of Shargai Noyon Baabai and the many shaman spirits he sends throughout the world for the healing and blessing of all mankind. After all, in the *gol*, what is the difference between Buryats and other nationalities? We are all one![3]

THE STRUCTURE OF THE MONGOLIAN SHAMANIST PANTHEON

Here I present a summary of the main deities of the Mongolian pantheon as a guide for those of you who are following a Mongolian/Siberian shamanic practice or who would like to have a better understanding of the great variety of spirits whom you can invoke for specific purposes. It is typical for shamans to keep lists of these spirits and their properties in order to tailor their invocations according to the purpose of their rituals. As mentioned earlier, each of these beings is known to be helpful for certain types of healing, protection, or magic, and invoking a spirit under the proper circumstances can summon great power for what a shaman intends to do.[4]

The Two Chief Deities

Tenger Esege (ten-ger eh-tsek): Also known as Huhe Munhe Tenger, the eternal blue sky, the source of the energy flowing from the sky to the earth that sustains all living things, the ultimate determiner of the fate of everything.

Gazar Eej (gah-zur ehj): Mother Earth, earth as the mother and nurturer of all life, the source of the energy flowing from earth to sky that sustains all living things. She is also known as Ulgen Ehe, or Itugen, words that describe her fertility. The name Itugen is related to the words *udagan* ("shamaness") and *utegen* ("womb"). She has seventy-seven *itugen* goddesses associated with her and in shamanic invocations she is sometimes addressed as "mother Itugen and the seventy-seven *itugen*." See also the section on the mother goddesses on pages 228–230.

The Nine Sons of the Sky

The nine sons of the sky are considered to be the eldest of the sky spirits and the ancestors and elders to all of the others. They comprise the chiefs of the four directions, Khan Sogto (north), Atai Ulaan (east), Aligan Sagaan (south), and Han Hormasta (west); the heavenly grandfathers Ubgen Yuruul and Esege Malaan; and the three patrons of religion, magic, and shamanism, Golto Sagaan, Shargai Noyon, and Buuluur Sagaan.

Ubgen Yuruul Tenger (oob-gen yoo-rool ten-ger): The eldest and most mysterious of the male deities, he was the mate of Ekhe Ekhe Burhan and the forefather all of the other *tenger*. He is said to be responsible for making the number three one of the basic principles of shamanic-magical practice. Esege Malaan Tenger, Khan Sogto Tenger, and Shargai Noyon Tenger are his three sons. He is not very active in the affairs of mankind at this time.

Esege Malaan Tenger (e-seg-eh mah-lahn ten-ger): The highest-ranking male sky spirit, he is regarded as responsible for the appearance of humans on earth. He is the spiritual father of all the sky spirits and has the greatest authority in their affairs.

Khan Sogto Tenger (hahn sog-ta ten-ger): Also known as Ariun Sagaan Tenger (*tenger* of purity), he is chief of the seventy-seven northern *tenger*. He is spiritual father to Huherdei Mergen and Hultei Hatan, patrons of storms.

Shargai Noyon Tenger (shahr-gai no-yun ten-ger): Shargai Noyon descended to earth to take residence in the Sayan Mountains in order to establish the present order of Siberian shamanism.

Aligan Sagaan Tenger (ahl-i-gen sah-gahn ten-ger): The leader of the ninety-nine sky spirits of the south and the father of Han Hormasta Tenger, Golto Sagaan Tenger, Buuluur Sagaan Tenger, and Atai Ulaan Tenger.

Han Hormasta Tenger: See "The Fifty-Five *Tenger*," below.

Golto Sagaan Tenger (gol-ta sah-gahn ten-ger): Meaning "white *tenger* of the *gol*," he is the patron of all religions and helper of all types of religious leaders, regardless of their tradition. He is the bringer of the eight wisdoms of the world and the leader of one thousand benevolent *burhan* spirits who assist in magical work.

Buuluur Sagaan Tenger: See "The Fifty-Five *Tenger*," below.

Atai Ulaan Tenger: See "The Forty-Five *Tenger*," on page 225.

The Fifty-Five *Tenger* of the Western Skies

1. **Han Hormasta Tenger** (hahn hor-mus-tah ten-ger): The second *tenger* to lead the western *tenger* after Esege Malaan Tenger. He is the father of Zasa Mergen Baatar, Bukhe Beligte (also known as Bukhe Tugelder or Abai Geser), and Habata Gerel (among others). His wife is Gere Sesen Ibii (her name means "mother wise in the house").

2. **Udaa Munhe Tenger** (oh-dah moon-heh ten-ger): The father and creator of the spirits of the waters of the western white tribe of sky spirits.

3. **Segeen Sebdeg Tenger** (say-gayn seb-deg ten-ger): Also known as Hahacaata Sagaan Tenger, he is the god of blue ice (winter). He is married to Ugan Sesen (oh-gun sehsun, "first

wisdom") and the father of Sesegen Nogoon (seh-seh-gehn naw-gone), goddess of spring. His daughter married Zasa Mergen Baatar, Abai Geser's older brother. In very ancient times he wavered in allegiance between the western *tenger* led by Han Hormasta and the eastern *tenger* led by Atai Ulaan. He is the spiritual father of the white-headed eagle, who is a messenger of the gods and helper of mankind. His oldest son has a fiery eye on the top of his head and a single tooth. His residence is in the high heavens of Oyor Sagaan Tenger, whose synonym is Garbal Tenger (*tenger* of ancestry).

4. **Buudal Uhan Huhe Tenger** (bow-dul oh-hun hoo-heh tenger): Creator and protector of all the earth's springs of medicinal or healing water.

5. **Homon Huhe Tenger** (hah-mun sah-gahn ten-ger): Another name for Hotoi Sagaan Tenger, spiritual father of Han Hormasta's son Uta Sagaan Noyon, who is master of Olkhon Island in Lake Baikal.

6. **Ugaal Sagaan Tenger** (oh-gahl sah-gahn ten-ger): Also known as Doloon Ungete Huhe Tenger (Seven-Colored Blue Heaven), who has control over when rain will fall; his name also recalls the seven colors of the rainbow. *Ugaal* means "cleansing," for he represents the cleansing power of rain on earth.

7. **Huhe Manhan Tenger** (hoo-heh mahn-hen ten-ger): Protector of human souls and of livestock. He gives blessing for reproduction and the increase of herds.

8. **Shara Hasar Tenger** (shah-ruh hah-ser ten-ger): Protector of the Sharyaat, Sharanut, and Hangilov clans.

9. **Buuluur Sagaan Tenger** (boo-loor sah-gahn ten-ger): Shamanic protector and spiritual father of the sky spirits and of shamans and elders. The great shaman of the heavens.

10. **Dabaan Joloo Tenger** (dah-bahn joh-lah ten-ger): Creator and father of the Darkhan Sagaan *Tenger* (the blacksmith gods), father of Bojintoi and his nine smiths and of their sister.

11. **Odon Sagaan Tenger** (aw-dun sah-gaan ten-ger): He is concerned with the highest levels of the *tenger*. He is the patron of the *sahius* spirits (shamanic protector spirits) of the biosphere and the informer of Han Hormasta *Tenger*. He watches all passages and entrances between the worlds and is aware of all offerings and worship made to the *tenger*.

12. **Khan Buudal Tenger** (hahn bow-dul ten-ger): Patron and administrator of ninety crucibles. He also has the name Khan Hyaha Ulaan Tenger (Red King Tenger of the Crucible). He lives in the northwestern direction. He loves the descendants and creations of the *tenger* on earth. Red colts are sacrificed to him or mares are dedicated to him and his wife,"Ulaan Noyon and Ulaajin Hatan." He is patron of the entrance to the upper world called *Tenger Sheree*, altar of the *tenger*, which is another symbol of the *gol*.

13. **Oyor Sagaan Tenger** (oh-yer sah-gahn ten-ger): Also known as Garbal Tenger (*tenger* of ancestry), he has a neutral position with regard to the authority of Esege Malaan Tenger, having his own power and authority. He is concerned with the education of souls for their spiritual growth and obtaining a more fortunate existence as they reincarnate. Offerings are made to his protégé Amitai Noyon (prince of shamanic tools), who is the patron of all shamanic attributes.

14. **Uurag Sagaan Tenger** (oh-rug sah-gahn ten-ger): Meaning "White Tenger of the First Milk." He is patron of the Hongoodor tribe. He is spiritual father to the Buudal *ongon* of the Hongoodor tribe, called Ulaan Zalaa Mergen Degei (Warrior of the Red Symbol), who has his dwelling place at Urig Pass-Arhag Mountain by the Urig River in the Sayan

Mountains. He sends wealth to the earth via his messengers, the swans.

15. **Bisalgan Sagaan Tenger** (bih-sil-gahn sah-gahn ten-ger): Also known as Pison Sagaan Tenger or Bajir Tenger Buudal, he is a patron of the Bargut tribe.

16. **Zada Sagaan Buudal Tenger** (zah-duh sah-gahn bow-dul tenger): Controls storms in the heavens. He sends *buudal udha* (shamanic initiator spirits sent directly from the sky) down to earth via certain meteorite stones called *zadai shuluun*, some of which can be used for the treatment of illness. These *zadai* stones are also used for weather magic—to bring rain or stop a storm.

17. **Budarguu Sagaan Tenger** (bow-dur-gee sah-gahn ten-ger): *Tenger* of the snowy sky, he is the patron of the Bulagat tribe and is said to be the father of three children—Uhaa Solbon Tenger, Bukha Noyon Baabai, and Sahyaadai Noyon (who with his wife Sahala Hatan is a deity of fire).

18. **Ishkhii Bayan Tenger** (ish-hee bah-yun ten-ger): Patron of wealth, abundance, and prosperity on earth.

19. **Hurei Bayan Tenger** (hoo-ray bah-yun ten-ger): Giver of descendants and patron of human reproduction and growth of families.

20. **Uhaa Solbon Tenger** (oh-hah sol-bun ten-ger): Creator of horses, known by the name Uuden Tenger (*tenger* of the gate) in sacrificial rituals, predestines shamans to the ninety-nine shamanic heavens, spirit of the evening and morning stars—Venus *(Solbon)*.

21. **Huhei Noyon Tenger** (hoo-hey no-yun ten-ger): Also known as Huhe Noyon Tenger (Blue Prince Tenger), he is the patron of the shamanic lineage Daibagarov. The shamans Ulaazar, Bahuunai, and their descendants Bugdan, Tangaraan, Balhai, who are honored in the Unga valley and Alar regions as the Goloi Turgeshuul (fast ones of the river)

at the *tailgan* called Turgeshuul, responsible for the shamanic spirits of the Unga, Osinsk, and Ilinsk valleys.

22. **Sahilgaan Sagaan Tenger** (sah-hil-gahn sah-gahn ten-ger): *Tenger* of white lightning, patron of all Mongols and Buryats, having thirteen aspects known as Buudal, the shamanic spirits conveyed by lightning *(neriyeer udha)*. Patron of the Khori-Tumet tribe, he watches over all living things of the earth. He keeps seventy-seven agents on earth in the form of Mongol blacksmiths. His protégé is Dayan Dabaanai Darkhat Mongol Khan ("Mongol Darkhat Khan of the Dayan Pass"). He is also the keeper of the light of the southwest direction and has thirteen *buudal* spirits in the Baikal region.

23. **Hute Buumal Tenger** (huu-teh bow-mul ten-ger): *Tenger* of milk, son of Esege Malaan Tenger, patron of all dairy products on earth.

24. **Buumal Sagaan Tenger** (bow-mul sah-gahn ten-ger): Patron of the Bulut clan and patron of the shaman spirits that descend to earth through meteors and other heavenly objects.

25. **Mender Zalaa Tenger** (men-dur zah-lah ten-ger): *Tenger* of hail. As patron and controller of hail and meteors, he has an executive and punitive office.

26. **Hundari Sagaan Tenger** (hohn-da ree sah-gahn ten-ger): Patron of marriages and matchmaking.

27. **Gutaar Bayan Tenger** (go-tahr bah-yun ten-ger): *Zayaasha* ("creator of destiny") for the shamanic *udha* and patron of morality and honor. He also has a punitive function.

28. **Khan Sagaan Tenger** (hahn sah-gahn ten-ger): White king *tenger*, patron and guide of the Buryat people, patron of nomads and travelers, spiritual father of Dalai Daiban Noyon.

29. **Noyon Sagaan Tenger** (no-yun sah-gahn ten-ger): White prince *tenger*, patron of royalty and politics, has authority over political office and fate. Patron of the shaman Noyon

Boo ("prince shaman"), he has authority over thirteen *khans* of the north; provider of the spirit of the Kuda Buryat *ongon* Ergil Buga Noyon Tunkhoo Galzuu, which contains five human souls (this *ongon* is also known as Holongoto Ubgen). The original spirit of this *ongon*, Ergil Buga Noyon, was the ancient reformer of Buryat shamanist practice.

30.   **Hun Sagaan Tenger** (hoon sah-gahn ten-ger): White man *tenger*, the manager of the *suld* souls of human beings, when they will be conceived. Arranges for the birth of the "shadow body" *(suld)*, arranges the birth of shamans, has authority over the physical body. In the *aranga* ceremony (funeral for shamans), he is referred to as "Eagle Feather."

31.   **Gal Ulaan Tenger** (gahl oh-lahn ten-ger): *Tenger* of the fiery red sky, he is the patron and shaper of fate for smiths. He has authority over the technological development of mankind and endows craftsmen with creative talent. He is also a determiner of *karma*.

32.   **Manha Malaan Tenger** (mahn-ha mah-lahn ten-ger): Patron and teacher of hermits and mystics, he also has authority over the intellectual development of children.

33.   **Oir Munhe Tenger** (oyr moon-heh ten-ger): Controls the ripening of fruit and the battle with harmful insects.

34.   **Zayaan Buudal Tenger** (zah-yahn bow-dul ten-ger): *Tenger* of fate, fights against evil spirits, is patron of *sahius* spirits (shamanic protector spirits), and controls success and fortune of human beings.

35.   **Altan Tenger** (ahl-tun ten-ger): *Tenger* of gold, controls the wealth buried in the earth, where deposits are located in the ground, sends nuggets. He also helps with education.

36.   **Huhe Zalaa Tenger** (hoo-heh zah-lah ten-ger): *Tenger* of the blue badge, controls growth of vegetation on earth. He is the patron of Bayan Hangai (master of the forest) and Oron Delhei (master spirit of earth).

37.   **Hajir Sagaan Tenger** (hah-jir sah-gahn ten-ger): Controls the
      biological energy of humans and is the patron of doctors
      and bonesetters (chiropractors).

39.   **Dun Sagaan Tenger** (dohn sah-gahn ten-ger): Controller of
      wealth, treasurer of the *tenger,* he is worshiped in the
      Hunshuulge and Tohon *duhaal* (dripping of butter)
      ceremonies.

40–43. **Hultei Halhin Tenger** (hool-tay hahl-heen ten-ger):
      Masters of the four west winds.

44–47. **Durben Emeershe Tenger** (door-ben eh-mehr-shun ten-ger):
      Tenger of the four breezes (gentle winds) of the west.

48.   **Oyodol Sagaan Tenger** (oh-yuh-dul sah-gahn ten-ger):
      Creates and sends to earth the *toli* (shaman mirrors) and
      controls their clarity and accuracy.

49.   **Somol Huhe Tenger** (saw-mul hoo-heh ten-ger): Controls
      geologically active zones on the earth and zones of turbu-
      lence in the sky.

50.   **Ohiruu Sagaan Tenger** (aw-hee-row sah-gahn ten-ger): Has
      authority over the shaman's *orgoi* (costume), patron and
      informer of who has been chosen by the spirits, calls
      meetings of the *tenger,* maintains connections between the
      tenger and the ten thousand *burhans* of the earth in the
      capacity of an envoy. He has control over the jurisdictions
      of the *tenger* and authority over the nine Garbal Tenger—
      Heer Noyon, Hoilongo Noyon, Huur Noyon, Hohim Noyon,
      Erite Noyon, Erdem Noyon, Gurel Noyon, Yashil Noyon, and
      Amitai Noyon.

51.   **Amitai Sagaan Tenger** (ahm-ih-tai sah-gahn ten-ger): A son
      of Ohiruu *Tenger,* he has authority over the Kurultai
      ("assembled") shamans, *noyons* (master spirits of the earth),
      and *buudals* (shaman spirits descended from the sky).

52.   **Yashil Sagaan Tenger** (yah-shil sah-gahn ten-ger): Has
      authority over those chosen to be political leaders, functions

as *ongon tenger* (*tenger* of inspiration), influences dreams of elected officials, shows the future to certain people, shows where mankind needs to go.

54. **Uran Sagaan Tenger** (oh-run sah-gahn ten-ger): White artistic *tenger,* the spirit of creativity, creates the elite group of actors, artists, astrologers, and composers. He controls the quality of architecture, landscaping, and sculpture and is present wherever there needs to be energy for creativity or healing.

55. **Urhe Uuden Tenger** (oor-heh oo-den ten-ger): *Tenger* of the gate and smoke hole, he carries out all commands of Esege Malaan Tenger, mediates between the *tenger* and mankind, and is closely associated with the *tengeriin uuden* (gateway between earth and the upper world).

The Forty-Four *Tenger* of the Eastern Skies

1. **Atai Ulaan Tenger**: (ah-tye-ah-lahn ten-ger) Also known as Galta Ulaan Tenger, he is the husband of Mayas Hara Toodei, and they are invoked together with the phrase *"Dulete Ulaan Atai, doshkhon Mayas Toodei!"* ("Fiery Atai Ulaan and fierce Mother Mayas"). He is the hard governor of punishments and the patron of horses and cattle. According to some myths, Abai Geser married his daughter Gaguurai Nogoon.

2. **Khan Boomo Tenger** (hahn baw-muh ten-ger): Also known as Makha Tenger or Makhasha Tenger, he is the patron of thirteen types of epidemic diseases of humans and animals, including plague and anthrax *(boomo).* He protects humans against all kinds of illnesses.

3–11. **Yuhen Shuhan Tenger** (yoo-hen show-hen ten-ger): The nine blood *tenger,* patrons of the blood of humans and animals and of sacrifices. They can be invoked when addressing problems of blood, heart, liver, or kidney disease.

12–24. **Asarangi Arban Gurban Tenger** (ahss-ren-gee ahr-bun gohr-bun ten-ger): The thirteen Asarangi Tenger, patrons

and governors of the activities of shamans, doctors, and
sorcerers. They function as a unity of patrons and protectors
of magic. They are honored by the placement of the *zuld*
(head, heart, and lungs) of game or livestock on the *aranga*
(platform for ceremonial burial).

25–33. **Hojiroi Doloon Tenger** (haw-jeer-oy daw-lawn ten-ger):
The seven Hojiroi Tenger, agents of Gujir Gunger Tenger,
giver of profit, plunder, and game (in hunting). They include
Godli Ulaan Tenger (Red Arrow *Tenger*), giver of the souls
of domestic animals; Zulhe Ulaan Tenger (Red Flow Tenger),
patron of war and defense; and Hara Maxa-Gal Tenger (Black
Flesh and Fire Tenger), father of the seven blacksmiths of
the east (and the seven stars of the Big Dipper). The remaining *tenger* of this group are the Bolinguud Tenger, patrons of
shamans, bards, and magicians.

34.   **Uhin Hara Tenger** (oh-hin hah-ra ten-ger): Manager of
diseases of girls and women as well as venereal disease.

35.   **Haraan Buudal Tenger** (hah-rahn bow-dul ten-ger): Patron
of clairvoyance and clairaudience.

36.   **Helin Hara Tenger** (hel-een heh-ra ten-ger): Also known as
Burhuu Hara Tenger, he is the controller of all kinds of
magic and has power over the energetic field of the human
spiritual body.

37.   **Gug Hara Tenger** (goog hah-ra ten-ger): Controller of the
two *udha* spirits known as Hara Mongol *udha* (Black Mongol
udha) and *Hiidan Manjur udha* (Kidan Manchu *udha*). He is
patron of the Evenk and Orochen tribes.

38.   **Tad Hara Tenger** (tahd hah-ra ten-ger): Patron of the eastern
blacksmiths of the heavens and of the shamans and girls of
the reindeer herders of the taiga forest.

39–41. **Gurban Manan Tenger** (gohr-bun mahn-un ten-ger): The
three *tenger* that control fogs, smoke, and mist.

42–44. **Gurban Boroon Buudal Tenger** (gohr-bun boh-rohn bow-dul ten-ger): The three *tenger* controlling rainstorms.

Other Important *Tenger:*

Bayan Hangai (bah-yun hahn-gai): The patron of the natural environment, he is pleased when drink offerings are made to him and when people clean the environment. He is offended by pollution, disrespect of plants and animals, and irresponsible hunting and harvesting of plants. He is so powerful that the other *tenger* do shamanic rituals to honor him. He is also known as Bayan Ahaa ("rich older brother"). Shrines are made to him by carving his face into a tree. Sometimes he will appear in the forest in the form of an unusual large game animal known as Orboli Sagaan Noyon (Prince White Deer).

Bukhe Beligte Tenger (boo-he beh-lik-tuh ten-ger): Son of Han Hormasta, he incarnated on earth as Abai Geser in order to save mankind and the environment from destruction. As Abai Geser he was the possessor of great shamanic power, and the stories of his exploits are a means of teaching shamanic tradition (the words of the epic stories are believed to possess magical power). He is the patron of justice and truth—his name means "all wise"—and he has great love and compassion for all living things. His consort is Alma Mergen Hatan (see *"Khans, Zayaans, and Master Spirits,"* below).

Dayan Deerh Tenger (die-yun dayrkh ten-ger): Patron of shamans, "the invincible," he represents the wild and aggressive aspects of shamanic practice. He is worshiped at a cave in the foothills of the Sayan Mountains in the Huvsgul region of Mongolia. Allthough *ongons* are not made for him, shamanists honor a drawing of him on horseback wearing armor and carrying a warrior's weapons.

Doloon Ubged (doh-lohn ub-gud): The Seven Old Men, the spirits of the seven stars of the Big Dipper. They represent the seven smiths of the eastern heavens and are patrons of black shamans.

Daichin Tenger (die-chin ten-ger): Patron *tenger* of soldiers and battle.

Dulen Tenger (dool-en ten-ger): *Tenger* of fireglow, northern lights, mysterious fires, radiation.

Eriin Tenger and **Hani Tenger** (ehr-een ten-ger, hahn-ee ten-ger): These *tenger* are worshiped as a pair. They are the patrons of male and female romantic love and sexual attraction. Shamans usually honor them by making offerings to a picture or sculpture of a man and woman.

Gujer Tenger (goo-jer ten-ger): *Tenger* in control of insults, gossip, lies, and slander.

Huherdei Mergen Tenger (hoo-her-day mayr-gun ten-ger): Brother of Han Hormasta, uncle of Bukhe Beligte *Tenger*, he is the head of the seventy-seven t*enger* of the northern skies. Lightning may be the manifestation of his arrows shot from the sky, especially when lightning strikes unexpectedly. Where his arrows strike, objects of great shamanic power are created. He is said to ride through outer space in a wagon drawn by winged horses. One of his wives is Sesegen Nogoon, daughter of Segeen Sebdeg Tenger (see above).

Tatai Tenger (tah-tie ten-ger): The *tenger* of storms, burns, and shocks. He has tremendous power for stopping storms, and Buryats invoke him when they suffer burns or electrical shocks. He is actually an aspect of Huherdei Mergen (see above).

The Great Mothers

Ekhe Ekhe Burhan (ehe yihe bohr-hun): The first of all the gods, she created the earth by having a duck bring mud from the depths of the ocean and placing it on the back of a turtle. She created all living things, then gave birth to her daughters, Manzan Gurme Toodei and Mayas Hara Toodei. When her daughters became mature, she retired to the highest heavens and now has little involvement in human affairs.

Golomt Eej (gol-umt eej): The mother of the place of the fire, also known as Golomto or Ut, she is an aspect of the mother goddess Umai as well as the patroness of the *gol*. As the mother goddess of the *gol*, she is revealed as being a manifestation of all the great mothers. In her aspect as Umai her name means "womb." Her other names are Nayinai and Omosi Mama (goddess of earth and mother of the *ami* souls).

Manzan Gurme Toodei (mahn-zun goor-meh too-day): Elder daughter of Ekhe Ekhe Burhan, ancestress of the fifty-five western *tenger*. She is the possessor of the greatest power and knowledge of all the sky spirits.

Mayas Hara Toodei (mah-yus hah-rah too-day): Younger daughter of Ekhe Ekhe Burhan, ancestress of the forty-four eastern *tenger*.

Khans, Zayaans, and Master Spirits (Ezen)

This is not a complete list of all these spirits, but it represents the most commonly honored ones. Each shaman will discover and work with many more than you see here.

Alma Mergen Hatan (ahl-ma mir-gen ha-tun): The daughter of Uha Loson (see below) and the consort of Bukhe Beligte Tenger (Abai Geser). She was one of the earliest and most powerful shamanesses in the history of mankind as well as a famous warrior woman. She is a patroness of battle and hunting and of shamanesses.

Erleg Khan (air-lek hahn): The master of the lower world, the judge of human souls. He determines where and when human souls reincarnate. He is said to have *besheeshe*, record keepers, who keep track of the karma of individuals so that each person gets assigned to a new life fairly and justly.

Gerel Noyon and **Tuyaa Hatan** (gehr-ul no-yun and toya hat-un): Uha Loson's son and his partner are water spirits, spirits of bright sparkling water.

Guruushe Noyon and **Guruushe Hatan** (goo-roo-sha no-yun and goo-roo-sha hat-un): Patrons of fishing with tackle.

Sahiaadai Noyon and **Sahal Hatan** (sah-hee-ya-dai no-yun and sa-hul hat-un): The spirits of the kindling of fire, being patrons of the flint and steel used to create fire and of the flames of the fire itself. They represent the lightning (flint) principle of the sky and the steel and fuel principle of female earth. They are different from Golomt Eej, who is the goddess of the fireplace as the site of the *gol*.

Uha Loson Khan and **Uhan Daban Hatan** (oh-hah low-sun hahn and oh-hun daw-bun hat-un): The chief of the *lus* spirits (master spirits of the waters) and his wife. Their daughter is Alma Mergen Hatan (see above). They are honored as chiefs of the nature spirits of the waters and are invoked while facing south.

Uir Sagaan Noyon and **Yotogor Sagaan Hatan** (oor sah-gahn no-yun and yo-toh-gor hat-un): The patron spirits of farmers.

Urgeshe Zayaan (oor-ge-sheh zah-yaan): *Zayaan* who controls trickery and gossip.

Ongons

This is a sampling of *ongons* that have widespread use among shamans, but it is by no means a comprehensive list, for many *ongons* are localized or are discovered by individual shamans during their work.

Abgaldai (ab-gul-dye): The bear ancestor *ongon*, this *ongon* is in the form of a copper mask that may be worn by the shaman on occasion. The mask usually is decorated with horsehair to represent bushy eyebrows, a mustache, and a beard.

Adaguusha (ada-goosh): *Ongon* of humor, an *ongon* made to bring blessing to those who perform comedy as a profession.

Altatan (ahl-ta-tun): A female *ongon* spirit for whom an *ongon* is created for the protection of young animals or children.

Anda Bars (ahn-da bahrss): A legendary shaman and hunter who is a patron of hunting. It is traditional to invoke him when game animals are killed. It is said that if he is ignored, he will cause hunters to get lost in the forest or suffer other hunting accidents. His name means "friend tiger." An important custom with regard to this *ongon* is not to feed it alcohol, because Anda Bars did not drink while he was alive and will be offended if it is offered to him.

Baljid (bahl-jid): The *ongon* of the daughter of the legendary shaman Burtu, her *ongon* is made to protect mothers and children at the time of birth and to protect infants from sudden crib death.

Ergil Buga (air-gyl boh-guh) or **Holongoto Ubgen** (haw-long-gaw-tuh oob-gun): *Ongon* of the legendary reformer of Siberian shamanism, his *ongon* is made of a skunk or sable skin. See page 214 for a more detailed account of his significance.

Gohosho (go-ho-sho): Patron *ongon* of fishermen.

Tur Khan (toor hahn): The patron *ongon* of the fertility of the earth, usually represented on *ongons* by a black horse.

Zar Zargaach (zahr zar-gotch): The spirit of wisdom and justice, this *ongon* is represented as a man without legs. His animal form is the porcupine. He is a protector when he is represented with porcupine quills. When he is represented as a regular *ongon*, he is a bringer of wisdom and success in lawsuits and other legal matters. His name means "judge and lawgiver," and he is a patron of lawyers, judges, and others involved in the practice and enforcement of law.

Zol Zayaach (zol zye-aahch): An *ongon* that brings good luck and protection to a household. It is created for families or for businesses to bring good fortune and success. Zol Zayaach is usually depicted as a man and woman standing side by side, representing the spirits Zayaasha Baabai (father of fate) and Zarlig Toodei (mother of justice). This *ongon* is decorated to commemorate good things that happen.

APPENDIX 3

The Nine Degrees
of Buryat Shamanic
Initiation

Known as *shanar*, there are nine degrees of Buryat shamanism, each
with its own initiation, attributes, and mastery of certain skills.
This does not mean that the instruments and skills associated with
certain degrees will not be used sooner, but it has been observed
from many generations that the full manifestation of these skills
comes over a period of eighteen years represented by the various
degrees and symbolized by the nine branches of the World Tree
(turge):[1]

1. ***Manjilaitai boo*** (newly initiated shaman): The first level has
    as its attributes a wooden staff (usually made of birch
    wood), fir bark for purification, and flint and steel for
    making ceremonial fires. This rank lasts three years and
    marks the beginning of doing shamanic work.

2. ***Noitolhon boo*** (baptized shaman): The shaman of the
    second degree is washed with the waters from nine differ-
    ent springs, preferably from his own ancestral homeland.

The attribute of this degree is a staff made from a gnarled branch. The shaman of this degree is entitled to perform sacrifices of sheep on behalf of his clan. This rank lasts three years.

3.   *Jodooto boo* (fir-tree shaman): The shaman of the third rank can freely contact any ancestral spirits from his own lineage as well as associate with and communicate freely with the master spirits of the place from which he derives his power, including the areas around it. A shaman of this degree is able to perform marriages. The attributes are the pipe and tobacco pouch and shaman whip. This rank lasts one year.

4.   *Shereete boo* (shaman with an altar): The fourth degree is actually an increase of the powers acquired in the third. A shaman strengthens his connection with the spirits associated with the previous level and is now able to communicate freely with the *khans* and *zayaans* that control the destiny of his nation as well as of his ancestral homelands and of the homeland of the *udha*. The attributes are the shamanic bell or cymbals (or *tingsha*), the *zele* (a rope made of natural animal hair used to lead or capture spirits), and the *sheree*, a chest to store shamanic tools that can be used as an altar. This rank lasts three years.

5.   *Hesete boo* (shaman with drums): The shaman of this degree has perfected the skill of merging with the *ongon* spirits. In recognition of this, he receives three drums—one made of cowhide, one of deer hide, and one of goat hide— as well as a drumstick. This rank lasts one year.

6.   *Horiboto boo* (shaman with a staff): The sixth rank, like the fourth, represents an increase in skill in performing the skills of the previous degree. A shaman will now no longer need musical instruments to induce the state of being

ongod orood. The attribute is a metal staff topped with a horse's head. The shaman will merge with the *ongons* while holding only the staff. This rank lasts three years.

7. **Tengeriin orgoito boo** (shaman with heaven's costume): The initiation of this degree involves a second baptism with *arshaan* that has been boiled with a stone from Lake Baikal that has been heated until it is red-hot. Afterward, the shaman is baptized with vodka and will worship Uha Loson Khan, master of the waters. He then receives the metal shaman crown and three more drums. The shaman of this rank can communicate freely with all of the spirits of the earth and sky. This rank lasts three years.

8. **Tengeriin orgoito buheli boo** (completed shaman with costume): The shaman of the eighth degree has mastered knowledge of all traditions and shamanic skills. He is fully capable of controlling wind, rain, and storms; can travel freely in all three worlds; and has fully mastered the skills of trance and meditation. The attributes are a wooden horse-headed staff decorated with jingle cones and ribbons of many colors and a hat decorated with the symbols of sun and fire. This rank lasts one year.

9. **Tengeriin tabilgatai zaarin boo** (great shaman with the mandate of heaven): This is the shaman who has fully mastered all shamanic and magical powers. He can control all types of weather, transport himself to any place while merged with the *ongon* spirits, and communicate with any being in physical or spiritual form anywhere in the universe. When a shaman achieves this degree, he receives three large drums with heads made of cow-, deer-, and goatskin. The attribute is a hat adorned with the sun and moon.

I would like to remind you of the importance of the "inner shamanic initiation." If you think about the amount of time that has elapsed since you acknowledged your shamanic calling and started doing shamanic work, you can look at the ranks listed above and judge for yourself (after all, only you and your *udha* know) which rank you have achieved. You may want to address some of the issues associated with the ranks you have already achieved. You may also feel moved to acquire the attributes of those degrees and use them as your *udha* directs.

Prayer to Abai Geser Bogdo Khan

This invocation is a very precious remnant of the literature of Mongolian shamanism. In the past there were many books of shamanic knowledge and invocations, but most of them were destroyed during the persecution of shamans by Tibetan lamas and Russian Orthodox missionaries. This invocation of Abai Geser was found in the remote village of Orlik in the Sayan Mountains by A. Dyrzhinov, a relative of Bayar Dugarov. What follows is a translation from the ancient Mongolian text, which I prepared with the assistance of Bayar Dugarov.

Invocations of Abai Geser are done for very specific reasons. They are used to stop drought, to stop epidemic diseases, and to protect the community from harm. In these turbulent times of human history he can be invoked to bring healing and peace to our troubled world as he did in the past. Abai Geser is powerful, wise, and honest. Do not invoke him carelessly. Invoke him with a focused mind; light a smudge bowl and offer him sacred smoke as you invoke him in a reverent and purposeful manner. This invocation is called a *sang*, which means that it is read while a smudge bowl or incense is burning in order to draw the spirit in and get his attention. Remember that sacred smoke is also used in *ariulga*, which is why the invocation repeatedly says "making a pure offering for cleansing," and you will see that the herbs normally used in this ceremony are specifically named within it. You can also use this invocation as a model for the shamanic invocations you may develop for your work in the future.

INCENSE-BURNING PRAYER FOR HOLY GESER KHAN

Om maahan! Om maahan! Om maahan!
You of the red lineage,
You with the reddish brown face,
With the golden topknot,
With one face and two fists,
With an arrow with the sign of the thunderbird in the right hand,
With a bow with the sign of the tiger in the left hand,
With a helmet like the sun,
With a shield like the moon on your shoulder,
With armor like the stars on your body,
With a sharp sword of knowledge in your hand,
With a saddle studded with lapis,
On your bay horse Beligen,
Holy Geser Khan,
I invite your from your pure land at this moment!
Abai Geser with the [mighty] name,
With your thirty warriors,
With your 360 leaders of your army I invoke you,
I gather the essence of a hundred billion beings
I offer a beautiful pure offering for cleansing.
I offer juniper, sandalwood, azalea, sage, thyme, and rhododendron,
I offer this to the lord of the ten directions,
Benevolent Geser Khan.
You who conquered the whole world,
Hubilgaan of the high tenger,
I offer a beautiful offering for cleansing.
You who have the power of all the burhans in your upper body,
You who have the power of eight lus and mountain spirits,

To Geser Khan I make a purifying offering.
To you who crushed the ferocious demons,
To mighty Geser Khan I make a purifying offering.
So that the deeds of religion and of the state are not confused,
I make an offering to Geser of the [mighty] name.
To him who exterminates and annihilates the enemies
That trouble the state and religion,
To Geser Khan I make a purifying offering.
In danger from fire you are like water,
In danger from wind you are like a mountain,
In danger from water you are like a boat,
In the face of the enemy you are like a thunderbolt,
To you fearsome Geser Khan I make a purifying offering.
In times of competition you are the giver of windhorse,
In times of shooting arrows you are the giver of accuracy,
In times of battle you are the giver of extra strength,
To you benevolent Geser Khan I make a purifying offering.
You gave speed to my favorite horse,

The author prays at the shamanist temple to Abai Geser near
Khujir in the eastern Sayan Mountains.

You became the spirit of my weak body,
You protected me like a hat,
You followed me majestically like a shadow,
To you benevolent holy Geser Khan I make a purifying offering.
To he who rides the blood red horse on the red cliff,
To [Daichin Tenger's] hubilgaan I make a purifying offering.[1]
To they who have a yellow dog going before and a flying raven
I worship the nine Dalha Tenger of the standard,[2]
To the guardian of limitless power of the white direction,
To the master of Donjing Garabuu Mountain [3]
I make a purifying offering.
To the tenger, water spirits, *and nature spirits of this mountainous world*
I make a purifying offering.
To Dayan Deerh of unequaled power and his companions
I make a purifying offering.
Devastate the enemies of the state.
Annihilate the enemies of religion.
Grant us peace and happiness.
Make windhorse spread.
May you make buyan *increase.*
In business grant magic power to increase profit,
In our travels grant us opportunity for gain.
On the hunt may we find game
And may the saddle straps be full.
Please make all these things happen quickly.
Gi gi suu suu lha-a yi luu
Gundu saravan duu duu hum.
Bajar ayuki suuha.[4]
Manggalam.

Glossary and List of Magical Phrases

Note: All Mongolian words are accented on the first syllable except when the second syllable has a double vowel (such as the words *joroo* and *shigshuur*), in which case the second syllable is stressed. This is especially important to remember when you are using magic words because they must be pronounced correctly in order to be effective.[1]

aba (ah-buh): Psychic power, paranormal abilities.

Abai Geser (ah-bai geh-sur): The name of Bukhe Beligte Tenger when he incarnated on earth in order to cleanse the world and save living things. As a shaman-hero, his actions illustrate the various techniques that shamans can use in their work. The epic about him is the chief teaching story of shamanism and the closest thing that Siberian shamanists have to a holy book, although it was traditionally transmitted orally from shaman to shaman. Unfortunately, the persecution of shamanism under Soviet rule resulted in the loss of the Geser epic among most Siberian peoples and it was written down (and thereby preserved) only by the Buryats, Mongols, and Tuvans. The most complete version is that of the western Buryats. A translation of the Geser epic into the English language will be published soon.

abaral (ah-bah-rul): Divination and performing magic.

ahanad (ah-ha-nahd): The leading shaman in a ritual in which several shamans are participating. Traditionally the *ahanad* is the oldest or most experienced shaman.

aikha (eye-haa): Sacred grove used for shamanic ceremonies. It is forbidden to cut trees from such a place except for making wooden objects for shamanic ritual.

alba (ahl-ba): Meaning "performing of duty," this is a ceremony asking the spirits to protect male members of the family.

ami (em): The upper-world soul of human beings, passed down through families.

amiluulah (em-i-low-lakh): The process of awakening the master spirit of an item, usually *ongons* or drums, with spiritual power.

amin tahalha (em ta-hul-ha): The separation of the *ami* from the body, meaning soul loss or death.

amitai (em-eh-teh): Meaning "alive," this refers to the living nature of an object that has been awakened (see **amiluulah**).

ara ner (ahra ner): The professional name of a shaman, which is usually different from his birth name. The *ara ner* is usually given to the shaman by his spirit helpers.

aranga (ahr-un-gah): The platform on which shamans were traditionally buried with their equipment. Because bears are believed to be shamans among the animals, the skull and bones of a bear are also placed on the *aranga*.

ariulga (ahr-ee-oh-luk): Spiritual purification, done with smudging of sacred smoke, application of energized water *(arshaan)*, or sometimes other substances.

ariun (ahr-ee-yohn): Spiritually clean.

arsa (ahr-sah): See **juniper**.

arshaan (ahr-shahn): Energized liquid, used in purification and healing.

arza (ahr-zah): The traditional ceremonial liquor of Siberian shamanism. It is distilled from fermented milk. Vodka now is used instead because *arza* has become rare.

ataatai boo (ah-tah-tie boo): A shaman who practices black magic; a malevolent shaman.

ayagtai boo (ayug-tie boo): A shaman with a creative and emotionally sensitive nature.

baabgain naadam (baab-ga-yin nah-dum): The bear dance, in which the shaman imitates the bear while merged with the spirits.

barisaa (bear-ih-sah): Sacred tree; a tree shrine representing the World Tree and established through tradition or by shamanic ritual as a representation of the World Tree.

Bear: One of the two great shaman animals, Bear and Eagle. Bear, associated with the east, is a conductor of souls on their way to the lower world after death.

bohirson (baw-her-sun): Being in a condition of spiritual pollution.

boo (buu): Male shaman. Female shamans are called *udagan* (see below).

boolehe (buu-le-he): To shamanize, to act in the role of a shaman.

bookholdoi (baw-hul-die): A haunting spirit, responsible for poltergeist activity, usually an unsettled *suns* or (rarely) the *suld* soul of a dead person.

burhan (bohr-hun): A type of nature spirit, usually very strong. *Burhan* exist in all three worlds. Some are benevolent, others are destructive.

butur (boo-toor): A shaman who has not responded to the calling of the spirits.

buumal (bow-mul): Something considered to have been sent down from the spirits for use by shamans. The heavenly origin of these things gives them great power. *Buumal* objects are usually meteorites, lightning-struck stones, or ancient artifacts. Some *buumal* objects are sent down from the sky as a way of bringing new *udha* spirits into the world.

buyan (boy-in): Spiritual merit, accumulated by benevolent and constructive actions. Accumulation of *buyan* raises a person's windhorse.

buzar (bow-zur): See **bohirson**.

chotgor (shoot-gur): A destructive spirit, usually a human *suns* soul that has failed to return to the lower world after death. *Chotgor* are a common cause of disease.

dalbuur (dahl-bohr): A shaman's spirit fan, usually made of horsehair tied to a forked stick or from a feather fan.

dallaga (dah-la-gah): A ritual to gather in spiritual power and blessing, performed by moving the hands clockwise before the body with the palms up while saying the magic words *"hurai, hurai, hurai!"* If the *dallaga* is done for a family or group, offerings of food and money may be put onto plates or into bags and participants will follow the shaman in doing the *dallaga* while holding the bags or plates. The offerings will please the spirits and thus will be endowed with spiritual power (becoming a type of *arshaan*).

Dolbor (dahl-bur): The World River, running from the upper world to the lower world, representing the flow and merging of spiritual consciousness. Each shaman has access to this river in journeying.

dom (dom): Magically empowered action or magic spell.

domtoi (dom-toy): An object that is imbued with magical power.

durdalga (dor-dul-gah): A shamanic invocation consisting of naming of the spirits the shaman wants to be present and then a statement of the shaman's intentions; literally, "calling."

Eagle: Eagle is believed to have been the first shaman. The white-headed eagle was sent down to earth by Segeen Sebdeg Tenger in very ancient times to bring healing when illness first appeared on earth.

erih (airkh): String of beads used for bead divination.

ezen, ezed (ez-en, ez-ed): An *ezen* is the nature spirit inhabiting a certain place or object such as a tree or stone. *Ezed* is the plural of *ezen*.

ezetei (ez-e-tay): An object or place that has an *ezen*, such as shamanic tools, trees, or rocks.

fir: Known as *jodoo* in Mongolian, this is a smudging herb used only by shamans. Both fronds and pieces of bark are used for smudging. Bark from firs scratched by bears is considered to be especially powerful.

gal (gahl): Literally, "fire." The word comes from the same root as *gol*.

galab (gah-lup): Very ancient times, thousands of years ago when Abai Geser and Shargai Noyon lived on earth and established the shamanic traditions.

gavia (gah-vee-yah): Merit gained from serving one's community. *Gavia*, like *buyan*, adds to windhorse.

gazar humihe (gah-zur hoo-mee-heh): Bending space and time in order to travel quickly in the spiritual or physical world.

gazarai urhe (gaz-er-ai ur-he): Literally, "smoke hole of the earth," the tunnel connecting the earth with the lower world. Also see **tengeriin uuden**.

ger (geer): The traditional dwelling in Mongolia and Siberia. Its layout, oriented to the four directions, is the same as that of the shamanic ritual space and reflects the traditional view of the structure of the universe.

gol (gohl): The center, the world center, the center of all existence where all time, places, and possibilities meet. It is represented by fire, the *oboo*, the World Tree, Humber Uula, and Dolbor.

golomt: See **gulamta**.

guideg (gwee-deg): Meaning "course" or "pathway," the process of reincarnation of human souls.

gulamta (gohl-um-ta): Also known as *gal gulamta*, the place of the fire, a symbol for the *gol*. This is also spelled *golomt* or *golomto* in some dialects.

habatai boo (hah-bah-tie boo): A shaman who has greater-than-normal extrasensory perception or magical powers; a wizard.

hadag (hah-duk): A strip of white or blue silk, usually about a foot wide and three to six feet long, used in shamanic ritual. *Hadags* are attached to sacred objects, and gifts to the shaman are usually presented with *hadags*. A blue *hadag* honors a low-ranking shaman; a white *hadag* honors a highly respected shaman.

hanhinuur (hah-hee-noor): Also known as a *holbogo*; a type of bell resembling the jingle cones that adorn some types of Native American clothing. It is attached to a shaman's clothing, drums, and other shamanic equipment.

has temdeg (hahss tem-dek): Also known as **has tamga**, this symbol resembles the swastika but its alignment of lines is vertical and horizontal rather than rotated 45 degrees, as in the Nazi symbol. It represents the rotation of the Big Dipper around the polestar and also represents the sun. The sun symbol has a variant consisting of two swastikas drawn over each other, one with a vertical alignment and another rotated 45 degrees. This creates a sunburst effect with eight lines radiating from the center, representing the *naiman hultei naran eej,* "mother sun of eight rays."

helme (hell-meh): Also known as *selem,* the magical knife-sword of the shaman.

hese (heh-suh): Also called *hengereg* (hen-gur-ek), this is the name of the shaman drum. The shaman drum is also called a *dungur* (doon-goor) in some parts of Mongolia and Buryatia and in Tuva.

hiimori (hee-mur): Literally, "windhorse"; personal spiritual energy.

hoimor (hoy-mur): The sacred place within the ritual circle; the location of the altar, normally situated on the north side.

holongo (haw-lon-goh): Also called *solongo* (saw-lon-goh), "rainbow." Rainbows are bridges between the earth and the heavens.

Hongoodor (hawn-gaw-der): Buryat tribe native to the eastern Sayan Mountains.

hoomei (hoo-mee): Throat singing, consisting of a base tone and whistling overtones representing the merging of spiritual and physical worlds within the shaman. *Hoomei* was traditionally used in worship; now, however, Mongolian and Tuvan singers perform *hoomei* in a nonreligious context.

horiboo (hoe-ri-boh): The shaman staff. It has several different forms and magical properties.

hubilgaan (hoh-bill-gahn): Meaning "transformation," this refers to the different forms that shamans and other spirits shape-shift into during shamanic work. *Hubilgaan* also means "reincarnation," for in every life human souls occupy a body with a different form.

huch (hooch): Spiritual power or force.

Humber Uula (hoom-ber ohl): The mythical mountain at the center of the world, it connects the earth, the upper world, and the lower world. It is one of the symbols for the *gol*.

huraaha (hoh-rah-kha): Gathering, symbolized by the circular gesture during shamanic ritual. *Huraaha* uses the magical word *hurai*, which is said three times while moving the hands clockwise in a gesture of gathering energy.

huur (hohr): The instrument used by a shaman in shamanic work.

id shid (id shid): Magical power; these words are usually used together as a phrase.

ilbe (ill-beh): Psychic-spiritual energy, the ability to hypnotize.

ili biye (ila bee-yuh): Literally, "brief body." This refers to the physical or visible aspect of a person's body.

ilibe biye (ili-beh bee-yuh): The spiritual aspect of a person's body. This phrase is related to the word *ilbe*, which means "psychic power," for the spiritual body can be manipulated by spiritual/psychic forces.

joroo (joh-roh): The custom of sharing the food and drink offerings brought to a ceremony among the participants in order to share in the spiritual energy that the spirits have put into them.

juniper: The chief smudging herb of Mongolian and Siberian shamanism. It is used both for cleansing and for pleasing the spirits with the offering of its smoke. Juniper from the homeland of the shaman using it or from mountainous regions is believed to have the greatest spiritual power.

khan (hahn): One of the types of upper-world spirits, less powerful than the *tenger* but stronger than human souls. Khans are invoked for help in shamanic work.

lus (lowss): Spirits of the waters. *Lus* are especially important in black shamanic tradition but are honored by all shamans. They may appear in human form or in the form of fish, snakes, or dragons. Their leader is Uha Loson (see page 230). They are very powerful and can exact terrible revenge in response to acts polluting water.

magtaal (mahg-tahl): A shaman song in praise of the spirits. The most skilled and talented shamans compose their own *magtaal* and can improvise new *magtaal* during rituals, but there are many traditional *magtaal* passed down from ancient times. *Magtaal* often alternate regular singing with *hoomei* (throat singing).

maihabsha (my-hub-shuh): The antlered crown of the advanced shaman.

mense (men-seh): The money given to a shaman for his services. It is forbidden for a shaman to state a price; each person must determine for himself according to his ability to pay. The *mense* is not believed to be compensation for the shaman; rather, it is a gift to the spirits in gratitude for their help. In addition to money, food, shamanic implements, fur, or cloth will be given to the shaman as part of the *mense*.

minaa (mih-naah): See **tashuur**.

mur (moor): Literally, "trail." Related to the word *murun*, which means "river."

mushin (moo-shin) or **mushid** (moo-shid): The Pleiades, the home of Manzan Gurme Toodei and the meeting place of the sky spirits. The Pleiades have six stars and the Big Dipper has seven, adding up to the magic number thirteen. The shamanic practice of burning thirteen sticks of incense in ceremonies honors the western *tenger*, who are associated with the Pleiades, and the eastern *tenger*, who are associated with the Big Dipper. In Siberian tradition the Pleiades bring the cold weather of winter when they appear in the sky; thus they are also known as *Ulger* (the holes in the sky), which bring the coldness of outer space to the earth. The sacred teaching story of Abai Geser is recited only when the Pleiades are visible in the night sky.[2]

muu shubuun (moe shoh-bohn): Meaning "bad bird," this is a type of *chotgor* usually found in the forest. It appears as a bird with a human head and is a manifestation of a female spirit who died tragically and did not return to the lower world.

naadan (naa-dun): Literally, "play." This word has two meanings in shamanic ritual. The first is "dance," there being several different shaman dances. They include the **yohor** (see below), the bear dance (see above), the goat dance, the wolf dance, the eagle dance, the dance of breaking the horse, the bee dance, and the grouse dance. With the exception of the *yohor*, all of these dances are imitative, for it is believed that the shaman merges consciousness with the animal whose name is associated with these various dances. In the dance of breaking the horse, for example, the shaman imitates a rider taming a wild horse. The second meaning of *naadan* is the games of archery, wrestling, and horse racing. When a large ceremony is done at an *oboo*, it is customary to perform all three— three people will race horses, someone will shoot three arrows, and there are three wrestling matches.

naiguur (nai-goor): A shamanic ritual for people who are depressed. The shaman and many people in addition to the depressed person will sing, swaying and dancing, until all reach an ecstatic state. This was an effective treatment for depression in Siberia before the advent of modern psychiatry.

naija (nai-zha): Literally, "friend"; a *naija* is like a shamanic godparent, a shaman pledged to the spiritual protection and health of a child. The *naija* is also called *boo baabai* ("shaman father") or *boo baatar* ("shaman hero") in recognition of his vital role in guaranteeing spiritual safety and long life for the child.

Nishan (nee-shahn): A legendary shamaness said to have lived in Inner Mongolia hundreds of years ago.[3]

nugeltei (noo-gel-tay): "Taboo," "sinful," meaning that a thing is harmful to one's *buyan*.

oboo (oh-boh): An *oboo* is a shamanic shrine that symbolizes Humber Uula, the World Tree, and the *gol*. *Oboos* can be made out of a pile of stones or from one or more wooden poles.

ochir: Also known as a *dorji*, the *ochir* is a piece of brass representing lightning that is usually sold together with Tibetan bells. In Mongolian and Siberian shamanic tradition it is a channel for spiritual energy and is held upright between the thumb and index finger or thumb and middle finger while the bell is being rung. The word *ochir* means "lightning."

ongod orood (on-gud or-ahd): The shamanic state of having one or more shamanic helper spirits in possession of the shaman's body.

ongon (on-gun): A physical object that is used as a representation of the presence of a certain shamanic spirit. This word also refers to shamanic spirits, as in the expression *ongod orood*.

ongon hirbee daida (on-gon heer-bay dai-dah): "The sacred land," a phrase acknowledging that the land is sacred because it is inhabited by the spirits of the ancestors and by the nature spirits who protect and maintain the ecology of the natural world.

orba (ohr-bah or ohr-ruv): The shaman's drumstick, which has its own uses outside of drumming. A shaman may use the *orba* without the drum for certain ritual actions.

orgoi (oar-goy): The ceremonial costume of the shaman used for journeying and other high rituals.

Owl: Owl is believed to be a patron of shamans, especially the eagle-owl of Siberia. Owl feathers as well as eagle feathers adorn shamans' headdresses. Owl feathers are also believed to have great power for protecting newborn children and will be placed near the cradle.

porcupine: The animal manifestation of the *ongon* Zar Zargaach, an animal of great wisdom and protective power.

sab-shim (sahb-shim): Meaning "container and essence," this is an analogy of the physical body *(ili biye)* to the spiritual body *(ilibe biye)*.

sabdag (sahb-dug): *Ezen* spirits of a hill or mountain, either male or female. They are often invoked together in the phrase *"lus sabdag nar,"* meaning "spirits of the waters and mountains," a collective address for all nature spirits.

Sagaan Ubgen (sah-gahn oob-gun): Meaning "white old man," a representation of **Esege Malaan Tenger** (see 217). He is often represented in Mongolian and Buryat art as an old man carrying a staff similar to a shaman staff adorned with a carving of a dragon head.

sahius (sah-hee-ohss): Literally, "protector spirit." This is another term for shamanic helper spirits. This word also refers to the shaman's medicine bag because the bag is imbued with the power of the helper spirits.

Sayan Mountains: A mountain range located in western Buryatia, Tuva, and Siberia and in the northern part of the Huvsgul region of Mongolia. This is the core homeland of Mongolian and southern Siberian shamanic traditions (see the story of the origin of shamanism in appendix 2).

serge (sayr-geh): A wooden post six or more feet high with a pointed head that may be used as an *oboo*, a representation of the *gol*. Other types of *serge* were historically used as hitching posts. Ribbons and horsehair are tied to the *serge* when people pray to the spirits.

serjim (sayr-jim): A magical ritual that invokes power through the scattering of various substances as offerings to the spirits.

seterleh (seh-ter-lekh or heh-ter-lekh): The giving of an animal to the spirits in lieu of butchering it and offering the meat. This is a preferable, nonviolent alternative to the old custom of making sacrifices. The shaman ties as many as nine colors of ribbons on the fur of the animal and the animal is allowed to run free without being ridden or shorn (depending on whether it is a horse, sheep, goat, or reindeer). At least blue and white *hadags* are tied onto the animals; ideally there should be nine colors of ribbon, including white, blue, red, green, yellow, and black. When the animal gets old it may be butchered and eaten, but a shaman may do a ceremony to dedicate another animal if the spirits desire it. In some cases the animal is a living *ongon* of a certain spirit, such as in the *shara tekhe* ceremony in which the protector spirit of boys is brought into a yellow billy goat to protect the boy until he reaches maturity.

setgel (set-gul or hed-khel): The center of human consciousness and spiritual power located in the chest. It is like the *gol* of the spiritual body.

sheree (shih-ray): A table used for the placement of ritual objects, *ongons*, and offerings to the spirits. The *sheree* is one of the important tools of a shaman, for a shaman's own *sheree* is a trunk or chest in which sacred objects are stored between rituals.

shigshuur (shig-shoor): Shaman's rattle.

Shoshoolog (shaw-shaw-lik): The highest-ranking shamanic clan. In rituals, a Shoshoolog shaman is *ahanad* even if he is not the eldest or most experienced, in deference to his connection with the founders of shamanic traditions.

shuleye abtaha (shoo-laya ab-ta-ha): Loss of spiritual energy and power due to attack by a spirit or hostile shaman.

smudge: A bundle or burning bowl of aromatic herbs that are burned for the purpose of clensing and raising windhorse for ritual. In Mongolian this is known as *utalga*, "sacred smoke."

snake: Snakes represent the connection between the shaman and other worlds. The tassels that adorn the shaman costume in Mongolia and Siberia are called snakes *(mogoi)*. The whip of the shaman is visualized as a magical snake, and the spiritual steed of the shaman sometimes takes the form of a giant snake. Snakes are thought to be manifestations of the *lus* (water spirits). The earth is believed to be the home of one or more giant yellow snakes, whose tracks created the courses of rivers in ancient times.

suld (soold): The non-reincarnating soul of humans. It resides at the crown of the head. After death it lives on as a nature spirit.

suns (soonss): The human soul that originates in the lower world. It can reincarnate anywhere and does not follow lineages.

suns daraad (soons dah-rahd): Soul repression.

suns geeh (soons gaykh): Soul loss.

sunsnii mur (soonss-nee moor): Literally, "trail of the spirit." This is the lineage of successive shamans associated with a certain *udha* spirit.

sunwise: In a clockwise motion, for this direction is held by most native peoples to reflect the movement of the sun.

tahil or *tahilga* (ta-khil or ta-khil-gah): General term for a shamanic ceremony done for a household or small group. If the ceremony is performed for an entire community, it may be referred to as a *tailgan* (tile-gun). In a *tailgan* several shamans may work together. More than one shaman may work in a *tahil*, but usually no more than two.

tailgan: See *tahil.*

tamga (tahm-guh): The personal power symbol of the shaman. During his initiation, a shaman will make a mark of his *tamga* on the World Tree as confirmation of the shamanic calling. Each shaman's *tamga* is unique, and it is revealed to the shaman by the spirits as part of the shamanic calling.

tarim (teh-rim): Shamanic exorcism, or shamanic treatment of an illness done in conjunction with treatments by an herbalist.

tashuur (tah-shore): The shaman's magic whip, also known as a *minaa*, often made from a horsetail with a handle fashioned of willow or tamarisk wood.

tayag (tah-yuk): See **horiboo.**

tegsh (tegsh): The principle of balance in one's personal life or in the world.

tenger (ten-gur): The most powerful upper-world spirits, they are believed to belong to four groupings associated with the four directions. They should not be confused with Tenger Esege, Father Heaven.

tengeriin uuden (ten-ger-een oo-den): The gateway between the earth and the upper world. See **gazarai urhe.**

Terte (tur-teh): Shamanic lineage to which the author belongs. The Terte clan has its origins in the Huvsgul region of Mongolia.

togoljin (to-gul-jin): Ward *ongons* set at the four directions in the shamanic ritual space.

toiroho (toy-roh-ho): The shamanic practice of walking around the ritual circle sunwise in multiples of three (usually three, nine, or twenty-seven). *Toiroho* means "to go around." In doing fire or *oboo* rituals, the shaman will walk around the fire or *oboo.*

toli (toyl): The shaman mirror, circular in form, usually made of bronze, iron, silver, or nephrite.

tonog (taw-nuk): The equipment used by the shaman.

tonogoi ezen (toh-nog-oy ez-un): The master spirits of shamanic equipment. An important part of shamanic initiation is to contact and identify the *ezen* of the various pieces of equipment a shaman uses.

tsats (tsots): See **zolig**.

tsatsal (tsaat-sul or sah-sul): The ceremonial spoon used in *tsatsah*, the sprinkling of liquids to the spirits in shamanic ritual and in the magical act called *serjim*. In some rituals the spoon may be thrown toward the sky for divination and to send messages to the upper-world spirits.

tsog (tsok): Spiritual energy, perceptible as fire or electricity.

turge (toor-geh): The World Tree, linking all three worlds, a symbolic representation of the *gol*. This also refers to a ceremonial tree representing the world's *turge* that is erected in some shamanic rituals. The difference between a ritual *turge* tree and a *barisaa* is that the *turge* is a cut or uprooted tree while a *barisaa* is a living tree. This tree is also known as *toroo* (toh-roh).

twaalah (twaah-lakh): The gentle rocking movement of shamans in trance.

udagan (ohd-gun): Female shaman, also spelled *odigon*.

udha (ohd-hah): The chief helper spirit of a shaman that chooses, instructs, and initiates. An *udha* will draw in additional helper spirits for the shaman. Some *udha* are compound spirits with one entity most dominant.

Umai (oh-my): The womb goddess. Umai sends *ami* souls from the upper world into babies being born. Also see **Golomt Eej** on page 229.

windhorse: Personal spiritual power, the source of psychic abilities and personal dynamism. Windhorse is increased by *buyan*, the merit earned by doing things to help other people and to restore balance in the world.

World Tree: See **turge**.

yabdal (yahb-dul): Shamanic journey; also called *ayalal*.

yohor (yo-hohr): A shamanic round dance in which the participants join hands in a circle and then dance clockwise around a sacred tree, a fire, or a shaman. It raises a spiral of energy that empowers the dancers and aids the shaman on his journey.

zaarin (zai-run): A shaman who has been initiated into all nine degrees of shamanism.

zadai (zah-dye): A stone used for weather magic. It is either an unusual stone or a stone taken from the stomach of an animal (bezoar).

zagalmai (zah-gul-mai): Cross symbol representing a flying hawk or the winged deer of the goddess Umai (the swan-deer).

zalaa (zah-lah): Strips of ribbon or animal fur that adorn shaman costumes or sacred objects. Ribbons made of squirrel fur or from the fur of members of the weasel family are the badge of a shaman. In Siberia, the type of fur used is determined by the tribe of the shaman.

zasal (zah-sul or zah-hul): Literally, "repair." This is the action a shaman must take to solve a particular problem.

zayaa (zah-yaah): Fate, karma, a person's destiny.

zayaan (zah-yaahn): A type of upper-world spirit, *zayaans* are believed to have the power to determine a person's destiny. Many *zayaans* were shamans in a past human incarnation.

zolig (zoh-lik): A representation of a person or dog that is used as a temporary *ongon* to receive a disease spirit or malevolent spirit during the process of a healing. The *zolig* is destroyed as a part of the exorcism ritual.

zuheli (zoo-hel-ee): The head and hide of an animal that was cooked as an offering to the spirits. The hide is put on a pole so that the head looks up toward the sky.

zulai (zoh-lie): The crown chakra, the point at which energy from the sky enters the body. Working with the *zulai* can have beneficial effects in healing, but touching the *zulai* of other people is taboo because interfering with it can cause harm.

zuld (zoold): The head, throat, heart, and lungs of an animal. When an animal is butchered in the traditional way, this is removed as one piece because it is believed to contain the *ami* soul of the animal and not damaging the *zuld* will ensure its quick reincarnation. In shamanic ritual, when animals are offered to the spirits the *zuld* is believed to be the meat most beloved.

Magical Phrases

Buugit! (bow-geet): This phrase is used when the shaman is calling the *ongon* spirits. Literally "come down," it means that the shaman is encouraging the spirits to merge consciousness with him.

Chok! (chok): Also *seeg* (seyg) or *suug* (sook), this word is said three times at the beginning and end of shamanic invocations. A ritual may include multiple invocations and this phrase is uttered with each one. This word may also be said at the end of a shamanic journey.

Dom, dom, dom!: A phrase said before an invocation to tell the spirits that the shaman intends to cast a spell *(dom)*.

Eh hairhan! (eh hayr-hahn): Used in shamanic invocations to express great respect, usually inserted between phrases of the invocation.

Em dom bolo! (em doom bah-look): Literally, "become medicine and a spell!" This phrase is said after the shaman has created a *domtoi* object in order to imbue it with the intention and energy of the spell.

Hoyor sagai negende! (hoh-yur saag-ay neh-gun-deh): "Two times becoming as one." This is perhaps the most powerful magical phrase of Buryat shamanism. The shouting of these words unites the time of intention with the time of manifestation through the power of the *gol.* This can also be said as *Ene sagahaa hoisho hoyor sagai negende,* meaning "From this time onward, two times becoming as one."

Hurai, hurai, hurai! (hooray, hooray, hooray): This phrase is accompanied by the gesture of moving one or both hands in front of the body in a clockwise direction, going once around for each time *hurai* is pronounced. The word and gesture together gather energy. This may be repeated several times during an invocation following each statement of a specific intention, thereby direct-ing energy to each intention. Some Siberian peoples say this as *Ai hurai, ai hurai, ai hurai!* but it has the same meaning and effect

Ikra! (ee-krah): An untranslatable phrase usually said while the shaman is merged with the spirits, meaning that the spirits desire something to drink or a pipe to smoke.

Manggalam! (man-gah-lam): A word used to conclude a series of statements of intention in an invocation. It always precedes the use of *chok* or *om maahan* and follows the use of *hurai.*

Muu yum saashaa! (moe yoom sah-shah): Literally, "Bad things go away!" This phrase has great power in expelling negative energy and averting sudden danger, especially if said three or nine times.

Om maahan! (ohm maa-hun): An adaptation of the Tibetan phrase *om mani padme hum* ("jewel in the lotus"), which is known throughout Asia for its magical power. It is usually pro-nounced three times before and after statements of intentions in order to energize them with spiritual power. This phrase may be also said as *aa hum* (ah hoom).

Seer! (sayr): "May it be forbidden!" meaning that something is *nugeltei* (defined above).

Tooreg! (too-rek): This word is shouted when a shaman throws the ritual liquid out of the cup when doing *serjim*. It tells the spirits to reveal information about the results of the *serjim* in the pattern of the splash of the liquid. A shaman may instead throw the cup for a simple yes-no answer and will shout *"Tooreg!"* In this case, if the cup lands right-side up the answer is yes; otherwise it is no.

Uragshaa burhan zailuul! (oh-rug-shah bore-hun zai-lool): Literally, "Go forward, may the spirits repel bad things!" This is used to repel danger and the arrival of bad spirits. Some Buryats say this phrase after someone sneezes so that *chotgor* will not attack the person who is sick. *Uragshaa* means "Go ahead into the future," implying going bravely forward with the power of the spirits, and it is in itself a powerful phrase.

Urshoo! (oor-shoo): Often said three times, it is usually repeated several times during shamanic prayers in the transition from the calling of the spirits to the stating of the shaman's intention. This phrase means "Forgive me, pay attention to what I ask."

Notes

Introduction

1. In fact, as you read this book and *Riding Windhorses*, you may notice that I do incorporate some quotes and practices that are Yakut and Evenk in origin. The reason is that both of these peoples were heavily influenced by Buryat shamanic traditions. In fact, in more recent times, when Buryat shamans were persecuted by Russian Orthodox missionaries and Tibetan Buddhist lamas (then finally by the Communists), some Buryat shamanic traditions were lost or corrupted. The Evenks, whose shamanism was largely adapted from the Buryat tradition, live in more remote areas and therefore have preserved some old Buryat customs and traditions. This is also true, to some extent, of the Yakuts. In the case of the Tuvans and Altaians, who along with the Buryats were part of the old Mongolian Empire until a few centuries ago, the connection with Buryat Mongolian shamanism is a direct one. Their shamanic practices are almost identical to those of the Mongols, even though they speak Mongolized Turkic languages rather than Mongolian.

2. Chimitdorjiev, V. Sh. *Buryaadai tuukhe besheguud* (Ulan-Ude: Rossin naukanuudai akademi Sibiriin tahag Buryaadai erdemei tub mongol shenjelelgiin, buddologi ba tibetologiin erdemei institut, 1999), pp. 133–36.

Chapter 1

1. Chadwick, Nora K., and Victor Zhirmunsky, *Oral Epics of Central Asia* (Cambridge: University Press, 1969), p. 242.

2. Humphrey, Caroline, and Urgunge Onon, *Shamans and Elders: Experience, Knowledge, and Power among the Daur Mongols* (Oxford: Clarendon Press, 1996), p. 185.

Chapter 2

1. Dioszegi, V., and N. O. Sharakshinova, "Songs of Bulagat Buriat Shamans," in *Mongolian Studies*, ed. Louis Ligeti (Budapest: Akademiai Kiado, 1970), p. 108.

2. Humphrey and Onon, *Shamans and Elders*, p. 185.

3. Potapov, L. P., and M. G. Levin, *The Peoples of Siberia* (Chicago: University of Chicago Press, 1964), p. 278.

4. Sanjeev, Garma, "Weltanschauung und Schamanismus der Alaren-Burjaten," in *Anthropos*, vol. 22 (1927), p. 607.

5. Chabros, Krystyna, *Beckoning Fortune: A Study of the Mongolian dalalga Ritual* (Wiesbaden: Otto Harrassowitz, 1992), pp. 144–49.

6. I especially recommend *Instrumental & Vocal Music from Buryatia* by the group Uragsha, which is available from Amazon.com. This album contains *hoomei* (throat singing) as well as *magtaal* and *yohor* music styles. These types of music are traditionally associated with shamanic ritual.

Chapter 3

1. Vasilevich, G. M., "Shamanistic Songs of the Evenki (Tungus)," in *Popular Beliefs and Folklore Tradition in Siberia*, ed. V. Dioszegi (The Hague: Mouton and Company, 1968), p. 360. This is an invocation asking the spirits to merge with the shaman. Note the phrase "center of the earth," which refers to the concept of the *gol*, the source of shamanic power and the gateway to other worlds, which will be discussed in chapter 4.

2. How people handle balance in Mongolian shamanism is aptly explained by Urgunge Onon: "Balance is the center of its surrounding world, and each human being should be like this. . . . Maybe weaker, maybe stronger, but each one must be its own light." Humphrey and Onon, *Shamans and Elders*, p. 82.

3. Sanjeev, "Weltanschauung und Schamanismus der Alaren-Burjaten," p. 949.

Chapter 4

1. Vasilevich, G. M., "Early Concepts about the Universe among the Evenks (Materials)," in *Studies in Shamanism*, ed. Henry N. Michael (Toronto: University of Toronto Press, 1965), pp. 56–57.

2. Wasilewski, Jerzy, "Space in Nomadic Cultures: A Spatial Analysis of the Mongol Yurts," in *Altaica Collecta: Berichte und Vortraege der XVII. Permanent International Altaistic Conference, 3–8 June 1974, in Bonn/Bad Honnef*, ed. Walther Heissig (Wiesbaden: Otto Harrassowitz, 1976).

3. Kihm, Walter, *Zur Symbolik im Schamanismus*, Ph.D. diss., University of Freiburg im Breisgau, 1974, p. 189.

4. Humphrey and Onon, *Shamans and Elders*, p. 125.

5. Another example is found in an Evenk shaman song:

> *The distance grows blue,*
> *Down, down, down,*
> *Like a peg top, like a peg top,*
> *Like a peg top, like a peg top,*
> *Like a peg top, like a peg top,*
> *Down, down,*
> *Like a peg top it is whirling . . .*
>
> —FROM VASILEVICH, G. M., "SHAMANISTIC SONGS OF THE EVENKI (TUNGUS)."

This Evenk song, in which the shaman is calling in the *ongon* spirits to merge with him, aptly describes the vortexlike nature of the *gol*. This section falls toward the end of the lengthy shaman song quoted at the beginning of chapter 3.

Chapter 5

1. Kenin-Lopsan, Mongush B., "Tuvan Shamanic Folklore," in *Shamanic Worlds: Rituals and Lore of Siberia and Central Asia*, ed. Marjorie Mandelstam-Balzer (Armonk, N.Y.: North Castle Books, 1997), p. 111. Note how the shaman begins his journey with the *ariulga*. In the second verse the "galloping with my shoulder blades" shows that the riding of the steed refers to drumming; the cloak and "head with the bird feathers" refer to the shaman's clothing.

2. Alekseev, N. A., "Shamans and Their Religious Practices," in *Shamanic Worlds: Rituals and Lore of Siberia and Central Asia*, ed. Marjorie Mandelstam-Balzer (Armonk, N.Y.: North Castle Books, 1997), pp. 57–58.

3. Purev, Otgony, *Mongol boogiin shashin* (Ulaanbaatar: Mongol Ulsyn Shinjlekh Ukhaany Akademiin Tuukhiin Khureelen, 1999), p. 71.

4. Kalweit, Holger, *Shamans, Healers, and Medicine Men* (Boston: Shambhala, 1992), p. 14.

5. The Dolbor journey is described in Humphrey and Onon, *Shamans and Elders*, and in Nowak, Margaret, and Stephen Durrant, *The Tale of the Nishan Shamaness: A Manchu Folk Epic* (Seattle: University of Washington Press, 1977). The journey described here, however, is based primarily on my own experiences of doing the Dolbor journey for the purpose of soul retrieval.

6. The journey along the Birds' Way is beautifully described and illustrated in V. V. Napolskikh's "Proto-Uralic World Picture: A Reconstruction," in *Northern Religions and Shamanism*, eds. Mihaly Hoppal and Juha Pentakainen (Budapest: Akademiai Kiado, 1992), pp. 3–20.

Chapter 6

1. Bazarov, B. D., *Tainstva y praktika shamanizma (Boge murgel-on niguca nugud) Kniga 2: Tainstva y praktika shamanizma* (Ulan-Ude: Buryaad Unen, 2000), pp. 172–73. The Shoshoolog are the most ancient and respected clan of the Hongoodor Buryats. That the shamans have nine drums apiece denotes that they are of the highest rank, *Tengeriin tabilgatai zaarin boo*, "great shamans with the mandate of Heaven" (see appendix 3). In shamanic lore the present system of shamanism was founded by Shargai Noyon Baabai, who came down from the upper world and initiated the first Shoshoolog shamans. In Buryat shamanism, many *zayaan* spirits are the souls of great shamans of the past who continue their work by helping living shamans.

2. Kihm, Walter, *Zur Symbolik im Schamanismus*, pp. 187–91; Basilov, V. N., "Chosen by the Spirits," in *Shamanic Worlds: Rituals and Lore of Siberia and Central Asia*, ed. Marjorie Mandelstan-Balzer (Armonk, N.Y.: North Castle Books, 1997), p. 24.

3. Shirokogoroff, S. M., *Psychomental Complex of the Tungus* (London: Kegan Paul, Trench, Trubner and Company, 1935), p. 141.

Chapter 7

1.   Sanjeev, Garma, "Weltanschauung und Schamanismus der Alaren-Burjaten," p. 582. When there is a soul loss, the shaman will usually first try to call the soul back with invocations before journeying to find it. Calling the soul is often all that is needed to recover it if it is still in the middle world. The Alar Buryats are a branch of the Hongoodor tribe.

2.   Ibid., pp. 581–82.

Chapter 8

1.   Dugarov, Bayar S., *Sagaan-Dali*, translated by Laurie Daniels and privately published by Ecologically Sustainable Development, 1997, p. 13.

2.   With the exception of Sagaalgan and Ulaan Tergel, the descriptions of traditional holidays in this section are based on the ceremonial calendar described by the Buryat shaman Sagaan Boitog in Bazarov, B. D., *Tainstva y praktika shamanizma (Boge murgel-on niguca nugud) Kniga 1: Taina pocvyasheniya v shamany* (Ulan-Ude: Buryaad Unen, 2000), p. 48.

3.   Humphrey and Onon, *Shamans and Elders*, p. 147.

4.   The Clean Tent ritual is described in some detail in Potapov, *The Peoples of Siberia*, p. 578. The version of the ritual presented here has been adapted for my own shamanic practice and I describe it as I perform it.

Chapter 9

1.   Kenin-Lopsan, Mongush B., *Shaman Songs and Myths of Tuva* (Budapest: Akademiai Kiado, 1995), p. 27.

2.   Dioszegi, V., "Ethnogenic Aspects of Darkhat Shamanism," in *Acta Orientalia Scientiarum Hungaricae* 16 (1962), p. 57.

3.   Bazarov, B. D., *Tainstva y praktika shamanizma (Boge murgel-on niguca nugud) Kniga 1*, p. 34.

4.   Hoppal, Mihaly, "The Life and Works of Benedek Barathosi Balogh, a Hungarian Researcher of Manchu-Tunguz Shamanism," in *Shaman*, vol. 7 (1999), p. 13.

5.   Humphrey and Onon, *Shamans and Elders*, p. 256.

6.   Bazarov, B. D., *Tainstva y praktika shamanizma (Boge murgel-on niguca nugud) Kniga 1*, p. 32.

7.   Bazarov, B. D. *Tainstva y praktika shamanizma (Boge murgel-on niguca nugud) Kniga 2: Tainstva y praktika shamanizma* (Ulan-Ude: Buryaad Unen, 2000) pp. 93–94.

8.   Ibid., p. 95.

9.   Holmberg, Uno, *The Mythology of All Races*, vol. 4: *Finno-Ugric, Siberian* (New York: Cooper Square Publishers, 1964), Plate XLV.

10. Okladnikova, L. A., "The Shamanistic Aspect of the Crystal Magic," in *Shamanism Past and Present* (part 2) (Los Angeles/Fullerton: International Society for Trans-Oceanic Research, 1989), p. 344.

11. My retelling of the Abai Geser legend is based on the version told by the shaman Peochon Petrov of the Hangin clan (Unga Buryats).

12. Shaman costumes are often referred to in folklore as silver on the front and gold on the back. This is related to the Mongolian shamanic custom of wearing gold and silver rings to represent the female and male principles, the sun and moon. The lark can there- fore be considered to be an animal shaman.

Appendix 2

1.   I have learned the legends that follow from many sources. Those about Shargai Noyon Baabai, Buhe Noyon Baabai, and Khan Khemegshen Toodei can be found in Sanjeev, "Weltanschauung und Schamanismus der Alaren-Burjaten," 576–613, 933–55. Sanjeev, himself a Buryat from a shamanic lineage, learned these stories from the bard and shaman Papa Tushemilov.

2.   The story of Holongoto Ubgen is recounted by Jeremiah Curtin in *A Journey in Southern Siberia: The Mongols, Their Religion, and Their Myths* (Boston: Little, Brown, and Company, 1909), pp. 105–6.

3.   The story of the prophecy of Dorji Banzarov was recounted to me by Bayar Dugarov.

4.   The most complete description of the Mongolian pantheon was written by the Buryat shaman Sagaan Boitog. This section is based on my translation of his description (in Bazarov, B. D., *Tainstva y praktika shamanizma [Boge murgel-on niguca nugud] Kniga 2*, pp.

30–34, 53–66) with additional comments and observations based on my own shamanic knowledge. The *khans* and *ongons* listed at the end of this section are mainly those that I use in my own shamanic practice and are the ones most commonly invoked by Mongolian shamans. The number of *khans, zayaans,* and *ongons* is so huge that it would be impossible to list all of them here.

Appendix 3

1. The descriptions of the nine levels of shamanic initiation are a summary of the explanations in Bazarov, *Tainstva y praktika shamanizma (Boge murgel-on niguca nugud) Kniga 1,* pp. 31–35.

Appendix 4

1. Daichin Tenger is the *tenger* of war, his name meaning approximately "defeater of enemies."

2. The Dalha Tenger are a group of nine *tenger* associated with the nine-tailed war standard of Chinggis Khan.

3. The master of Donjing Garabuu Mountain, also known as the Bogd Uul, which is south of Ulaanbaatar in Mongolia, is Geser's brother Zasa Mergen.

4. These magic words are untranslatable. As always the accent is on the first syllable. Say each syllable clearly and distinctly in order to achieve the maximum magical effect.

Glossary

1. The definitions in this glossary are either drawn from my own knowledge or taken from Zomonov, M. D., and I. A. Manjigeev, *Kratkii slovar' buryatskogo shamanizma* (Ulan-Ude: Buryatskoye knijnoye izdatel'stvo, 1997), unless noted otherwise.

2. Mandoki, L., "Two Asiatic Sidereal Names," in *Folk Beliefs and Shamanistic Traditions in Siberia,* ed. Vilmos Dioszegi (Budapest: Akademiai Kiado, 1996), pp. 168–69. This article has some interesting information about Siberian Pleiades folklore.

3. Humphrey and Onon, *Shamans and Elders,* p. 306.

Bibliography

Alekseenko, E. A. "Some General and Specific Features in the Shamanism of the Peoples of Siberia." In *Shamanism in Eurasia*, ed. Mihaly Hoppal. Paris: Edition Herodot, 1984.

Alekseev, N. A. "Shamans and Their Religious Practices." In *Shamanic Worlds: Rituals and Lore of Siberia and Central Asia*, ed. Marjorie Mandelstam-Balzer. Armonk, N.Y.: North Castle Books, 1997.

Amschler, Wolfgang. "Ueber die Tieropfer (besonders Pferdeopfer) der Telengiten im Sibirischen Altai." In *Anthropos*, vol. 28 (1933): 305–13 [in German].

Anisimov, A. F. "Cosmological Concepts of the Peoples of the North." In *Studies in Shamanism*, ed. Henry N. Michael. Toronto: University of Toronto Press, 1965.

Anonymous. *Monggol's Tree Worship*. Unpublished ms. 1990 (?).

Anttonen, Veikko. "Transcending Bodily and Territorial Boundaries: Interpreting Shamanism as a Form of Religion." In *Shaman*, vol. 2 (1994): 99–107.

Atkinson, Thomas Witlam. *Oriental and Western Siberia: A Narrative of Seven Years' Explorations and Adventures in Siberia, Mongolia, the Kirghis Steppes, Chinese Tartary, and Part of Central Asia*. Philadelphia: J. W. Bradley, 1860.

Baecker, Joerg. "'Do Mergen und Chinihua Hato': Schamanenheldinnen und Unterweltsreise bei den Daghuren." In *Fragen der mongolischen Heldendichtung*, vol. 3, ed. Walther Heissig. Wiesbaden: Otto Harrassowitz, 1985 [in German].

————. "Himmelshund, Zobelmaedchen und Zielen auf dem Himmelsburchan-Mythologie und Maerchen im Daghurischen Heldenepos." In *Fragen der mongolischen Heldendichtung*, vol. 4, ed. Walther Heissig. Wiesbaden: Otto Harrassowitz, 1987 [in German].

Baldaev, S. P. *Abai Geser bogdo khaan: Buryaadai morin uliger*. Ulan-Ude: Bugede Buryaadai undehen soyoloi eblel, 1995 [in Buryat].

Baldano, Namjil. *Abai Geser khubuun: Buryaad aradai uliger*. Ulan-Ude: Buryaadai nomoi kheblel, 1959 [in Buryat].

Banzarov, Dorji. "The Black Faith, or Shamanism among the Mongols." Translated from the Russian by John R. Krueger. In *Mongolian Studies*, vol. 6 (1980): 53–89.

————. *Sobranie Sochinenii*. Moskva: Izdatel'stvo akademii nauk SSSR, 1955 [in Russian].

Bartha, Antal. "Myth and Reality in the Ancient Culture of Northern Peoples." In *Northern Religions and Shamanism*, eds. Mihaly Hoppal and Juha Pentakainen. Budapest: Akademiai Kiado, 1992.

Basilov, V. N. "Chosen by the Spirits." In *Shamanic Worlds: Rituals and Lore of Siberia and Central Asia*, ed. Marjorie Mandelstam-Balzer. Armonk, N.Y.: North Castle Books, 1997.

Bauwe, Renate. "Jagdkult und seine Reflexion in der mongolischen Dichtung." In *Altaica Berolinensia: The Concept of Sovereignty in the Altaic World, Permanent International Altaistic Conference 34th Meeting, Berlin 21–26 July 1991*, ed. Barbara Kellner-Heinkele. Wiesbaden: Harrassowitz Verlag, 1993 [in German].

Bawden, C. R. *Confronting the Supernatural: Mongolian Traditional Ways and Means*. Wiesbaden: Harrassowitz Verlag, 1994.

————. "Mongol: The Contemporary Tradition." In *Traditions of Heroic and Epic Poetry*, vol. 1: *The Traditions*, ed. A. T. Hatto. London: The Modern Humanities Research Association, 1980.

————. "Some 'Shamanist' Hunting Rituals from Mongolia." In *Central Asiatic Journal*, vol. 12 (1968): 101–43.

————. "Vitality and Death in the Mongolian Epic." In *Fragen der mongolischen Heldendichtung*, vol. 3, ed. Walther Heissig. Wiesbaden: Otto Harrassowitz, 1985.

Bazarov, B. D. *Tainstva y praktika shamanizma (Boge murgel-on niguca nugud) Kniga 1: Taina pocvyasheniya v shamany*. Ulan-Ude: Buryaad Unen, 2000 [in Russian].

————. *Tainstva y praktika shamanizma (Boge murgel-on niguca nugud) Kniga 2: Tainstva y praktika shamanizma*. Ulan-Ude: Buryaad Unen, 2000 [in Russian].

Berglie, Per-Arne. "Spirit-Mediums and the Epic: Remarks on Gesar and the Epic among Spirit-Mediums in Tibet and Ladakh." In *Shaman*, vol. 4 (1996): 17–26.

Bese, Louis. "Ueber die Struktur des Burjatischen Pantheons." In *Traditions religieuses et para-religieuses des peuples Altaiques: Communications présentées au XIIIe Congrès de la "Permanent Altaistic Conference," Strasbourg, 25–30 juin 1970*. Paris: Presses universitaires de France, 1972 [in German].

Bira, Sh. "The Monggol-un Niguca Tobciyan and the Legend and Folktale Contacts of Nomadic Peoples." In *Altaic Religious Practices and Beliefs: Proceedings of the 33rd Meeting of the Permanent International Altaistic Conference, Budapest, June 24–29, 1990*, eds. Geza Bethlenfalvy, Agnes Birtalan, Alice Sarkozi, and Judit Vinkovics. Budapest: Research Group for Altaic Studies, Hungarian Academy of Sciences, 1990.

Birtalan, Agnes, and Alice Sarkozi. *Dayan Degereki: The Protector Deity of a Bayit Shamaness*. Unpublished ms., 1997.

Bischoff, Friedrich A., and Walter Kauffman. "Die Melodie der Gesaenge des Bulgan Schamanen." In *Zentralasiatische Studien* 10 (1976): 311–21 [in German].

Boyle, John Andrew. "The Thirteenth-Century Mongols' Conception of the After-life: The Evidence of Their Funerary Practices." In *Mongolian Studies*, vol. 1 (1974): 5–13.

Brands, Horst Wilfrid. "Bemerkungen zu einer tuvanischen Variante des Geser-Motivs." In *Zentralasiatische Studien*, vol. 11 (1977): 265–75 [in German].

Bulag, Uradyn E. *Nationalism and Hybridity in Mongolia*. Oxford: Clarendon Press, 1998.

Bulgakova, T. D. "An Archaic Rite in Nanai Shaman Ceremonies." In *Shaman*, vol. 3 (1995): 67–79.

Campbell, Joseph. *The Masks of God: Primitive Mythology*. New York: Viking Press, 1959.

Cerensodnom, D. "Ueber den Brauch der Verehrung des Baumes in den mongolischen Epen." In *Fragen der mongolischen Heldendichtung*, vol. 5, ed. Walther Heissig. Wiesbaden: Harrassowitz Verlag, 1992 [in German].

———. "Zu Fragen der Herkunft des Names der Epengestalt Chan Charanchuj." In *Fragen der mongolischen Heldendichtung*, vol. 3, ed. Walther Heissig. Wiesbaden: Otto Harrassowitz, 1985 [in German].

Chabros, Krystyna. *Beckoning Fortune: A Study of the Mongolian dalalga Ritual*. Wiesbaden: Otto Harrassowitz, 1992.

———. "An East Mongolian Ritual for Children." In *Altaic Religious Practices and Beliefs: Proceedings of the 33rd Meeting of the Permanent International Altaistic Conference, Budapest, June 24–29, 1990*, eds. Geza Bethlenfalvy, Agnes Birtalan, Alice Sarkozi, and Judit Vinkovics. Budapest: Research Group for Altaic Studies, Hungarian Academy of Sciences, 1990.

———. "Space and Movement in Mongolian Culture." In *Journal of the Anglo-Mongolian Society*, vol. 11 (1988): 30–37.

Chadwick, Nora K., and Victor Zhirmunsky. *Oral Epics of Central Asia*. Cambridge: University Press, 1969.

Chernetsov, V. N. "Concepts of the Soul among the Ob Ugrians." In *Studies in Siberian Shamanism*, ed. Henry N. Michael. Toronto: University of Toronto Press, 1965.

Chichlo, Boris. "Les métamorphoses du héros épique." In *Fragen der mongolischen Heldendichtung*, vol. 1., ed. Walther Heissig. Wiesbaden: Otto Harrassowitz, 1981 [in French].

Chimitdorjiev, V. Sh. *Buryaadai tuukhe besheguud*. Ulan-Ude: Rossin naukanuudai akademi Sibiriin tahag Buryaadai erdemei tub mongol shenjelelgiin, buddologi ba tibetologiin erdemei institut, 1999 [in Buryat].

Chiodo, Elisabetta. "The Jarud Mongol Ritual 'Calling the Soul with the Breast.' In *Zentralasiatische Studien*, vol. 26 (1996): 153–71.

Choi, Han-Woo. "On the Turkic Shamanic Word Bogu." In *Altaic Religious Practices and Beliefs: Proceedings of the 33rd Meeting of the Permanent International Altaistic Conference, Budapest, June 24–29, 1990*, eds. Geza Bethlenfalvy, Agnes Birtalan, Alice Sarkozi, and Judit Vinkovics. Budapest: Research Group for Altaic Studies, Hungarian Academy of Sciences, 1990.

Curtin, Jeremiah. *A Journey in Southern Siberia: The Mongols, Their Religion, and Their Myths*. Boston: Little, Brown, and Company, 1909.

Czaplicka, Marie A. *Aboriginal Siberia: A Study in Social Anthropology*. Oxford: Clarendon Press, 1908.

Damdinsuren, C. "Explanation of Some Personal Names in Mongolian Epos about Geser." In *Religious and Lay Symbolism in the Altaic World and Other Papers: Proceedings of the 27th Meeting of the Permanent International Altaistic Conference, Walberberg, Federal Republic of Germany, June 12–17, 1984*, eds. Klaus Sagaster and Helmut Eimer. Wiesbaden: Otto Harrassowitz, 1989.

Damdinsuren, Ts. "Mongolskii epos o Geser-Khane." In *Archiv Orientalni*, vol. 23 (1955): 52–62 [in Russian].

David-Neel, Alexandra, and Lama Yongden. *The Supernatural Life of Gesar of Ling*. Boulder, Colo.: Prajna Press, 1981.

Diakonova, Vera P. "Shamans in Traditional Tuvinian Society." In *Ancient Traditions: Shamanism in Central Asia and the Americas*, eds. Gary Seaman and Jane S. Day. Niwot: University Press of Colorado, 1994.

Dioszegi, V. "Ethnogenic Aspects of Darkhat Shamanism." In *Acta Orientalia Scientiarum Hungaricae* 16 (1962): 55–81.

———. "How to Become a Shaman among the Sagais." In *Acta Orientalia Scientiarum Hungaricae* 15 (1962): 87–96.

———. "The Origins of the Evenki 'Shaman Mask' of Transbaikalia." In *Acta Orientalia Scientiarum Hungaricae* 20 (1967): 185–201.

Dioszegi, Vilmos. *Tracing Shamans in Siberia*. Oosterhout: Anthropological Publications, 1968.

Dioszegi, V., and N. O. Sharakshinova. "Songs of Bulagat Buriat Shamans." In *Mongolian Studies*, ed. Louis Ligeti. Budapest: Akademiai Kiado, 1970.

Djakonova, V. P. "The Vestments and Paraphernalia of a Tuva Shamaness." In *Shamanism in Siberia*, eds. V. Dioszegi and M. Hoppal. Budapest: Akademiai Kiado, 1978.

Dugarov, Bayar S. *Sagaan-Dali*. Translated by Laurie Daniels and privately published by Ecologically Sustainable Development, 1997.

Dugarov, D. S. "K probleme proiskhojdeniya khongodorov." In *Etnicheskaya instoriya narodov: Yujnii sibirii I tsentralnoi azii*, ed. B. R. Zoriktuyev. Novosibirsk: Nauka, 1993 [in Russian].

Dugarov, Dash-Nyamaa S. *Istoricheskiye korny buryatskogo shamanizma*. Moscow: Nauka, 1991 [in Russian].

Dulam, S. *Darkhad Boogiin Ulamjlal dahi Belgedel bui*. Unpublished ms., 1999 [in Mongolian].

Dumas, Dominique. "Die 'Feuergottheiten' der Mongolen." In *Synkretismus in den Religionen Zentralasiens*, eds. Walther Heissig and Hans-Joachim Klimkeit. Wiesbaden: Otto Harrassowitz, 1987 [in German].

Eliade, Mircea. *Myth and Reality*. New York: Harper Colophon Books, 1975.

———. *Shamanism: Archaic Techniques of Ecstasy*. New York: Pantheon Books, 1964.

Emsheimer, E. "Schamanentrommel und Trommelbaum." In *Ethnos*, vol. 11 (1946): 166–79.

Even, Marie-Dominique. "Chants de chamanes Mongols," vol. 19–20 (1988–1989), of *Études mongoles et sibériennes* [in French].

———. "Dajan Deerx invoque." In *Journal of the Anglo-Mongolian Society* 9 (1984): 12–18 [in French].

———. "The Shamanism of the Mongols." In *Mongolia Today*, ed. Shirin Akiner. London: Kegan Paul International, 1991.

Fedotov, Alexander. "On Shamanistic Trends in 'The Secret History of the Mongols.'" In *Proceedings of the 38th Permanent International Altaistic Conference (PIAC), Kawasaki, Japan, August 7–12, 1995*, ed. Giovanni Stary. Wiesbaden: Harrassowitz Verlag, 1996.

Frye, Richard N. *The Heritage of Central Asia: From Antiquity to the Turkish Expansion*. Princeton: Markus Wiener Publishers, 1996.

Galdanova, G. P., N. L. Zhukovskaya, and G. N. Ochirova. "The Cult of Dayan Derkhe in Mongolia and Buryatia." In *Journal of the Anglo-Mongolian Society*, vol. 8 (1984): 1–11.

Gomboin, D. D. "Obrazii zooantropomorfniikh vragov v ekhirit-bulagatskikh uligerakh." In *Poetika janrov buryatskogo fol'klora*. Ulan-Ude: Akademiya nauk SSSR sibirskoye otdeleniye buryatskii filial, 1982 [in Russian].

Grim, John A. *The Shaman: Patterns of Siberian and Ojibway Healing*. Norman: University of Oklahoma Press, 1983.

Gungarov, B. Sh. "Toponimicheskie legendii I predaniya khori-buryat." In *Poetika janrov buryatskogo fol'klora*. Ulan-Ude: Akademiya nauk SSSR sibirskoye otdeleniye buryatskii filial, 1982 [in Russian].

Halen, Harry. "Altan Khan and the Mongolian Geser Epic." In *Altaica Osloensia: Proceedings of the 32nd Meeting of the Permanent International Altaistic Conference, Oslo, June 12–16, 1989*, ed. Bernt Brendemoen. Oslo: Universitetsforlaget.

Haltod, Magadburin. "Ein Schamanengesang aus dem Bulgan-Gebiet." In
*Collectanea Mongolica: Festschrift fuer Professor Dr. Rintchen zum 60.
Geburtstag*, ed. Walther Heissig. Wiesbaden: Otto Harrassowitz, 1966
[in German].

Hamayon, Roberte. "Abuse of the Father, Abuse of the Husband: A
Comparative Analysis of Two Buryat Myths of Ethnic Origin." In
Synkretismus in den Religionen Zentralasiens, eds. Walther Heissig and
Hans-Joachim Klimkeit. Wiesbaden: Otto Harrassowitz, 1987.

———. "Are 'Trance,' 'Ecstasy' and Similar Concepts Appropriate in the
Study of Shamanism?" In *Shaman*, vol. 1 (1993): 3–25.

———. *La chasse à l'âme: Esquisse d'une théorie du chamanisme sibérien*.
Nanterre: Société d'ethnologie, 1990 [in French].

———. "Dérision lamaique du chamanisme, dérision pastorale de la chasse
chez les bouriates de Bargouzine." In *Documenta Barbarorum:
Festschrift fuer Walther Heissig zum 70. Geburtstag*, eds. Klaus Sagaster
and Michael Weiers. Wiesbaden: Harrassowitz Verlag, 1983 [in French].

———. "Game and Games, Fortune and Dualism in Siberian Shamanism."
In *Shamanism and Northern Ecology*, ed. Juha Pentikainen. Berlin:
Mouton de Gruyter, 1996.

———. "The Hunter, the Shaman and the Bard: Three Types of Narrative
Speech." In *Fragen der mongolischen Heldendichtung*, vol. 5, ed.
Walther Heissig. Wiesbaden: Harrassowitz Verlag, 1992.

———. "Is There a Typically Female Exercise of Shamanism in Patrilinear
Societies Such as the Buryat?" In *Shamanism in Eurasia* (part 2), ed.
Mihaly Hoppal. Paris: Edition Herodot, 1984.

———. "The One in the Middle: Unwelcome Third as a Brother, Irreplace-
able Mediator as a Son." In *Fragen der mongolischen Heldendichtung*,
vol. 3, ed. Walther Heissig. Wiesbaden: Otto Harrassowitz, 1985.

———. "The Relevance of the Marriage of the West Buryat Epic Hero to
Hunting and Shamanism." In *Religious and Lay Symbolism in the Altaic
World and Other Papers: Proceedings of the 27th Meeting of the
Permanent International Altaistic Conference, Walberberg, Federal
Republic of Germany, June 12–17, 1984*, eds. Klaus Sagaster and Helmut
Eimer. Wiesbaden: Otto Harrassowitz, 1989.

———. "Shamanism in Siberia: From Partnership in Supernature to
Counter-Power in Society." In *Shamanism, History, and the State*, eds.
Nicholas Thomas and Caroline Humphrey. Ann Arbor: University of
Michigan Press, 1994.

———. "Tricks and Turns of Legitimate Perpetuation, or Taking the Buryat *Uliger* Literally as 'Model.'" In *Fragen der mongolischen Heldendichtung*, vol. 1, ed. Walther Heissig. Wiesbaden: Otto Harrassowitz, 1981.

———. "Tricks and Turns of Legitimate Perpetuation (Continuation)." In *Fragen der mongolischen Heldendichtung*, vol. 2, ed. Walther Heissig. Wiesbaden: Otto Harrassowitz, 1982.

Harle-Silvennoinen. "In the Land of Song and the Drum: Receiving Inspiration from Tuvan Shamans." In *Sacred Hoop*, vol. 25 (1999): 10–15.

Harva, Uno. *Die Religioesen Vorstellungen der Altaischen Voelker.* Helsinki: Werner Soederstroem Osakeytio, 1938 [in German].

Hatto, A. T. *Traditions of Heroic and Epic Poetry*, vol. 2: *Characteristics and Techniques.* London: The Modern Humanities Research Association, 1989.

Heissig, Walther. "Banishing of Illnesses into Effigies in Mongolia." In *Asian Folklore Studies*, vol. 49 (1990): 33–43.

———. "Das Epenmotiv von Kampf Gesers mit dem schwarzgefleckten Tiger." In *Motiv und Wirklichkeit*, ed. Walther Heissig. Wiesbaden: Harrassowitz Verlag, 1993 [in German].

———. *Erzaehlstoffe rezenter mongolischen Heldendichtung Teil I.* Wiesbaden: Otto Harrassowitz, 1988 [in German].

———. "Ethnische Gruppenbildung in Zentralasien im Licht muendlicher und schriftlicher Ueberlieferung." In *Studien zur Ethnogenese.* Opladen: Westdeutscher Verlag, 1985 [in German].

———. "Felsgeburt (Petrogenese) und Bergkult." In *Motiv und Wirklichkeit*, ed. Walther Heissig. Wiesbaden: Harrassowitz Verlag, 1993 [in German].

———. "Gedanken zu einer strukturellen Motiv-Typologie des mongolischen Epos." In *Die mongolischen Epen: Bezuege, Sinndeutung, und Ueberlieferung*, ed. Walther Heissig. Wiesbaden: Otto Harrassowitz, 1979 [in German].

———. "Geser Khan als Eselmensch." In *Motiv und Wirklichkeit*, ed. Walther Heissig. Wiesbaden: Harrassowitz Verlag, 1993 [in German].

———. "Geser-Khan Rauchopfer als Datierungshilfen des mongolischen Geser-Khan Epos." In *Zentralasiatischen Studien*, vol. 12 (1978): 89–135 [in German].

——. "Geser-Kongruenzen." In *Motiv und Wirklichkeit,* ed. Walther Heissig. Wiesbaden: Harrassowitz Verlag, 1993 [in German].

——. *Geser-Studien: Untersuchungen zu den Erzaehlstoffen in den "neuen" Kapiteln des mongolischen Geser-Zyklus.* Opladen: Westdeutscher Verlag, 1990 [in German].

——. *Heldenmaerchen versus Heldenepos?* Opladen: Westdeutscher Verlag, 1992 [in German].

——. "Historical Realities and Elements in the Mongol Heroic Epic." In *Motiv und Wirklichkeit,* ed. Walther Heissig. Wiesbaden: Harrassowitz Verlag, 1993 [in German].

——. "Innere Logik und historische Realitaet des Erzaehlmodells: die Toetung von Mangusmutter und Mangussohn." In *Fragen der mongolischen Heldendichtung,* vol. 3, ed. Walther Heissig. Wiesbaden: Otto Harrassowitz, 1985 [in German].

——. "Motivveraenderungen im oralen Erzaehlen der Mongolen." In *Motiv und Wirklichkeit,* ed. Walther Heissig. Wiesbaden: Harrassowitz Verlag, 1993 [in German].

——. "Das Oeloetische Kurzepos 'Waisenmaedchen Noedei' (Oenoechin Noedei): Versuch einer Interpretation." In *Zentralasiatische Studien 27* (1997): 121–87 [in German].

——. *Oralitaet und Schriftlichkeit.* Kleve: Westdeutscher Verlag, 1992 [in German].

——. "Recent East Mongolian Shamanistic Traditions." In *Shamanism and Northern Ecology,* ed. Juha Pentikainen. Berlin: Mouton de Gruyter, 1996.

——. *The Religions of Mongolia.* Berkeley: University of California Press, 1980.

——. "Schamanenlegenden und ihr historischer Hintergrund." In *Gedanke und Wirkung: Festschrift zum 90. Geburtstag von Nikolaus Poppe,* eds. Walther Heissig, Klaus Sagaster, Veronika Veit, and Michael Weiers. Wiesbaden: Otto Harrassowitz, 1989 [in German].

——. "Schlange und Stier im mongolischen Epos." In *Religious and Lay Symbolism in the Altaic World and Other Papers: Proceedings of the 27th Meeting of the Permanent International Altaistic Conference, Walberberg, Federal Republic of Germany, June 12–17, 1984,* eds. Klaus Sagaster and Helmut Eimer. Wiesbaden: Otto Harrassowitz, 1989 [in German].

——. "Shaman Myth and Clan-Epic." In *Shamanism in Eurasia* (part 2), ed. Mihaly Hoppal. Paris: Edition Herodot, 1984.

——. "Von der Realitaet zum Mythos: der Daumen im mongolischen Epos." In *Religious and Lay Symbolism in the Altaic World and Other Papers: Proceedings of the 27th Meeting of the Permanent International Altaistic Conference, Walberberg, Federal Republic of Germany, June 12–17, 1984,* eds. Klaus Sagaster and Helmut Eimer. Wiesbaden: Otto Harrassowitz, 1989 [in German].

——. "Wiederbeleben und Heilen als Motiv in mongolischen Epos." In *Motiv und Wirklichkeit,* ed. Walther Heissig. Wiesbaden: Harrassowitz Verlag, 1993 [in German].

——. "Zu zwei evenkisch-daghurischen Varianten des mandschu Erzaehlstoffes 'Nishan shaman-i bithe.'" In *Central Asiatic Journal* 41 (1997): 200–230 [in German].

——. "Zur Frage der Homogenitaet des ostmongolischen Schamanismus." In *Collectanea Mongolica: Festschrift fuer Professor Dr. Rintchen zum 60. Geburtstag,* ed. Walther Heissig. Wiesbaden: Otto Harrassowitz, 1966 [in German].

Herrmanns, Matthias. *Das National-Epos der Tibeter Gling Koenig Ge Sar.* Regensburg: Josef Habbel, 1965 [in German].

——. *Schamanen, Pseudo-Schamanen, Erloeser und Heilbringer: Eine vergleichende Studie religioeser Urphaenomene.* Wiesbaden: Franz Steiner Verlag, 1970 [in German].

Hesse, Klaus. "On the History of Mongolian Shamanism in Anthropological Perspective." In *Anthropos* 82 (1987): 403–13.

Holmberg, Uno. *The Mythology of All Races,* vol. 4: *Finno-Ugric, Siberian.* New York: Cooper Square Publishers, 1964.

Hoppal, Mihaly. "Changing Image of Eurasian Shamans." In *Shamanism Past and Present* (part 2). Los Angeles/Fullerton: International Society for Trans-Oceanic Research, 1989.

——. "The Life and Works of Benedek Barathosi Balogh, a Hungarian Researcher of Manchu-Tunguz Shamanism." In *Shaman,* vol. 7 (1999): 3–23.

——. "Shamanism: An Archaic and/or Recent System of Beliefs." In *Studies on Shamanism,* eds. Anna-Leena Siikala and Mihaly Hoppal. Helsinki: Finnish Anthropological Society, 1992.

——. "Shamanism in a Post-Modern Age." In *Shaman,* vol. 4 (1996): 99–107.

Horloo, P. "Traditions and Peculiarities of Mongolian Heroic Epic." In *Fragen der mongolischen Heldendichtung*, vol. 3, ed. Walther Heissig. Wiesbaden: Otto Harrassowitz, 1985.

Hultkrantz, Ake. "Ecological and Phenomenological Aspects of Shamanism." In *Shamanism in Siberia*, eds. Vilmos Dioszegi and Mihaly Hoppal. Budapest: Akademiai Kiado, 1996.

———. "A New Look at the World Pillar in Arctic and Sub-Arctic Religions." In *Shamanism and Northern Ecology*, ed. Juha Pentikainen. Berlin: Mouton de Gruyter, 1996.

———. "The Shaman in Myths and Tales." In *Shaman*, vol. 1 (1993): 37–55.

Hummel, Siegbert. *Mythologisches aus Eurasien im Ge-sar Heldenepos der Tibeter*. Stuttgart: Fabri Verlag, 1993 [in German].

Humphrey, Caroline. "A Fragmentary Text of Curative Magic." In *Journey of the Anglo-Mongolian Society*, vol. 9 (1984): 27–33.

———. "The Host and the Guest: One Hundred Rules of Good Behaviour in Rural Mongolia." In *Journal of the Anglo-Mongolian Society*, vol. 10 (1987): 42–53.

———. "Notes on Shamanism in Ar-Hangai Aimag." In *Journal of the Anglo-Mongolian Society*, vol. 4, no. 1 (1980): 95–99.

———. "Shamanic Practices and the State in Northern Asia: Views from the Center and Periphery." In *Shamanism, History, and the State*, eds. Nicholas Thomas and Caroline Humphrey. Ann Arbor: University of Michigan Press, 1994.

Humphrey, Caroline, and Urgunge Onon. *Shamans and Elders: Experience, Knowledge, and Power among the Daur Mongols*. Oxford: Clarendon Press, 1996.

Isono, Fujiko. "More About the *Anda* Relationship." In *Journal of the Anglo-Mongolian Society*, vol. 8 (1983): 36–47.

Jacobson, Esther. *The Deer Goddess of Ancient Siberia*. Leiden: E. J. Brill, 1993.

Jagchid, Sechin. "Chinggis Khan in Mongolian Folklore." In *Essays in Mongolian Studies*, ed. Sechin Jagchid. Provo, Utah: Brigham Young University, 1996.

———. "Shamanism among the Dakhur Mongols." In *Essays in Mongolian Studies*, ed. Sechin Jagchid. Provo, Utah: Brigham Young University, 1996.

———. "Traditional Mongolian Attitudes and Values as Seen in the 'Secret History of the Mongols' and the 'Altan tobchi.'" In *Essays in Mongolian Studies*, ed. Sechin Jagchid. Provo, Utah: Brigham Young University, 1996.

Jagchid, Sechin, and Paul Hyer. *Mongolia's Culture and Society*. Boulder, Colo.: Westview Press, 1979.

Janhunen, Juha. "On the Role of the Flying Squirrel in Siberian Shamanism." In *Shamanism Past and Present* (part 1). Los Angeles/Fullerton: International Society for Trans-Oceanic Research, 1989.

Jankovics, M. "Cosmic Models and Siberian Shaman Drums." In *Shamanism in Eurasia* (part 2), ed. Mihaly Hoppal. Paris: Edition Herodot, 1984.

Jinwen, Zhong. "Shamanism in Yughur Folk Tales." In *Shaman*, vol. 3 (1995): 55–66.

Joki, Aulis J. "Die Tungusen und ihre Kontakte mit anderen Voelkern." In *Studia Orientalia*, vol. 47 (1991): 109–19 [in German].

Kalweit, Holger. *Shamans, Healers, and Medicine Men*. Boston: Shambhala, 1992.

Kara, Gyorgy. "Chants de chasseur oirates dans la recueil de Vladimirtsov." In *Collectanea Mongolica: Festschrift fuer Professor Dr. Rintchen zum 60. Geburtstag*, ed. Walther Heissig. Wiesbaden: Otto Harrassowitz, 1966 [in French].

———. Review of the book *La Chasse à l'âme: Esquisse d'une théorie du chamanisme sibérien* by Roberte Hamayon. In *Shaman*, vol. 7 (1999): 167–72.

Kaschewsky, Rudolf. "Vergleiche als Stilmittel in Gesar-epos." In *Fragen der mongolischen Heldendichtung*, vol. 3, ed. Walther Heissig. Wiesbaden: Otto Harrassowitz, 1985 [in German].

Kaschewsky, Rudolf, and Pema Tsering. "Zur Frage der Historizitaet des Helden Gesar." In *Religious and Lay Symbolism in the Altaic World and Other Papers: Proceedings of the 27th Meeting of the Permanent International Altaistic Conference, Walberberg, Federal Republic of Germany, June 12–17, 1984*, eds. Klaus Sagaster and Helmut Eimer. Wiesbaden: Otto Harrassowitz, 1989 [in German].

Kenin-Lopsan, Mongush B. *Shaman Songs and Myths of Tuva*. Budapest: Akademiai Kiado, 1995.

———. "Tuvan Shamanic Folklore." In *Shamanic Worlds: Rituals and Lore of Siberia and Central Asia*, ed. Marjorie Mandelstam-Balzer. Armonk, N.Y.: North Castle Books, 1997, p. 111.

Khisamatidinova, Firdaus G. "Bashkir Concepts of Souls." In *Shaman*, vol. 4 (1996): 109–14.

Kihm, Walter. *Zur Symbolik im Schamanismus*. Ph.D. diss., University of Freiburg im Breisgau, 1974 [in German].

Kister, Daniel A. "A Korean Shaman Folktale and Ritual Skits in Honor of the Grandmother Spirit of Childbirth." In *Shaman*, vol. 4 (1996): 115–30.

Klimkeit, Hans-Joachim. "Das Manichaeische Koenigtum in Zentralasien." In *Documenta Barbarorum: Festschrift fuer Walther Heissig zum 70. Geburtstag*, eds. Klaus Sagaster and Michael Weiers. Wiesbaden: Otto Harrassowitz, 1983 [in German].

Kohalmi, Katharina U. "Die brave Schwester, die boese Schwester und die weisse Hase." In *Fragen der mongolischen Heldendichtung*, vol. 3, ed. Walther Heissig. Wiesbaden: Otto Harrassowitz, 1985 [in German].

——. "Geser Khan in tungusischen Maerchen." In *Acta Orientalia Scientiarum Hungaricae*, vol. 34 (1980): 75–83 [in German].

Krader, Lawrence. "Shamanism: Theory and History in Buryat Society." In *Shamanism in Siberia*, eds. V. Dioszegi and M. Hoppal. Budapest: Akademiai Kiado, 1978.

Krippner, Stanley. "The Use of Dreams in Shamanic Traditions." In *Shamanism Past and Present* (part 2). Los Angeles/Fullerton: International Society for Trans-Oceanic Research, 1989.

Krueger, John R. "Jeremiah Curtin as a Scholar of Mongolian Folklore." In *Studia Orientalia*, vol. 47 (1991): 131–35.

Lattimore, Owen. *The Mongols of Manchuria*. New York: The John Day Company, 1934.

Laude-Cirtautas, Ilse. "Der Held in der Gestalt eines armseligen Jungen." In *Fragen der mongolischen Heldendichtung*, vol. 1, ed. Walther Heissig. Wiesbaden: Otto Harrassowitz, 1981 [In German].

——. "Zu den Einleitungsformeln in den Maerchen und Epen der Mongolen and der Tuerkvoelker Zentralasiens." In *Central Asiatic Journal* 27 (1983): 211–48 [in German].

Leeming, David Adams, and Margaret Adams Leeming. *A Dictionary of Creation Myths*. New York: Oxford University Press, 1995.

Lincoln, Bruce. *Priests, Warriors, and Cattle: A Study in the Ecology of Religions*. Berkeley: University of California Press, 1981.

Lorincz, Laszlo. "Bewaehrungsproben als Motive in der mongolischen Folklore." In *Fragen der mongolischen Heldendichtung*, vol. 1, ed. Walther Heissig. Wiesbaden: Otto Harrassowitz, 1981 [in German].

———. "Die Burjatischen Geser-Varianten." In *Acta Orientalia Scientiarum Hungaricae*, vol. 29 (1975): 55–91 [in German].

———. "Die Heldenepik der Altai-Tuerken: Inhaltlich-typologische Analyse." In *Tractata Altaica*, eds. Walther Heissig, John R. Krueger, Felix J. Oinas, and Edmond Schuetz. Wiesbaden: Otto Harrassowitz, 1976 [in German].

———. "Die mongolische Mythologie." In *Acta Orientalia Scientiarum Hungaricae* 27 (1972): 103–26 [in German].

———. "Der Mythische Hintergrund der burjatischen und mongolischen Epen." In *Die mongolischen Epen: Bezuege, Sinndeutung, und Ueberlieferung*, ed. Walther Heissig. Wiesbaden: Otto Harrassowitz, 1979 [in German].

———. "Natur-und Gebrauchsgegenstaende als uebernatuerliche Elemente in den Heldenliedern von Manshut Emegenov." In *Documenta Barbarorum: Festschrift fuer Walther Heissig zum 70. Geburtstag*, eds. Klaus Sagaster and Michael Weiers. Wiesbaden: Otto Harrassowitz, 1983 [in German].

———. "Sonnenmythos, Sonnen- (Solar) Heros und Kulturheros in der mongolischen Mythologie." In *Acta Orientalia Scientiarum Hungaricae* 31 (1977): 365–89 [in German].

Lot-Falck, Eveline. "À propos d'Atugan: Déesse mongole de la terre." In *Revue de l'histoire des religions*, vol. 149 (1956), no. 2: 157–96 [in French].

Louis, Roberta, and Jan van Ysslestyne. "Shamanic Healing Practices of the Ulchi." In *Shaman's Drum*, vol. 53 (1999): 51–60.

Luvsanvandan, C. "Das Heldenepos der Mongolen und der Begriff des Volkes vom Schoenen." In *Fragen der mongolischen Heldendichtung*, vol. 5, ed. Walther Heissig. Wiesbaden: Harrassowitz Verlag, 1992 [in German].

Mandoki, L. "Two Asiatic Sidereal Names." In *Folk Beliefs and Shamanistic Traditions in Siberia*, ed. Vilmos Dioszegi. Budapest: Akademiai Kiado, 1996.

Marrazzi, U. "Remarks on the Siberian Turkic Shamans' Secret Language." In *Shamanism in Eurasia* (part 2), ed. Mihaly Hoppal. Paris: Edition Herodot, 1984.

Mikhailov, Vasilii Andreevich. *Religioznaya mifologia*. Ulan-Ude: Soyol, 1996 [in Russian].

Mikhailovskii, V. M. "Shamanism in Siberia and European Russia." In *Journal of the Royal Anthropological Institute of Great Britain and Ireland*, vol. 24 (1894): 62–158.

Mikhajlov, T. M. "Evolution of Early Forms of Religion among the Turco-Mongolian Peoples." In *Shamanism in Eurasia*, ed. Mihaly Hoppal. Paris: Edition Herodot, 1984.

Mingchao, Ma, and Guo Chonglin. "Typen und kulturelle Beziehungen der Epen der nordasiatischen Voelker in der Endphase." In *Gedanke und Wirkung: Festschrift zum 90. Geburtstag von Nikolaus Poppe*, eds. Walther Heissig, Klaus Sagaster, Veronika Veit, and Michael Weiers. Wiesbaden: Otto Harrassowitz, 1989 [in German].

Molnar, Adam. *Weather-Magic in Inner Asia*. Bloomington, Ind.: Research Institute for Inner Asian Studies, 1994.

Mote, Victor L. *Siberia: Worlds Apart*. Boulder, Colo.: Westview Press, 1998.

Nachtigall, H. "Die erhoehte Bestattung in Nord- und Hochasien." In *Anthropos*, vol. 48 (1953): 44–70 [in German].

Nahodil, O. "Mother Cult in Siberia." In *Popular Beliefs and Folklore Tradition in Siberia*. The Hague: Mouton and Company, 1968.

Napolskikh, V. V. "Proto-Uralic World Picture: A Reconstruction." In *Northern Religions and Shamanism*, eds. Mihaly Hoppal and Juha Pentakainen. Budapest: Akademiai Kiado, 1992.

Narsu and Kevin Stuart. "Insects Used in Mongolian Medicine." In *Journal of the Anglo-Mongolian Society*, vol. 2 (1988): 7–13.

Neklyudov, S. Ju. "Animistiche Motive in Sujets vom Kampf mit dem Daemonen im mongolischen Epos." In *Fragen der mongolischen Heldendichtung*, vol. 3, ed. Walther Heissig. Wiesbaden: Otto Harrassowitz, 1985 [in German].

———. "Das mongolische Epos und das jakutische Olongcho." In *Fragen der mongolischen Heldendichtung*, vol. 4, ed. Walther Heissig. Wiesbaden: Otto Harrassowitz, 1987 [in German].

———. "Polistadialnii obraz dukha-khozyaina, khranitelya I sozdatelya ognya v mongolskoi mifologichekoi traditsii." In *Acta Orientalia Scientiarum Hungaricae* 46 (1992–1993): 311–21 [in Russian].

———. "Tyurskiye syujetii o gesere I ikh otnoshenie k mongol'skim versiyam." In *Documenta Barbarorum: Festschrift fuer Walther Heissig zum 70. Geburtstag,* eds. Klaus Sagaster and Michael Weiers. Wiesbaden: Harrassowitz Verlag, 1983 [in Russian].

———. "Zur Transformation eines mythologischen Themas in den ostmongolischen muendlichen Versionen der Geseriade." In *Die mongolischen Epen: Bezuege, Sinndeutung, und Ueberlieferung,* ed. Walther Heissig. Wiesbaden: Otto Harrassowitz, 1979 [in German].

Nimayev, D. D. "O srednevekobiikh khori I bargutakh." In *Etnicheskaya instoriya narodov: Yujnii sibirii y tsentralnoi azii,* ed. B. R. Zoriktuyev. Novosibirsk: Nauka, 1993 [in Russian].

Nowak, Margaret, and Stephen Durrant. *The Tale of the Nishan Shamaness: A Manchu Folk Epic.* Seattle: University of Washington Press, 1977.

Ohlmarks, Ake. *Studien zum Problem des Schamanismus.* Lund: C. W. K. Gleerup, 1939 [in German].

Okada, Hidehiro. "The Fall of the Uriyanqan Mongols." In *Mongolian Studies* 10 (1986): 49–57.

Okladnikov, A. P. *Istoriya y Kul'tura Buryatii: Svornik Statei.* Ulan-Ude: Buryatskoye Knizhnoye Izdatel'stvo, 1976 [in Russian].

Okladnikova, L. A. "The Shamanistic Aspect of the Crystal Magic." In *Shamanism Past and Present* (part 2). Los Angeles/Fullerton: International Society for Trans-Oceanic Research, 1989.

Oshibuchi, Hajime. "Origin of the Mongol-Tribe and the Question of the Mongolian Race." In *Palaeologia,* vol. 3 (1954): 1–18.

Pallisen, N. "Die alte Religion der Mongolen und der Kultus Tschingis-Khans." In *Numen,* vol. 3 (1956): 178–229 [in German].

Partanen, Jorma. "A Description of Buriat Shamanism." In *Journal de la Société Finno-ougrienne,* vol. 51 (1941): 3–34.

Paulson, Ivar. *Die primitiven Seelenvorstellungen der nordeurasiatischen Voelker.* Stockholm: 1958 [in German].

Poppe, Nicholas. "Betrayal and Murder in Mongolian Epics." In *Fragen der mongolischen Heldendichtung,* vol. 3, ed. Walther Heissig. Wiesbaden: Otto Harrassowitz, 1985.

———. "A Buryat Literary Source of the XIX Century on Shamanism." In *Traditions religieuses et para-religieuses des peuples Altaiques:*

Communications présentées au XIIIe Congrès de la "Permanent Altaistic Conference," Strasbourg, 25–30 juin 1970. Paris: Presses universitaires de France, 1972.

————. "On Some Diabolic Characters in Mongolian Epics." In *Religious and Lay Symbolism in the Altaic World and Other Papers: Proceedings of the 27th Meeting of the Permanent International Altaistic Conference, Walberberg, Federal Republic of Germany, June 12–17, 1984,* eds. Klaus Sagaster and Helmut Eimer. Wiesbaden: Otto Harrassowitz, 1989.

————. "Schamanenweihe bei den Aga-Burjaten." In *Fragen der mongolischen Heldendichtung,* vol. 4, ed. Walther Heissig. Wiesbaden: Otto Harrassowitz, 1987 [in German].

————. "Die Schwanenjungfrauen in der epischen Dichtung der Mongolen." In *Fragen der mongolischen Heldendichtung,* vol. 1, ed. Walther Heissig. Wiesbaden: Otto Harrassowitz, 1981 [in German].

————. "Zum Motiv der dankbaren Tiere in der mongolischen Volksdichtung." In *Documenta Barbarorum: Festschrift fuer Walther Heissig zum 70. Geburtstag,* eds. Klaus Sagaster and Michael Weiers. Wiesbaden: Harrassowitz Verlag, 1983 [in German].

————. "Zur Erforschung der mongolischen Epenmotive." In *Die mongolischen Epen: Bezuege, Sinndeutung, und Ueberlieferung,* ed. Walther Heissig. Wiesbaden: Otto Harrassowitz, 1979 [in German].

————. "Zur Shono Baatar Sage bei den Burjaeten." In *Collectanea Mongolica: Festschrift fuer Professor Dr. Rintchen zum 60. Geburtstag,* ed. Walther Heissig. Wiesbaden: Otto Harrassowitz, 1966 [in German].

Potapov, L. P. "The Shaman Drum as a Source of Ethnographical History." In *Shamanism in Siberia,* eds. Vilmos Dioszegi and Mihaly Hoppal. Budapest: Akademiai Kiado, 1996.

Potapov, L. P., and Dr. Menges. "Materialen zur Volkskunde der Tuerkvoelker des Altaj." In *Mitteilungen des Seminars fuer Orientalische Sprachen an der Friedrich-Wilhelms Universitaet zu Berlin Jahrgang 37,* ed. Hans Heinrich Schaeder. Berlin: Walter de Gruyter, 1934 [in German].

Potapov, L. P., and M. G. Levin. *The Peoples of Siberia.* Chicago: University of Chicago Press, 1964.

Purev, Otgony. *Mongol boogiin shashin.* Ulaanbaatar: Mongol Ulsyn Shinjlekh Ukhaany Akademiin Tuukhiin Khureelen, 1999 [in Mongolian].

Rasanen, Martti. "Regenbogen-Himmelsbruecke." In *Studia Orientalia,* vol. 14 (1947): 5–11 [in German].

Reichl, Karl. *Turkic Oral Epic Poetry: Traditions, Forms, Poetic Structure.* New York: Garland Publishing, 1992.

Revunenkova, E. V. "Shamanism and Poetry." In *Shamanism Past and Present* (part 2). Los Angeles/Fullerton: International Society for Trans-Oceanic Research, 1989.

Reynolds, Georgeanne Lewis. "The Prehistory of Mongolia and the Roots of Man in North America." In *Studies on Mongolia: Proceedings of the First North American Conference on Mongolian Studies.* Bellingham, Wash.: Center for East Asian Studies, Western Washington University, 1978.

Riasanovsky, Valentin A. *Customary Law of the Nomadic Tribes of Siberia.* The Hague: Mouton and Company, 1965.

Riftin, B. L. "Die Beschreibung der heldnischen Frau im ostmongolischen Epos." In *Fragen der mongolischen Heldendichtung*, vol. 3, ed. Walther Heissig. Wiesbaden: Otto Harrassowitz, 1985 [in German].

Rinchen.* "Doma dukhov u Shamanov Prikosogol'ya." In *Acta Orientalia Scientiarum Hungaricae* 15 (1962): 249–58 [in Russian].

Rintchen. "En marge du culte de Guesser Khan en Mongolie." In *Journal de la Société Finno-ougrienne*, vol. 60 (1958): 3–51 [in French].

Rintschen, B. "Die Seele in den schamanistischen Vorstellungen der Mongolen." In *Sprache, Geschichte, in Kultur der Altaischen Voelker: Protokollband der XII. Tagung der Permanent International Altaistic Conference 1969 in Berlin*, eds. Georg Hazai and Peter Zieme. Berlin: Akademie-Verlag, 1974 [in German].

Ripinsky-Naxon, Michael. *The Nature of Shamanism: Substance and Function of a Religious Metaphor.* New York: State University of New York Press, 1993.

Rona-Tas, A. "Dream, Magic Power and Divination in the Altaic World." In *Acta Orientalia Scientiarum Hungaricae*, vol. 25 (1972): 227–36.

Ronge, Veronika. "Vorkehrungen zum Schutze von Kleinkindern in Tibet un in der Mongolei." In *Documenta Barbarorum: Festschrift fuer Walther Heissig zum 70. Geburtstag*, eds. Klaus Sagaster and Michael Weiers. Wiesbaden: Harrassowitz Verlag, 1983 [in German].

---

*Rinchen (also spelled "Rintchen" or "Rintschen") was a Buryat who emigrated to Mongolia. He published in several different languages, which accounts for the variant spellings of his name, as it is transliterated somewhat differently in each language. He was one of the greatest scholars of Mongolian shamanism.

Rudnev, A. "A Buriat Epic." In *Memoires de la Société Finno-ougrienne*, vol. 52 (1924): 238–49.

Rupen, Robert A. *Mongols of the Twentieth Century*. Indiana University Publications Uralic and Altaic Series, vol. 37, part 1. The Hague: Mouton and Company, 1964.

Sagaster, Klaus. "Bemerkungen zum Begriff 'gut' im Alttuerkischen, Mongolischen, und Tibetischen." In *Die mongolischen Epen: Bezuege, Sinndeutung, und Ueberlieferung*, ed. Walther Heissig. Wiesbaden: Otto Harrassowitz, 1979 [in German].

Salga, Maria. "Erscheinungen in dem heutigen mongolischen Epos im Spiegel der Poetik." In *Religious and Lay Symbolism in the Altaic World and Other Papers: Proceedings of the 27th Meeting of the Permanent International Altaistic Conference, Walberberg, Federal Republic of Germany, June 12–17, 1984*, eds. Klaus Sagaster and Helmut Eimer. Wiesbaden: Otto Harrassowitz, 1989 [in German].

Salzman, Emanuel, Jason Salzman, Joanne Salzman, and Gary Lincoff. "In Search of Mukhomor, the Mushroom of Immortality." In *Shaman's Drum*, vol. 41 (1996): 36–47.

Sanjeev, G. D. "An Epic of the Unga Buriats." In *Mongolian Studies*, ed. Louis Ligeti. Budapest: Akademiai Kiado, 1970.

Sanjeev, Garma. "Weltanschauung und Schamanismus der Alaren-Burjaten." In *Anthropos*, vol. 22 (1927): 576–613, 933–55; vol. 23 (1928): 538–60, 967–86 [in German].

Sarkozi, Alice. "Horse-Sacrifice among the Mongols." In *Permanent International Altaistic Conference XVIth Meeting 21–26 October 1973, Ankara*. Ankara: Turk Kulturunu Arashtirma Enstitusu, 1979.

———. "Incense-Offering to the White Old Man." In *Fragen der mongolischen Heldendichtung*, vol. 5, ed. Walther Heissig. Wiesbaden: Harrassowitz Verlag, 1992.

———. "Mandate of Heaven: Heavenly Support of the Mongol Ruler." In *Altaica Berolinensia: The Concept of Sovereignty in the Altaic World, Permanent International Altaistic Conference 34th Meeting, Berlin, 21–26 July 1991*, ed. Barbara Kellner-Heinkele. Wiesbaden: Harrassowitz Verlag, 1993.

———. "A Mongolian Hunting Ritual." In *Acta Orientalia Scientiarum Hungaricae* 25 (1972): 191–208.

——. "A Mongolian Text of Exorcism." In *Shamanism Past and Present* (part 1). Los Angeles/Fullerton: International Society for Trans-Oceanic Research, 1989.

——. "Symbolism in Exorcising Evil Spirits." In *Religious and Lay Symbolism in the Altaic World and Other Papers: Proceedings of the 27th Meeting of the Permanent International Altaistic Conference, Walberberg, Federal Republic of Germany, June 12–17, 1984*, eds. Klaus Sagaster and Helmut Eimer. Wiesbaden: Otto Harrassowitz, 1989.

Schmidt, I. J. *Die Taten Bogda Gesser Khan's: Des Vertilger der Wuerzel der zehn Uebel in den zehn Gegenden.* Berlin: Auriga Verlag, 1925 [in German].

Schmidt, P. Wilhelm. *Der Ursprung der Gottesidee Band X: Die Asiatischen Hirtenvoelker.* Muenster: Aschendorffsche Verlagsbuchhandlung, 1952 [in German].

Schmidt, W. "Das Himmelsopfer bei den innerasiatischen Pferdezuechtervoelkern." In *Ethnos*, vol. 7 (1942): 127–48 [in German].

Schoene, Uta. "Einige Bemerkungen zum Frauenbild in der 'Geheimen Geschichte der Mongolen.'" In *Altaica Berolinensia: The Concept of Sovereignty in the Altaic World, Permanent International Altaistic Conference 34th Meeting, Berlin, 21–26 July 1991*, ed. Barbara Kellner-Heinkele. Wiesbaden: Harrassowitz Verlag, 1993 [in German].

Serruys, Henry. "A Mythological Animal in Central Asia." In *Central Asiatic Journal*, vol. 26 (1982): 119–21.

——. "The Silver Cup for Medical Treatment and Divination in Mongolia." In *Central Asiatic Journal*, vol. 26 (1982): 237–40.

Shelear and Kevin Stuart. "The Tungus Evenk" (abridged translation of Lu Guang Tian, "The Tungus Evenk" in *Evenk Social and Historical Investigation* [Hohhot: Inner Mongolia People's Press, 1986]). In *Journal of the Anglo-Mongolian Society*, vol. 12 (1989): 28–46.

Shirokogoroff, S. M. *Psychomental Complex of the Tungus.* London: Kegan Paul, Trench, Trubner and Company, 1935.

Shoolbraid, G. M. H. *The Oral Epic of Siberia and Central Asia.* Bloomington: Indiana University, 1975.

Sieroshevski, M. "The Yakuts." In *Journal of the Anthropological Institute of Great Britain and Ireland*, vol. 30 (1900): 65–110.

Siikala, Anna-Leena. *The Rite Technique of the Siberian Shaman.* Helsinki: Suomalinen Tiedeakatemia, 1978.

Skrynnikova, T. D. *"Sulde:* The Basic Idea of the Chinggis Khan Cult." In *Acta Orientalia Scientiarum Hungaricae,* vol. 46 (1992): 51–59.

Smolyak, A. V. "Some Elements of Ritual Attire of Nanai Shamans." In *Shamanism in Eurasia* (part 2), ed. Mihaly Hoppal. Paris: Edition Herodot, 1984.

Solomatina, S. N. "The Role of the Altaic Shaman In the Symbolic Protection of Childbirth." In *Shamanism Past and Present* (part 2). Los Angeles/Fullerton: International Society for Trans-Oceanic Research, 1989.

Stein, R.-A. *Recherches sur l'épopée et le barde au Tibet.* Paris: Presses Universitaires de France [in French].

Sternberg, Leo. "Der Adlerkult bei den Voelkern Sibiriens." In *Archiv fuer Religionswissenschaft,* vol. 28 (1930): 125–53 [in German].

Szynkiewicz, Slawoj. "On Kinship Symbolics among the Western Mongols." In *Religious and Lay Symbolism in the Altaic World and Other Papers: Proceedings of the 27th Meeting of the Permanent International Altaistic Conference, Walberberg, Federal Republic of Germany, June 12–17, 1984,* eds. Klaus Sagaster and Helmut Eimer. Wiesbaden: Otto Harrassowitz, 1989.

Taksami, A. M. "Survivals of Early Forms of Religion in Siberia." In *Shamanism in Eurasia* (part 2), ed. Mihaly Hoppal. Paris: Edition Herodot, 1984.

Tatar, Maria Magdalena. "Human Sacrifices in the Altay-Sayan Area: The Duck and Its People." In *Altaic Religious Practices and Beliefs: Proceedings of the 33rd Meeting of the Permanent International Altaistic Conference, Budapest, June 24–29, 1990,* eds. Geza Bethlenfalvy, Agnes Birtalan, Alice Sarkozi, and Judit Vinkovics. Budapest: Research Group for Altaic Studies, Hungarian Academy of Sciences, 1990.

———. "Mythology as an Areal Problem in the Altai-Sayan Area: The Sacred Holes and Caves." In *Shamanism and Northern Ecology,* ed. Juha Pentikainen. Berlin: Mouton de Gruyter, 1996.

———. "Tragic and Stranger *Ongons* among the Altaic Peoples." In *Altaistic Studies: Papers at the 25th Meeting of the Permanent International Altaistic Conference at Uppsala, June 7–11, 1982.* Stockholm: Almqvist and Wiksell International, 1982.

———. "Zur Fragen des Obo-Kultes bei den Mongolen." In *Acta Orientalia Scientiarum Hungaricae* 24 (1971): 301–30 [in German].

Taube, Erika. "Der Igel in der Mythologie Altaischer Voelker." In *Altaica Osloensia: Proceedings of the 32nd Meeting of the Permanent International Altaistic Conference, Oslo, June 12–16, 1989*, ed. Bernt Brendemoen. Oslo: Universitetsforlaget, 1989 [in German].

———. "Sardaqban in den Ueberlieferungen der Tuwiner im Altai." In *Altaic Religious Practices and Beliefs: Proceedings of the 33rd Meeting of the Permanent International Altaistic Conference, Budapest, June 24–29, 1990*, eds. Geza Bethlenfalvy, Agnes Birtalan, Alice Sarkozi, and Judit Vinkovics. Budapest: Research Group for Altaic Studies, Hungarian Academy of Sciences, 1990 [in German].

———. "South Siberian and Central Asian Hero Tales and Shamanistic Rituals." In *Shamanism in Eurasia* (part 2), ed. Mihaly Hoppal. Paris: Edition Herodot, 1984.

Taube, Erika, and Jakob Taube. "Maerchen im Dienste von Macht." In *Altaica Berolinensia: The Concept of Sovereignty in the Altaic World: Permanent International Altaistic Conference 34th Meeting, Berlin, 21–26 July 1991*. Wiesbaden: Harrassowitz Verlag, 1993 [in German].

Tenishev, E. R. *Abai Geser Khubuun:* Uliger. Moskva: Vostochnaya Literatura, 1995 [in Buryat].

Tserensodnom, D. "Mongol yaruu nairgiin zarim ner tome'yonii garal uucliin asuudald." In *Documenta Barbarorum: Festschrift fuer Walther Heissig zum 70. Geburtstag*, eds. Klaus Sagaster and Michael Weiers. Wiesbaden: Harrassowitz Verlag, 1983 [in Mongolian].

Tsydendambaev, Ts. B. "On the Language of the Mongol and Buriat Versions of the Geser Epic." In *Mongolian Studies*, ed. Louis Ligeti. Budapest: Akademiai Kiado, 1970.

Tugutov, I. E. "The *Tailagan* as a Principal Shamanistic Ritual of the Buryats." In *Shamanism in Siberia*, eds. V. Dioszegi and M. Hoppal. Budapest: Akdemiai Kiado, 1978.

Ulanjee. *An Introduction to the Music and Dance in Mongolian Shamanism*. Unpublished ms. translation of Chinese text of an article published in *Musicology in China*, vol. 3, 1992.

Ulanov, A. I. *Abai Geser.* Ulan-Ude: Akademia nauk SSSR sibirskoye otdelenie, 1960 [in Russian].

———. "O roli mifov v drevnem fol'klore buryat." In *Poetika janrov buryatskogo fol'klora*. Ulan-Ude: Akademiya nauk SSSR sibirskoye otdeleniye buryatskii filial, 1982 [in Russian].

Ulymzhiev, D. "Galsan Gomboyev, a Buryat Researcher." *Mongolian Studies* 18 (1995): 59–64.

Underdown, Michael. "Symbolism in Tungus Shamanism." In *Religious and Lay Symbolism in the Altaic World and Other Papers: Proceedings of the 27th Meeting of the Permanent International Altaistic Conference, Walberberg, Federal Republic of Germany, June 12–17, 1984*, eds. Klaus Sagaster and Helmut Eimer. Wiesbaden: Otto Harrassowitz, 1989.

Uray-Kohalmi, Kaethe. "Herd und Kessel in der epischen Dichtung der innerasiatischen und sibirischen Voelker." In *Religious and Lay Symbolism in the Altaic World and Other Papers: Proceedings of the 27th Meeting of the Permanent International Altaistic Conference, Walberberg, Federal Republic of Germany, June 12–17, 1984*, eds. Klaus Sagaster and Helmut Eimer. Wiesbaden: Otto Harrassowitz, 1989 [in German].

———. "Die Herren der Erde." In *Fragen der mongolischen Heldendichtung*, vol. 5, ed. Walther Heissig. Wiesbaden: Harrassowitz Verlag, 1992 [in German].

———. "Synkretismus im Staatskult der fruehen Dschingisiden." In *Synkretismus in den Religionen Zentralasiens*, eds. Walther Heissig and Hans-Joachim Klimkeit. Wiesbaden: Otto Harrassowitz, 1987 [in German].

Uther, Hans-Joerg. "Der Fuchs als Tierhelfer in mongolischen Volkserzaehlungen." In *Fragen der mongolischen Heldendichtung*, vol. 5, ed. Walther Heissig. Wiesbaden: Harrassowitz Verlag, 1992 [in German].

Vajnshtejn, S. I. "The *eerens* in Tuvan Shamanism." In *Shamanism in Siberia*, eds. Vilmos Dioszegi and Mihaly Hoppal. Budapest: Akademiai Kiado, 1996.

———. "The Tuvan (Soyot) Shaman's Drum and the Ceremony of Its Enlivening." In *Popular Beliefs and Folklore Tradition in Siberia*, ed. V. Dioszegi. The Hague: Mouton and Company, 1968.

van Deusen, Kira. "In Black and White: Contemporary Buriat Shamans." In *Shaman*, vol. 7 (1999): 154–66.

———. "The Flying Tiger: Aboriginal Women Shamans, Storytellers and Embroidery Artists in the Russian Far East." In *Shaman*, vol. 4 (1996): 45–77.

Vasilevich, G. M. "The Acquisition of Shamanistic Ability among the

Evenki (Tungus)." In *Popular Beliefs and Folklore Tradition in Siberia*, ed. V. Dioszegi. The Hague: Mouton and Company, 1968.

————. "Early Concepts about the Universe among the Evenks (Materials)." In *Studies in Shamanism*, ed. Henry N. Michael. Toronto: University of Toronto Press, 1965.

————. "Shamanistic Songs of the Evenki (Tungus)." In *Popular Beliefs and Folklore Tradition in Siberia*, ed. V. Dioszegi. The Hague: Mouton and Company, 1968.

Veit, Veronika. "Der Begriff 'bagatur' [Held] des mongolischen Epos als Topos in Biographien Mongolischer Nationalhelden." In *Die mongolischen Epen: Bezuege, Sinndeutung, und Ueberlieferung*, ed. Walther Heissig. Wiesbaden: Otto Harrassowitz, 1979 [in German].

————. "Einige Ueberlegungen zu natuerlichen und uebernatuerlichen Aspekten bezueglich des Pferdes in mongolischen Epos." In *Fragen der mongolischen Heldendichtung*, vol. 1, ed. Walther Heissig. Wiesbaden: Otto Harrassowitz, 1981 [in German].

————. "Muendliche Elements in der traditionellen mongolischen Historiographie des 13.-17. Jahrhunderts." In *Fragen der mongolischen Heldendichtung*, vol. 5, ed. Walther Heissig. Wiesbaden: Harrassowitz Verlag, 1992 [in German].

————. "Das Pferd-Alter Ego des Mongolen?" In *Fragen der mongolischen Heldendichtung*, vol.3, ed. Walther Heissig. Wiesbaden: Otto Harrassowitz, 1985 [in German].

von Gabain, A. "Iranische Elemente im Zentral- und Ostasiatischen Volksglauben." In *Studia Orientalia*, vol. 47 (1991): 57–70 [in German].

von Sadovszky, Otto J. "Linguistic Evidence for the Siberian Origin of the Central California Indian Shamanism." In *Shamanism Past and Present* (part 1). Los Angeles/Fullerton: International Society for Trans-Oceanic Research, 1989.

Waida, Manabu. "Central Asian Mythology of the Origin of Death: A Comparative Analysis of Its Structure and History." In *Anthropos 77* (1982): 662–97.

Wasilewski, Jerzy. "Space in Nomadic Cultures: A Spatial Analysis of the Mongol Yurts." In *Altaica Collecta: Berichte und Vortraege der XVII. Permanent International Altaistic Conference, 3–8 June 1974, in Bonn/ Bad Honnef*, ed. Walther Heissig. Wiesbaden: Otto Harrassowitz, 1976.

Willhelm, Hellmut. "A Note on the Migration of the Uriankhai." In *Studia*

Altaica: Festschrift fuer Nikolaus Poppe zum 60. Geburtstag am 8. August 1957. Wiesbaden: Otto Harrassowitz, 1957.

Winters, Clyde Ahmad. "The Dravidio-Harappan Colonization of Central Asia." In *Central Asiatic Journal* 34 (1990): 120–44.

Yongsiyebu, Rinchen.*"Everlasting Bodies of the Ancestral Spirits in Mongolian Shamanism." In *Studia Orientalia*, vol. 47 (1991): 175–80.

———. "White, Black, and Yellow Shamans among the Mongols." In *Journal of the Anglo-Mongolian Society*, vol. 9 (1984): 19–24.

Zhornickaja, M. Ja. "Dances of Yakut Shamans." In *Shamanism in Siberia*, eds. V. Dioszegi and M. Hoppal. Budapest: Akademiai Kiado, 1978.

Zomonov, M. D., and I. A. Manjigeev. *Kratkii slovar' buryatskogo shamanizma.* Ulan-Ude: Buryatskoye knijnoye izdatel'stvo, 1997 [in Russian].

---

*Rinchen Yongsiyebu may be the son of the Mongolian scholar Rinchen. Mongols often use their father's name as a first name.

Index